indian
instincts

MINIYA CHATTERJI

indian instincts

*Essays on Freedom
and Equality in India*

PENGUIN
VIKING

An imprint of Penguin Random House

VIKING

USA | Canada | UK | Ireland | Australia
New Zealand | India | South Africa | China

Viking is part of the Penguin Random House group of companies
whose addresses can be found at global.penguinrandomhouse.com

Published by Penguin Random House India Pvt. Ltd
7th Floor, Infinity Tower C, DLF Cyber City,
Gurgaon 122 002, Haryana, India

First published in Viking by Penguin Random House India 2018

ISBN 9780670089734

Typeset in Adobe Garamond Pro by Manipal Digital Systems, Manipal
Printed at Replika Press Pvt. Ltd, India

www.penguin.co.in

For Chirag

Contents

Introduction

During the course of writing this book, I became a parent. I watched with amazement as my baby boy, fresh out of my womb, learnt the need and technique of suckling, for surviving in his new environment. I found that he was not endowed with any primordial instinct to suck on my breast, but he learnt. Thus began his journey, wherein he would use his rational faculty to learn skills to survive in this world.

Survival is a primordial instinct, but most of our instincts or the spontaneous behaviours that we display are not innate. In fact, to deny this is to accept that a person's character is inherited, which is the basis of every xenophobic argument. Instead, I believe that instincts are a 'spontaneous rationality' (or irrationality) developed by our cognitive faculty in response to the environment. And the development of this rationality is volitional—we must want it, nurture it, and learn how to use it.

Thus, there is no predetermined 'Indian instinct'. In India, our spontaneous behaviour is a rational (or irrational) choice under the overwhelming influence of politics, ambition and religious fervour in the environment.

In every era and everywhere, governance structures—tribes, kingdoms, nation states—were created to provide resources such as food, shelter and safety for the people. Now, in India, we are besotted with the latest news, views, analyses and Twitter wars on party politics instead of the resources the state must provide. We created the concept of corporations and jobs so that we could earn ourselves a comfortable life, but it turns out that often the first half of our life is overpowered by the quest for building a curriculum vitae for a job, and thereafter by the inimitable 24/7 Indian corporate culture. Similarly, we invented religion as a framework by which to lead our lives, yet blinded by our faith we kill each other. A recent survey gives India a high rank in terms of religious hostility, putting it in the company of Syria, Nigeria and Iraq.[1]

This is why a certain hypothesis has haunted me for several years—that we are willingly entrapped in the institutions of our own making, having abandoned the rationality to realize that we have lost sight of the reasons these institutions were set up in the first place.

The central theme of this book is that, in India these institutions—the government, corporation, religion—have often become sources of the problem, increasing economic inequality and curbing our free will. It is to this environment that we Indians respond, sometimes with rationality and sometimes without. The fifteen essays of this book hold up a mirror to what we have thus become.

This book is not one that could have been written merely sitting at my study desk. Instead it is a consequence of taking on life's adventures. For this, I thank my parents and my brother for supporting three decades of my unlikely choices. I thank Chirag for sweeping me off my feet—this book is because of him, for him. Thank you, Naveen, for your friendship and for giving me wings in India. Laxman and Rajshree, thank you for your generosity. Sayem, thank you for showing me life. Neelini, I am grateful for your edits. Milee, thanks for your friendship, advice and patience.

---

[1] 'Religious restrictions vary significantly in the world's most populous countries' (Pew Research, 13 April 2017).

Part I

INSTINCTS

1

Survival

Almost 200 years ago, the Swiss-born natural historian Louis Agassiz invented the premise for every xenophobe's favourite argument. He said that the three major human races—Whites, Asians and Negroes, as he liked to categorize them—had risen independently from separate ancestral lineages.[1] This would mean that a person with a particular skin colour belonged to an altogether different species from someone with a different skin colour. 'The brain of the Negro is that of the imperfect brain of a seven months' infant in the womb of a White,'[2] Agassiz declared.

As a professor at Harvard University, Agassiz was one of the first to propose that Earth had endured an Ice Age, but he also used his public stature as a scientist to 'prove' racism. It was the era of scientific racism, which meant that there were others such as Samuel George Morton who used various so-called 'scientific' methods to 'rank' human races.[3] Despite these contentious claims, or perhaps because of them, Agassiz acquired fame, and at the

---

[1] Nott and Gliddon 1854.
[2] Hoeveler 2007, 57; Carmichael 2012.
[3] Menand 2001, 110.

time of his death in 1873 he was considered America's leading scientist. There is even a street in Cambridge, Massachusetts; an entire Swiss mountain; the Harvard zoology museum he founded; and a public school named after him.[4]

Fortunately for us, Agassiz's argument was debunked by his contemporary from the other Cambridge, in the United Kingdom—the academic Charles Darwin. Darwin suggested— now famously—that all of us had descended from one common ancestor in Africa.[5] 'We are all one family, in that sense,' he said. Needless to say, Agassiz detested Darwinism.[6]

But Darwin had actually spoken about apes, not modern man. Moreover, if we go back far enough, we will see that humans share a distant common ancestry with every living thing on Earth, including bacteria and mushrooms. Therefore, it might be more relevant to find out what happened *after* the first exodus of apes from Africa took place sixteen million years ago. Many apes left for South-East Asia to evolve into gibbons and orangutans, and the ones who stayed on in Africa evolved into gorillas, chimpanzees and humans.[7]

So what happened after that? How did humans not only survive in Africa from that point onwards, but also go on to inhabit the rest of the world? And if we all have descended from that one human in Africa, why do we talk about race? Why do we believe that people belonging to specific nationalities, religions and ethnicities display common characteristics, and that each such community is different from the others?

In India, thousands of diverse local communities are defined by the conviction that there is something unique shared among

---

[4] Stott 2013.
[5] Darwin 1859.
[6] Bergman 2011, 12.
[7] Grehan and Schwartz 2009, 1823.

the people of a particular community. We assume that we must naturally display some characteristics of the community to which we are connected by blood and heritage.

This belief among Indians—that we display a set of settled characteristics because of our membership by birth to a certain community—has far-reaching and varied effects on our thinking about ourselves and about others. It gives some of us a sense of mystic belonging to a community. We might believe that our behaviour can't be helped since our mannerisms were predetermined by birth as per that community. We might even forcefully emulate some of the community's established characteristics to feel divinely connected to it. This could also mean that we are left with hardly any place for choice or individuality.

For example, a Gujarati is supposed to be entrepreneurial by blood. Now, if a young Gujarati boy is told this from the day he can distinguish language from random sounds, that is likely to be the ambition he will grow up with—emulating the characteristics of his fellow Gujarati business wizards, and feeling a sense of community bonding. Similarly, when a Parsi or a Sindhi meets another Parsi or Sindhi for the first time in any corner of the world, there is often an immediate sense of familiarity and trust between them. The bond between two members of the same community is often accompanied by a willingness to help the other out. To cite another example, the cultural cliché is that Bengalis are good at the arts, that they make good writers, musicians, painters and so on. How does that cliché affect a young Bengali child in Kolkata in terms of the education she or he receives and the expectations from the community? When this child grows up, she or he can probably leverage the instant 'community bond' with fellow Bengalis in creative fields to land a similar job.

I had no such luck. I am a native Bengali speaker, but my Hindi language skills are just as good. My family does not belong to the business or academic community, yet I belong to both. In fact, even though I am an Indian by nationality, I also feel like the offspring of at least two more of the eight countries I have lived in for education, work and love. However, I do share an immense liking for sweets with most of my fellow Bengalis.

These differences as well as similarities which I share with the various communities that I am supposed to be a part of 'by birth'— Indian, Hindu, Brahmin, Bengali—were what made me first wonder about the origins of such supposedly shared characteristics. Has the idea of 'community characteristics' been forced upon us?

My father was a pilot in the Indian Air Force, and every three or four years, I moved with him, my mother and my younger brother from one military camp to another in various far-flung regions of India. We lived in Agra in Uttar Pradesh, Jorhat in Assam, Chennai in Tamil Nadu, Dehradun in Uttarakhand, and in many other big and small towns. I changed nine schools across five states. The medium of instruction at each of them was in different languages, and we were taught several interpretations of India's history and culture. Perhaps because of this kind of upbringing, I did not develop the specific characteristics I was supposed to have inherited at birth. But living among various other communities in India made me more curious than ever about the truth of these clichéd 'community characteristics' within the remarkable diversity of the country.

I was a voracious reader—a habit inculcated in me by my mother who, given my father's peripatetic vocation, had taken to teaching high school English in every city we lived in. There was no Internet in those days, not even a landline telephone in most of the places we lived in. Moreover, I was a child and my access to the world was limited by the restrictions of each place my father was posted in. And so I tried to find the answers to all my questions about human diversity in books.

The books I found on the subject could be divided into two broad categories—historical and anecdotal. However, in both kinds, the respective authors only presented their own perception of our origins; none of them could give an adequate explanation in scientific terms.

Initially, I found oral histories interesting, but they were specific to distinct communities. When I was a pre-teen, palaeoanthropology provided me details of fascinating possibilities about our ancestry, but none that I could consider scientific. Later, I found that reading about human morphology—the practice of digging up and studying bones and skulls—was even more interesting. I learnt about Carl von Linne, a Swedish botanist who, in the eighteenth century, categorized about 12,000 species, and eventually coined the term homo sapiens, or 'wise man' in Latin.[8] In the post-Darwinian era, von Linne declared that humanity was divided into different categories—Africans, Americans, Asians, Europeans, and a blatantly racist category he called 'Monstrosus' in which he included deformed people and imaginary folk like elves! When I read about this, I was tempted to conclude that we must have no concrete details about our ancient past for von Linne and others to consider such obtuse possibilities about our origins.

We did not have a television at home, but my father would tell me about his travels to other countries. He had friends in Russia—the manufacturers and engineers of the Russian AN32 airplane that he flew—who would visit our home. At that time we lived in far-flung Assam, in the north-east of India. So strong was the Russian influence in our family that my younger brother was named Sasha, meaning 'little boy' in Russian. My father often travelled to Egypt and Muscat as well—for aircraft fuel—and he

---

[8] Wells 2007.

would come back with photographs and stories from those lands. Our home was full of the memorabilia he picked up from abroad; he even added significantly to my book collection. Through the gift of knowledge that my father gave me, I realized India was just a microcosm of the world, populated by many different types of people. The scope of my curiosity expanded from India to the diversity of the people of the world.

As I grew up, my curiosity gradually made me look for answers in the scientific discoveries of the time. I found in Agassiz's research, for example, that between 70,000 and 50,000 years ago, Earth was frozen. The ice caps were expanding as a result of a worldwide catastrophe that had occurred because of a monumental change in climate. Cold deserts in Africa expanded, sea levels everywhere dropped, prey became rare in the drought, and hunters desperately searched for food. But humanity, on the verge of extinction, was miraculously saved by a massive leap of development in the human intellect. In order to survive, a small group of humans living in the severely cold and parched Africa 50,000 years ago were able to think the unthinkable—they had the idea of leaving Africa forever. It was assumed that these earliest humans probably did so on foot, walking over frozen lands along the coast. It was the primordial survival instinct of humans in the Ice Age that kept our species alive.

For a long time, scientists tried hard to find proof of this journey, but archaeologists were unable to unearth any evidence of the route taken by the first humans out of Africa.

The answer was found in our own DNA by genetic scientists. Studies showed that the first modern humans left Africa in two distinct evolutionary migrations. The first wave apparently walked eastward along the coastline to reach Australia. The second wave was more successful—they moved northward to populate the Middle East, Asia, Europe and the Americas. As each group of people broke away to found a new community, like branches of a tree, it took along a sample of the parent population's genetic blueprint.[9]

So when did the first human from Africa reach India? And if we do indeed share one origin that lies in Africa, how did we end up looking and sounding so different from each other? What about all the communities in India? Is there any scientific basis for their different characteristics?

These were the questions that led me to talk to population geneticist Professor Ramasamy Pitchappan a few years ago. It had been a few months since I returned to India after fourteen years of living across the world, and I soon picked up my personal inquiry into the origins of India's diversity that had intrigued me as a child. I had read online about the Genographic Project, a formidable ten-year global collaborative study started in 2005 that had conducted an advanced DNA analysis of various indigenous communities around the world to find our origins. I tried to contribute to the global project by purchasing their gene kit online. It would be shipped to me in India, and I would use it to contribute a sample of the skin of my inner cheek and send it back so that my DNA and ancestry could be analysed. However, I was informed that it was forbidden to send genetic information and related material out of India. I was disappointed, but not disheartened, and continued to pursue my quest. Within days, I found that the Genographic Project had an India director— seventy-year-old Professor Pitchappan—who had researched more than 12,000 blood samples from ninety-one tribes and 129 castes in India for their genetic compositions.[10] I was excited beyond words.

---

[9] Culotta and Gibbons 2016.

[10] Author's interview with Ramasamy Pitchappan, 6 January 2016.

I got in touch with the professor, first through email and
then phone calls. He was friendly and gave me his time, patiently
explaining how DNA is a manual of life itself. It is in our blood
and all other cells, coordinating our life processes, strung together
in pairs of forty-six chromosomes in an incredibly long sequence.
If laid out, the DNA of a person can stretch from Earth to Moon
and back 3000 times.

'Because of its length, when it is inherited, DNA is prone
to developing certain glitches in its sequence similar to "copying
errors",' he explained to me on the phone. 'These copying errors
are called mutations—we all have them.'

'Copying errors?' I asked.

'You heard right—copying errors!' he confirmed.

He explained that this is how with each new generation the
chromosomes get chopped up and reordered, making each baby a
unique combination of its parents.

'Each generation inherits the X and Y chromosomes from the
mother and the father respectively, right?' I asked.

'Correct. But the Y chromosome, in fact, does not get
reordered in every generation,' he said. 'And so the Y chromosome
is the key to our history, since it passes unchanged from father to
son. If, once in an evolutionary blue moon, a genetic mutation
does occur, that mutation too gets passed on in the Y chromosome
to the next generation.'

'Okay, so in this way, every male progeny collects the genetic
mutations of his ancestors?'

'Yes, the collection of these mutations in our DNA writes our
ancestral history.'

The professor's research was done in his laboratory at
Madurai Kamaraj University in Tamil Nadu, the southernmost
state of India. I had learnt from what I had read about the
Genographic Project that at this laboratory he painstakingly

distilled blood samples to extract DNA, from which he traced Y chromosome mutations to find the ancestral trail to several communities and tribes in India.

In one of our conversations, he told me how one morning twenty years ago he heard from an old friend, fellow geneticist Spencer Wells from the University of Austin in Texas. Wells told him that he was looking for the route that the first human migrants had taken when they left Africa in the Ice Age about 60,000 years ago. So far, some of the major theories in genetic science held that the first migrant group from Africa reached Australia and much later the second migrant group walked northward to the Middle East, Europe, America and Asia.[11] But Wells was interested only in the first group. He wanted to know how they had travelled the entire distance to faraway Australia. Astonishingly, there were no archaeological traces of any such journey on that route.

The genetic mutation in the DNA of the San bushmen in Africa—who are considered the direct descendants of early man—was discovered in the blood of the Aborigines of Australia as well. This meant that the Australian Aborigines had inherited the ancient genetic mutation NRY HG C-M130, which can be traced back around 60,000 years ago to the African bushmen. The bushmen, though, have no trace of the Australian aboriginal mutations in their blood, which indicates that the migration was one way only: from Africa to Australia. While this discovery was spectacular, we still did not know how they got there. There was no evidence—archaeological or through DNA—of this human journey.

---

[11] Author's interview with Anu Acharya, CEO, Mapmygenome India Limited, 27 July 2017.

Professor Pitchappan agreed to help Wells with the DNA research. Immediately, he flew down to meet him in Madurai, and that was the starting point of the laborious process of sampling the blood of thousands of Indians across autochthonous communities in India.

After two years of arduous research, the genetic mutation NRY HG C-M130 appeared in the DNA of Virumandi, a man in his late twenties who lived in the Jothimanickam village of Tamil Nadu. This discovery completely turned on its head our earlier understanding of the origins of man. It demonstrated that the earliest man had arrived in India and expanded his family line in the Indian subcontinent thousands of years before setting foot in Europe, the Americas, or Central and East Asia. Virumandi was a direct descendant of the earliest man who had left Africa 60,000 years ago. Even more mind-boggling was the subsequent discovery that Virumandi's entire community carried the NRY HG C-M130 mutation.

This discovery is fascinating, as much for its unexpectedness as for the feat of the survival of the strain. This smallest and most ancient marker of human existence could have been eradicated by an endless number of events—migrations, caste wars, invasions. How could its continuation be explained, that too in a land that has consistently received as many travellers and traders as invaders, more than anywhere else in the world?

The fascinating survival stories of communities in the subcontinent are as compelling as the endurance of the idea of India itself. Is it by providence that the political boundaries of Chandragupta Maurya's India of 300 BC are remarkably much the same as that of modern India? Several stories that some Indians wanted to tell were composed into the 24,000 verses of the Ramayana and the 200,000 verses of the Mahabharata around 500 BC, and both epics don't just exist today; they are best-sellers. Ancient religions like Hinduism and Buddhism were born in this land and did not die—instead, they are the world's third and fourth largest religions today. I studied various accounts of the Indian subcontinent written by ancient travellers. Even the most ancient travelogues contain a glimpse of India as it is today.[12]

The character of India is a mix of the various cultures of the people who landed here. Over 3000 years ago, the Aryans, Turks, Afghans and Mughals arrived from the north to conquer the land. Despite the loot and plunder, they became part of our diversity, creating a hybrid Indo-Islamic civilization with languages such as Deccani and Urdu, which mixed the Sanskrit-derived vernaculars with Turkish, Persian and Arabic. The Europeans, meanwhile, started arriving in India from the end of the fifteenth century, and did not mingle with us. Instead, they remained aloof, ruled ruthlessly and prospered immensely. Subsequently, India's long and painful freedom struggle was as much about ousting the last of the imperial powers—the British and the Portuguese—as it was about ensuring that each of the disparate historical and cultural influences on the subcontinent would be part of the nation that was born in 1947.

---

[12] Ambassadors from Greece were sent to the Indian subcontinent with gifts for Emperor Chandragupta Maurya (321–298 BC), and in turn they also wrote accounts of what they saw. They described Stone Age tribes in the Himalayas, as well as the cities in the plains, and said that it was a land of 118 nations, rich and fertile, with rivers so wide that they could not see on the other side. One of the rivers, they said, was worshipped by all Indians. Another traveller, the Muslim polymath Al-Biruni, travelled through India nearly a thousand years ago, and wrote about the emphasis on the purity of fire and water, the avoidance of touching between communities, and that men wore earrings and a girdle passing from the left shoulder to the right side of the waist, that they spat out and blew their noses without any respect for the elders present. Al-Biruni could have been writing this same text about India now, and he would not be far from the truth (Mookerji 1966, 38; Wood 2008, 285).

So, at the time of Independence, there were an estimated 554 kingdoms in all that had to be integrated into a country. Each Indian kingdom was different, with its own unique social, ethnic and religious community. Opposers of Independence like Winston Churchill and supporters like Franklin D. Roosevelt had both been sceptical that a nation as fissiparous as India would be able to adopt a universal franchise.[13] But they were proved wrong.

Even in August 1947, when the British finally left after 200 years in India, it was decided that the subcontinent would be partitioned into two independent nation states—Hindu-majority India and Muslim-majority Pakistan. But the complication still continued (as it does even today) with Kashmir. The consequentially rough partition left everyone unhappy, and the Indian subcontinent imploded in violence caused by religious differences. Thereafter began one of the goriest migrations in human history, as Muslims trekked west and east, while Hindus and Sikhs headed in the opposite direction. In the process, villages were set afire and around 75,000 women were raped, kidnapped, abducted and forcibly impregnated.[14]

By 1948, between one and two million were dead.[15] Soon after, the nation was swayed by movements based on language. When this was sorted out by separating distinct linguistic groups into administrative units or states, India's unity was once again endangered by the Naga insurgency. In the 1960s, there were anti-Hindi protests in Tamil Nadu, while Naxal violence began in West Bengal and Andhra Pradesh. In the 1970s, India had

---

[13] French 2011, 18.
[14] Butalia 2000, 45.
[15] Dalrymple 2015.

to deal with the Emergency, followed by separatist movements in Assam and Punjab. In the 1990s, there were conflicts and bloodshed over caste and religious identities, which still continue. In the next decade, the bloodbath in Gujarat occurred, along with a rise in right-wing nationalist and religious sentiment, which grew in many other parts of the country as well. Perhaps it would take a miracle for the idea of India to survive and remain undisturbed.

The conflicts in India's history have thus brought about a violent need to ensure the survival of our 'identity', but at the same time, it made clear that our sense of belonging is accompanied by more volatility than is seen in most other parts of the world.

Much of this conflict, which has threatened to tear contemporary India apart, is located along the cracks separating the enormous number of communities that live here.

'Unscrupulous politicians make use of these cracks based on bogey theories of race, fanning whimsical thoughts in the minds of novice citizens and whipping up mass frenzy and fanaticism of various kinds,' Professor Pitchappan once angrily wrote to me.

This does not come as a surprise because the complex layers in our sense of belonging—to a place, a community or an idea— are more fraught than anywhere else in the world. We belong to several communities, to some more than to others depending on context and time, with a few occasionally overlapping or colliding among themselves. Identity is not static anywhere in the world, but in India, where the different aspects of identity often lead to fires being lit and doused, the friction can spark off a blazing inferno. The fascinating fact is that yet we hold together, with all our diversity, within this unlikely democracy that still survives.

India has been witness to much bloodshed over convictions about the superiority of one community over the other, and the belief that the inferior one must be driven out of certain political boundaries. The naive belief that each community has different bodily compositions because of race or ethnicity has been stretched to such an extent that we are ready to kill in its defence. But genetic science shows us that everyone—regardless of religion, region, caste or tribe—has originated from the same woman in Africa. The origin of the human population across all the communities in the world is the same. However, each of us has different characteristics, and for this reason we must accept that our characteristics or identities are by no means a derivative of our origins. This is the single most important truth that can stop a large amount of conflict in our country. 'Race', in fact, is a political concept that has been created by constructs of power and knowledge. Who determines what counts as knowledge? Who decides whose voice will be heard, whose stories will be remembered? If we agree that we are all born of the same woman in Africa, we must see clearly that the entire issue of race is about the way history has been written and validated by society, through violent conflicts as well as silent negotiations, over generations. Our identity thus has little to do with our origins—which are the same for all—but is a product of the cumulative experiences of a lifetime that change according to context. This is perhaps the reason that despite being a Bengali who has never lived in Bengal, I am unlikely to display many of the characteristics that my community would have expected to naturally just be 'in my blood'.

I had known Professor Pitchappan for several months but I finally got the chance to meet him when he invited me to the wedding of his granddaughter. I was surprised and grateful at his generous gesture.

The rational, clear-headed and patient man I had become acquainted with was as passionate about his family responsibilities as he was about his research. He had mentioned his family to me in several conversations. He told me he had grown up with two sisters in a village and that he now had three children, from whom he had two grandchildren each. His eldest granddaughter, Valli, was a medical doctor, he proudly announced. She was to get married in his native village about 200 kilometres away from Madurai to another medical doctor. He also told me that it was Virumandi who would receive me when I arrived in Madurai for the wedding.

Virumandi arrived with his cousin Ganesha, both dressed in loose trousers and checked cotton shirts. He was fairly broad, with a receding hairline that stretched his forehead further above his small eyes and large flat nose. While Virumandi had a calm demeanour and seemed eager to help, Ganesha spoke enthusiastically in Tamil—a language I had already told him I did not understand a word of. We sat down for some tea in the veranda of my hotel.

'In 2001, I was working as a laboratory assistant at Madurai Kamaraj University,' said Virumandi as soon as we sat down on a cane sofa. 'I was a regular blood donor anyway and had volunteered my blood to be sampled for Professor Pitchappan's gene project. I did not know the professor, and my blood sample was one of thousands that the professor was collecting from all over India for his research. One day, while I was away, my parents told me that the professor had come to my home in my village looking for me. I was perplexed. The next day, I went to his office at the university. Initially, his assistants would not let me in, but then the professor happened to see me. He took me to his chamber and explained that my genes matched the genes of the first man out of Africa.'

'At that time, did you know anything about genetic science?' I inquired.

'No. But within weeks, Spencer Wells from the US came home to meet me to confirm this discovery, and then he explained everything to me. Do you know Spencer Wells?' he paused to ask.

'Yes, I have heard of him,' I replied.

'When I first met him, I had many questions. He told me that we are all brothers, with a common ancestor born in Africa. He said that the whole world—Chinese, Americans, Europeans, Indians—is one family. I told him that what he was saying was correct, but I had a doubt because I was black and he was very fair. How is it possible that we are part of the same family?'

'What did he say?'

'He said that his last few ancestors lived in cold climatic conditions, so his genes had mutated further and the colour of his skin had changed from mine.'

'So generations and climate changes affect gene composition?'

'Yes, that is correct. But I had more questions for him,' Virumandi continued. 'I had read different things in different books. In some, I had read that humans were first born in India, and then they went from here to Africa. In some other books, I read that humans were first born in Australia. I asked Wells what the truth was.'

'Without scientific evidence, there can be many claims,' I remarked, to which Virumandi quickly nodded in agreement, and said, 'Yes, yes, Wells told me that people can write anything they want in general books, but scientific research has to be accurate.'

Virumandi continued, 'But then I asked Wells why this M130 was found in me. He explained that it was because firstly, mixed marriage was strictly forbidden in my community; secondly, all generations of my community had always lived in the same area; and three, the place we lived had a climate very similar to that of Africa, where man originated.'

We sat crammed, all three of us, on the back seat of a local taxi on our way to Virumandi's village, Jothimanickam, located about 25 kilometres from Madurai. En route, Virumandi explained that he and Ganesha both belonged to the autochthonous Piramalai Kallar tribe, which consisted of no more than fifty families, all of them living in the same village to which we were going.

Talking about personal affairs, he said that inspired by his association with Professor Pitchappan and all the scientists who were interested in his genes, Virumandi had been the first in his ancestral history to complete university education. In fact, he had submitted his PhD thesis a year ago at Madurai Kamaraj University, in which he had researched the possibilities of incorporating new technologies within the university's library documentation procedures. On the other hand, Virumandi's cousin Ganesha earned his livelihood through farming, the traditional practice of the tribe.

After reaching the village, we carried on the conversation in Virumandi's home, surrounded by his mother, his wife, his children and Ganesha. We were later joined by Virumandi's father. The family lived in a three-room shack with mud walls that were painted bright blue on the inside.

I found out that my two friends from the Piramalai Kallar tribe were both about the same age. However, while Virumandi had twins who were barely three years old, Ganesha's son was married. Virumandi explained to me that the tribe was so close-knit that even his young children knew every tribe member.

'How is that possible?' I asked.

'We have not mingled with other communities, so we remain very small. In ancient times—much before the caste system was established in India—the Piramalai Kallar tribe was isolated physically and culturally. Later, it was considered "dangerous" by the British, so much so that every male member was to appear at the police station at 6 p.m. each evening, submit a thumbprint, and sleep behind bars all night in police custody. In present times, our tribe, much like many other communities in the south of India, allows marriage only among cousins.'

'Is this to keep your community closed to any outside influence?'

'No, it is because we have a system,' Virumandi explained. 'We first look among the mother's side of the family for a cousin who is the same age as the prospective groom or bride. The community then comes together and discusses the match. If the community feels that their temperaments do not match, we look at the next in line on the mother's side of the family in order of age. If we find no one, then we look on the father's side.'

'Does the couple have to accept the marriage arranged by the community?' I asked.

'If a person refuses to marry the son or daughter of a maternal uncle as proposed by the community, there is a fine of Rs 1 lakh that this person has to pay to the rejected candidate,' Virumandi explained.

'Does anyone marry outside the tribe?'

'It has happened twice as far as I can remember. One time the couple soon committed suicide, and the other time they escaped from Tamil Nadu,' he said.

'How would you react if your son wished to marry a girl outside the tribe?' I asked Virumandi.

'I would not encourage it, but I would accept his choice. We have to change with the times,' he replied.

'How about you?' I turned to Ganesha, who had told me about his still unmarried younger son.

'I will not allow it,' he said in Tamil, which was translated for me by Virumandi.

'Why?' I asked. I had gathered by then that Ganesha could understand English, but could not speak it.

'Marriage for love fails. Just look around you. A young couple needs the support of the family to guide them during the ups and downs of life. If my son marries outside the community, he loses his tribe. This is the tradition,' Ganesha replied.

'So are there no divorces in your system?' I asked Virumandi.

'If the couple quarrels, the community comes together to counsel them both. If the quarrels continue and no mediation is possible, the community decides that the couple must separate. The court is never involved in the separation. A divorce is not recorded in the court,' he explained.

'What about remarriage?' I inquired. 'Does that happen?'

'Yes, of course. The community again looks for suitable partners for the separated girl and boy.'

'Is there a minimum age for marriage?' I asked.

'No. The community prefers to wait and find the right match rather than marry a person off in a hurry. We want to make sure that our children are handed over to good companions who will care for them after the parents die,' Virumandi replied.

The traditions by which life must be led in a community are different all over the world. But in India, thousands of diverse communities coexist—more than anywhere else—with distinct traditions and practices dating back thousands of years, and often passed down from generation to generation. The genetic analysis of India's population sheds some light on the reason for its social diversity. Many shared behaviours and physical characteristics, like the colour of one's skin, as well as the culture and traditions of members of a community, can be scientifically traced back to the variations produced not by separate origins, but ironically by the intermixing of genetic compositions, as well as local conditions such as weather and food. Let us see how.

Virumandi's ancestors first arrived in India (on their way to Australia) during the first coastal migration 60,000 years ago. This was a small group, and their progeny is still found in some parts of the Western Ghats, the eastern plains, and in some places across north-east and central India.

The second wave of migration that occurred about 50,000 years ago from Africa brought a different genetic mutation, NRY HG F*-M89, to India. This wave was more successful in spreading. The mutation is seen in many populations in the Deccan and in south India, and in some places in Gujarat and the north-east, interestingly, without any distinctions of castes and tribes.[16]

The third wave of migration consists of the majority of the early settlers in the Indian subcontinent. The subcontinent received many gene pools via migration from both the east and the west of India during the Neolithic period.[17] This explains the various languages and cultures found here. Males with the NRY HG O2a-M95 mutation arrived at the north-eastern Frontiers 10,000 to 5000 years ago from Laos, with their Austro-Asiatic language, to expand and give rise to the Munda language. From Central Asia to the west of India, many streams of Neolithic people carrying the M304 and M207 mutations arrived, bringing with them technology for rearing cattle, which became their

---

[16] Kumar, Prasad et al. 2012, 6.

[17] Recent research by Analabha Basu, Neeta Sarkar-Roy and Partha P. Majumder at the National Institute of Biomedical Genomics in Kalyani, West Bengal, says that Indians have five ancestral stocks, not two—one ancestral to all north Indians and the other to all south Indians—as was believed earlier. The three additional ancestries discovered were the Austro-Asiatic, the Tibeto-Burman, and an ancestral lineage dominant among the Jarawa and Onge tribals of Andaman and Nicobar Islands that was found to be similar to the present-day Pacific Islanders (Basu, Sarkar-Roy and Majumder 2016).

mode of subsistence as they settled. The largest expansion within the M 207 clade was of the people carrying the R1a1-M17 and R2-M124 mutations with their Indo-European language settling across the whole of the Indo-Gangetic region and north of the Vindhyas.[18] Each of these groups established their own traditions and ways of life, distinct from the others.

Professor Pitchappan's research shows that in the south of India, there had, in fact, been no intermixing, through migration or marriage, between the various subsistence-based Dravidian communities in the past 3000 years. The mode of subsistence, such as fishing on the coast, dryland farming in the interior regions in rain shadow, and hunting and gathering in the hilly tracts, played a dominant role in ensuring that the communities remained geographically fixed. This gave rise to a highly stratified society with distinct occupational communities in Tamil Nadu, which continues even today. And this much before the establishment of the caste system in the subcontinent!

Geographical and cultural isolation led the Dravidians to inbreed, which in turn resulted in the development of unique genetic signatures as well as cultural practices and traditions in each of them. Simply put, endogamy further sharpened the boundaries of these communities. So the M89 mutation remains concentrated in the hill tribes of the Western Ghats, the M20 mutation is found in 50 per cent of the population in Tamil Nadu and is characteristic of the Dravidian population, whereas the M17 and M205 mutations are found in the Vellala and Brahmin–related populations of south India.[19]

Much later, in the Bronze Age, the caste system or the varna scheme—the basis of the current practice of the Hindu

---

[18] Kumar, Prasad et al. 2015a, 546.
[19] Kumar, Prasad et al. 2015b, 493.

stratification of society according to birth—began to further divide communities by establishing for each a hereditary occupation, and the endogamy and preservation of its traditions. The strict ranking of the various castes prescribed by the caste system also created a general deference to hierarchy that ensured the continuation of these practices across generations.

The caste system often gives rise to the fallacy that different communities have separate origins—and it does so through a hymn! In the earliest instance of the social institutionalization of the varna system, the *Purusha Sukta* hymn of the Rig Veda (10.90)[20] said that the four social classes emerged from the Purusha, who was considered the original sacrificial victim. In the hymn, the Brahmins came from Purusha's mouth, the Kshatriyas (warriors) from his arms, the Vaishyas (merchants) from his loins, and the Shudras (servants) from his feet. Since Brahmins were said to have emerged from the mouth of the Purusha, it was assumed that they must enjoy the highest status. But there have been historical criticisms of the Brahmin claims to superiority. For instance, in about 500 BC the Buddha referred to the *Purusha Sukta* hymn, pointing out that anyone could see that the Brahmins had emerged not from the mouth of the Purusha, but from the same female bodily organ as everybody else. Yet the belief is prevalent among Hindus even today.

I will expand more on the subject of caste in a subsequent essay in this book, but for our present argument, it is important to note that even in the establishment of the caste system, communities were formed due to historical developments and

---

[20] The ancient hymns of the Vedas, transmitted orally from the Bronze Age (1500–1200 BC), were not written down until thousands of years later. One of the hymns, *Purusha Sukta*, mentions that the entire cosmos as well as human society came into being out of primordial sacrifice.

our interpretations of them. In reality, it is utterly needless to say that we have all indeed originated from the vagina of a woman in Africa. We continue to exist as a species today because the earliest humans in Africa decided to walk out of the country in order to survive the Ice Age. As far as geneticists know, those humans out of Africa arrived in the south of India 10,000 years before they even reached Australia, the Americas, Europe or the rest of Asia.

The following day, Virumandi and I, dressed in our finery and with gifts in hand, set out for the three-hour drive to Professor Pitchappan's native village for the wedding. By now, I had seen Virumandi in his many avatars: research specimen, family man, tribesman, fellow wedding guest and more.

'If you were to describe Virumandi, what would you say?' I asked him.

'It depends on who's asking,' he said and laughed. 'If it was someone asking me here in the market,' he said, pointing outside the window of our taxi, 'I would say Virumandi is a part of a tribe, speaks Tamil and lives in a village in Tamil Nadu. I would also explain the history of our community.' He paused and then added, 'But if someone in office asks me this question, I do not need to speak about my tribe.'

'And if you were to describe Virumandi to your own self, within a closed room, then what would you say?' I probed.

'You ask the most difficult questions!' Virumandi said with another laugh. 'I would say that Virumandi is an educated man who has a PhD in library sciences. He has learnt from each and every one of the researchers he has met because of M130, and he wants to rid his community of some bad things.'

He paused for a few moments, then added softly, 'You know, miss, we still kill our girl babies. I tell our community to stop this tradition, but it still happens.'

'Why are they killed?' I asked.

'It is a tradition that if the second child is a girl, she has to be killed within ten days. There are specific men in the tribe who know how to do it. They pluck leaves that secrete poison and feed them to the infant girl. She dies immediately,' he said.

'But how do parents allow this?'

'Parents do not want to pay the dowry for a girl when she gets married,' he explained. 'Dowry is a tradition,' he added as we got off the car.

'So tradition has its dark side?' I asked.

'Yes, and only education can cure us of these terrible things,' he replied.

'You are the only person in your tribe who is so educated. How has it helped you?'

'Education does not mean just knowing how to read or write. Education means understanding the other person's point of view. Sometimes there are quarrels among people in the community. Because of my education, I know how not to react impulsively and stay calm, and I tell people who are fighting to do the same thing. I am able to sort out problems in the community.'

The wedding venue was spread across three large, traditional Nattukottai Chettiar homes, discontinuously located on a single muddy pedestrian street that led to the village temple at the end. The large banners that proclaimed 'Dr Valli weds Dr Thiyagarajan' were hard to miss.

'The professor belongs to a wealthy trader community called Chettiar,' explained Virumandi as we walked towards the house where the main ceremony was to be. 'Most of his family members work in banks or are big businessmen.'

'And clearly the new generation is made up of well-educated doctors!' I added, pointing to the gigantic wedding banners around us.

The house had a columned veranda in front, where about a hundred guests—mostly men—were sitting on the floor. The pillars, I was told by Virumandi, were made of Burma teak, the style unique to the Chettiar community living in this 100-square-mile area. About 20 feet away was a second row of Burma teak pillars on another slightly more raised veranda.

We entered the wedding like a happy couple—Virumandi and I—getting photographs clicked with the family on the way into the spacious inner courtyard, where there were now mostly women. We walked towards the entrance to the centre.

The professor was standing at the entrance with his hands folded. 'Welcome, Miniya,' he said with a smile. He asked Virumandi if our journey to the venue was comfortable.

The courtyard had thin teak pillars and a series of rooms on all sides. Virumandi pointed ahead to the bride and the groom, and explained to me that this was an arranged marriage between cousins, as per the community tradition.

'Yes, the bride and the groom did not know each other at all till the match was suggested, and then they met in a hotel alone for a half-hour to evaluate each other. This happened three months before the wedding day,' Professor Pitchappan told me.

References

Basu, Analabha, Neeta Sarkar-Roy and Partha P. Majumder. 2016. Genomic reconstruction of the history of extant populations of India reveals five distinct ancestral components and a complex structure. *Proceedings of the National Academy of Sciences of the United States of America* 113.6.

Bergman, Jerry. 2011. Louis Agassiz: Anti-Darwinist Harvard Paleontology Professor. *Acts & Facts* 40.3, pp. 12–14.

Butalia, Urvashi. 2000. *The Other Side of Silence*, first edition (Durham: Duke University Press).

Carmichael, Mary. 2012. Louis Agassiz exhibit divides Harvard, Swiss group. *Boston Globe,* 27 June.

Culotta, Elizabeth, and Ann Gibbons. 2016. Almost all living people outside of Africa trace back to a single migration more than 50,000 years ago. *Science | AAAS,* http://www.sciencemag.org/news/2016/09/almost-all-living-people-outside-africa-trace-back-single-migration-more-50000-years.

Dalrymple, William. 2015. The great divide: The violent legacy of the Indian partition. *New Yorker,* 29 June.

Darwin, Charles. 1859. *The Origin of Species,* first edition (London: John Murray).

French, Patrick. 2011. *India: A Portrait* (New York: Vintage Books).

Grehan, John R., and Jeffrey H. Schwartz. 2009. Evolution of the second orangutan: Phylogeny and biogeography of hominid origins. *Journal of Biogeography* 36.10, 1823–44.

Hoeveler, J. David. 2007. *The Evolutionists: American Thinkers Confront Charles Darwin, 1860–1920* (Lanham: Rowman & Littlefield).

Kumar, Arun, Ganesh Prasad et al. 2012. Correction: Population differentiation of southern Indian male lineages correlates with agricultural expansions predating the caste system. *PLOS ONE* 28 November, http://journals.plos.org/plosone/article?id=10.1371/journal.pone.0050269.

Kumar, Arun, Ganesh Prasad et al. 2015b. Genome-wide signatures of male-mediated migration shaping the Indian gene pool. *Journal of Human Genetics* 60.9.

Kumar, Arun, Ganesh Prasad et al. 2015a. A late Neolithic expansion of Y chromosomal haplogroup O2a1-M95 from east to west. *Journal of Systematics and Evolution* 53.6.

Menand, Louis. 2001. Morton, Agassiz, and the origins of scientific racism in the United States. *The Journal of Blacks in Higher Education* 34, p. 110.

Mookerji. Radhakumud. 1966. *Chandragupta Maurya and His Times* (New Delhi: Motilal Banarsidass Publishers).

Nott, Josiah Clark, and George R. Gliddon. 1854. *Types of Mankind: Or, ethnological researches, based upon the ancient monuments, paintings, sculptures, and crania of races, and upon their natural, geographical, philological, and biblical history* (London: Trubner).

Stott, Rebecca. 2013. Under the Microscope. Review of *Louis Agassiz, Creator of American Science,* by Christoph Irmscher. *New York Times Book Review,* 31 January.

Wells, Spencer. 2007. A family tree for humanity. https://www.ted.com/talks/spencer_wells_is_building_a_family_tree_for_all_humanity.

Wood, Michael. 2008. *The Story of India* (Random House).

2

Evolution

While India was mounting its freedom struggle, many of the country's nationalist leaders were living and studying in Europe, where modernity was the essence of the times. The Europeans had developed a missionary zeal for social change ever since their fifteenth- and sixteenth-century explorers had brought back with them reports of the 'backward' societies they had discovered in the rest of the world, which badly needed to change their 'barbaric' ways and become civilized and 'modern'.[1]

---

[1] Within that framework, there had been many perspectives. Auguste Comte in France explained that social change occurs primarily as the outcome of intellectual development, while Herbert Spencer in Britain was influenced by Darwin's theory of evolution to show, with empirical data, that every society goes through a series of fixed stages of evolution as a consequence of some sort of cosmic design over which man has no control. Spencer had thus explained the superiority of the Western cultures over others, as the latter were at an earlier stage of evolution than the former (Spencer 1860, 9–27).

Even in the America of the nineteenth century, anthropologist Lewis Henry Morgan had applied evolutionary principles to social phenomena, to explain that society moved inexorably through stages he termed as 'savagery', 'barbarism', and 'civilization' (Bock 1955, 123).

Contrary to these beliefs in Europe, the march for social progress in India had a very distinct character in which tradition and modernity would not be divorced from each other. There was so much to fix when political freedom was gained, and it was felt that both tradition and modernity could help lift us out of our miserable condition. We were not just poor, we were infected with several social illnesses such as female infanticide, child marriage, dowry and sati. We were also burdened with a terribly hierarchical society divided by caste, and our wonderfully diverse communities had developed cracks along religious lines. In addition, our self-confidence had been battered by the British, who ruled us for two centuries with their misplaced assumption of racial supremacy. India's nationalist leaders, led by Prime Minister Jawaharlal Nehru, set aside their European learnings at least in this context; even though they agreed that some beliefs had to be discarded, the traditions that nurtured us and made us who we were had to be preserved.

In Europe, social evolution meant successive, homogeneous and graded stages of development—a view established by the British evolution scientist Charles Darwin and philosopher Herbert Spencer, among others. In India, however, we made a deliberate choice to plan social progress such that our diverse communities would retain their distinct characters. We created an unusual political structure, a federation of states, in which each state was defined territorially by the cultural characteristics of its people. We decided to make laws to protect our minorities and their rights to a distinct script and culture, as well as the right to establish their own educational institutions. We even chose twenty-two constitutionally recognized languages instead of one. Indeed, we were influenced by the West in our project of nationhood—more on that in a subsequent essay in this book[2]—but we did not borrow their normative social project of modernity.

---

[2] See Chapter 8 titled 'Nationalism'.

The Preamble of the Indian Constitution clearly laid out this objective. The aim, it said, was 'to secure to all its citizens social, economic and political justice; liberty of thought, expression, belief, faith and worship; equality of status and opportunity, and to promote among them fraternity so as to secure the dignity of the individual and the unity and integrity of the Nation'.[3]

How much of that objective have we achieved within our framework where tradition and modernity coexists?

According to India's most recent census almost four out of ten Indians were illiterate[4] in 2015 133.5 million families were earning less than Rs 500 per month[5] and by 2017 as many as 163 million people did not have access to safe drinking water.[6] Our girls are unsafe, in part because of the skewed sex ratio of 940 females per 1000 males,[7] and forty-five million women are missing in our country because we kill our girl babies.[8] There has also been progress. Famines have been eliminated, life expectancy at birth has doubled from 32 years in 1947 to 66 years in 2012[9] and literacy has risen from 16 per cent in 1951 to 74 per cent (but female literacy is still at 65 per cent).[10]

However, some of the most downtrodden sections of the population—lower castes, religious minorities, Dalits and tribals—have gained the least from the nation's progress.

In Hinduism, India's majority religion, the caste or varna of an individual is predetermined by birth. In addition to the four historical varnas, most Hindus also belong to about 3000 contemporary

---

[3] Pylee 2003, 64.
[4] Das 2002, 28; Census of India 2011.
[5] Tewari 2015; Socio-economic Caste Census 2011.
[6] Water.org.
[7] Census of India 2011.
[8] Bongaarts and Guilmoto 2015, 241; *The Economist* 2017.
[9] World Health Organization.
[10] World Bank 2017; Rana and Sugden 2013.

sub-castes or jatis, many of which are social, occupational—the cobbler and weaver castes, for example—or geographic.[11] Brahmins (priests, teachers) are at the top of the four-caste hierarchy, followed by Kshatriyas (landholders, warriors, rulers). Vaishyas or banias (businessmen) come third, while Shudras (labourers, artisans) are last. The three upper castes have governed the country for 3000 years, even though about half of India belongs to the Shudra caste.[12] Besides this, 8.6 per cent of the population is tribal, and more than 16 per cent is made up of the casteless or 'untouchables'. These are some of the communities that have barely seen an improvement in the quality of life in the past seven decades.

Nowhere else on earth is a human being considered so repugnant to be deemed untouchable. And no other society has a hierarchy as rigid as the Indian caste system. Given at birth as a public marker of one's status in society, a lower-caste name is carried around like a burden.

An 'untouchable' has no choice but to remain so all his life—in India, you can change your religion, but not your caste or 'castelessness'. What does progress mean to him, then? An improvement in his caste status is not possible, so what are the other ways in which he can improve his life? Essentially, the issue of choice in social 'progress' in India is highly problematic because it raises the moral question of who determines progress—the agent of social change or the subject of it? Who decides that progress is needed, the direction it should take, and what it should look like? If the choice of progress is made by the supposed agents of change—the government, the private sector, not-for-profit agencies, religious organizations and so on—does that not

---

[11] In the varna system, each of the jatis broadly fits into one of the varnas, giving Hindus membership to a varna and jati each at birth. People of one jati often share a traditional vocation, and usually do not marry or dine outside the jati.

[12] Das 2002, 140.

simultaneously restrict the freedom of choice of the subject, the individual or the community in question? Moreover, ironically, if others are making choices for the individual, where is the progress? Isn't progress the ability to make a well-informed choice?

In this context I will take up examples of the three most desperate communities in India—first, a socially ostracized one such as the Devadasis of south India; second, the Adivasis; and third, the Muslims. The evolution of a nation is not just about the growth of its gross domestic product (GDP)—progress must be measured in terms of how opportunities for individuals in society have expanded. I would further argue that there is a need to look at what progress has meant specifically for the most socio-economically disadvantaged communities, such as the ones I examine in this essay.

At the outset, I should clarify one more point. I have read that there are two Indias—one that is primarily rural and dominated by caste, superstition and traditional beliefs; the second, an urban, elite culture, more national in its outlook, for whom caste and other social hierarchies do not matter. The economist Amit Bhaduri has called this a politically correct cliché. He writes:

(one is) the India that shines with its rich neighbourhoods, corporate houses of breathtaking size, glittering shopping malls and high-tech flyovers over which flow a procession of new-model cars. These are the images from a globalized India on the verge of entering the first world. And then there is the other India. The India of helpless peasants committing suicide, Dalits regularly lynched in not-so-distant villages, tribals dispossessed of forest land and livelihood, and children too small to walk properly yet begging on the streets of shining cities.[13]

---

[13] Bhaduri 2009, 47.

Author Aravind Adiga also calls the 'two Indias' the 'India of light' and the 'India of darkness'.[14] However, my intimate association with both, the metropolis and rural India, has taught me that this concept of the 'two Indias' cannot be further from the truth. The underlying issue of inequality plagues cities as well as small towns and villages. Urban poverty is rampant, as is poverty in the villages. Discrimination based on caste and class is as prevalent in the cities and the 'high society' of metropolises as it is in smaller towns; this is further amplified in the villages. Discrimination against women and the girl child is prevalent across all societal classes, in varying degrees and in different ways. There is only one India, because despite the exterior differences between cities and villages, our social ailments flow through all strata.

It was the year 2011, and it had been two years since I quit my job as a hedge fund manager in Paris to create my not-for-profit organization that worked on improving the education and health of women in the Middle East and India. This step had been a choice I made to live a more useful life. I wanted to help alleviate some of India's social challenges rather than make the European ultra-rich even richer via the hedge fund, a job I had gradually realized was rather pointless and not worth my precious life.

At that time, I was living in the sleepy little Swiss town of Geneva, where I also worked at the World Economic Forum, an organization that brought together world leaders from all fields to solve critical global problems. I was the only employee in the history of the World Economic Forum to own and run, in parallel, a private not-for-profit organization.

My fledgling organization was running a project located in another continent, thousands of miles away from Geneva. The aim of the project was to improve the education and health

---

[14] Adiga 2008, 12.

of women and children in Nizamabad, a small district in the southern state of Andhra Pradesh (now in Telangana) in India with a population of just over 300,000. It is four hours away by road from the city of Hyderabad, where the nearest airport is. In this unusual arrangement I had crafted for myself, I would fly out from Geneva at least one weekend every month on a twenty-hour journey, by air and by road, to arrive at Nizamabad. Then, with my six-member team, I would work towards renovating and improving the facilities of dilapidated anganwadis—rooms with a courtyard built by the government of India four decades ago for providing education and nutrition to preschoolers and expecting mothers. I had partnered with a global technology company to provide the children with learning tools and games on electronic tablets. I had also brought on board a Chennai-based pharmaceutical company which had agreed to supply to me, at cost price, prenatal multivitamin tablets, which I distributed to women at the anganwadis.

I had a team in place to carry out this work, but I was also on the lookout for a local from Nizamabad to give a boost to our work. For this, I established a master's degree scholarship at King's College in London for one underprivileged girl who displayed extraordinary leadership skills in community service. I had negotiated with King's College to waive the tuition fee for this candidate. I had naively thought I would find such a candidate in Nizamabad in the hope that she would continue overseeing the development work after my organization left.

This was why Rajvi Naidu,[15] the vice principal of the local college in Nizamabad, introduced me to Swapna.

'Swapna is exactly whom you are looking for,' Rajvi told me.

'Who is she?' I asked.

---

[15] Identity withheld.

'An eighteen-year-old girl in her final year of a Bachelor of Arts degree in our college,' she said. 'She belongs to the Devadasi community here.'

Devadasi is not a caste, but an occupational community that sprung up because of the caste system. The tradition of the Devadasi community, found mostly in the south and west of India, dates back several hundred years, with its popularity reaching a peak in the eleventh and twelfth centuries.[16] The basic premise of the Devadasi tradition was to make girls who reached puberty dedicate their lives to the service of God. They took care of temple rites, danced and sang in their rites of worship.

However, during British rule, the kings who were the patrons of temples and temple arts became powerless. As a result, the Devadasis were left without their traditional means of support and patronage from the royal families. In desperation, they turned to prostitution to support themselves. Gradually the practice withered to such an extent that Devadasis were expected to have sexual intercourse with men in the community, an obligation that had no relation to religion.[17]

'I thought that the practice had been abolished,' I said. As far as I knew, the Devadasi practice had been outlawed in 1988 on the grounds that it was akin to prostitution.[18]

'Yes, it has been abolished by law, but not by society,' Rajvi said softly.

I met Swapna the following day at Rajvi's office. After exchanging greetings, Swapna and I stepped out to the college sports field for a walk.

---

[16] Kaminsky and Long 2011, 168.
[17] Dalrymple 2008.
[18] Colundalur 2011.

'Madamji, why are you here?' she asked me before I could inquire about her.

'To meet you!'

'You have come from Geneva?'

'Yes.'

'I went to America once.'

'What were you doing there?'

'I got myself admitted in school here. My mother did not want me to, but I managed. I do not know who my father is,' Swapna explained in slow, broken English with a smattering of Hindi and Telugu (which I did not understand). 'Then, when I was nine I thought that I should bring together all orphans in my school because they must have had difficulties to study like I did. So I started The Child's Club. All orphans in my school were part of The Child's Club and we met and played together. One American organization heard about it and they got me to America to give them a speech about the club. They gave me an award.'

'That is wonderful. But why did your mother not want you to go to school?' I asked.

'She wanted me to follow our Devadasi tradition!'

'How do you like it in college here?'

'I like it, but it is difficult to attend classes.'

'Why?'

'I am a Devadasi. My people and my mother still do not want me to study. Some other people think I am bad and they do not want me to be with their children,' she said.

'Then how did you manage to complete school and enrol in college?'

'I told everyone that I did not want to follow the Devadasi tradition. I wanted to go to school. I had to fight my people. I live with my mother far away, outside Nizamabad, near the fields. It was difficult to come to school every day,' Swapna told me.

'Here, in college, it is difficult to attend all the classes. But vice principalji helps me. She tells the teachers to give me extra classes. Sometimes, she even arranges for my exams to be held later, only for me, when I cannot come to college for them. Vice principalji is very kind,' she added.

Swapna's teachers at the college had told me that Swapna was a good student, but she had to deal with the wrath of her community to pursue an education. Her actions had caused mayhem at home and almost ruined Swapna's relations with her mother, who, from what Swapna told me, would much rather have her daughter follow the community's traditions.

Before returning to Geneva, with Swapna's consent and as a precursor to her education in London, I arranged to have her sent to train during the summer at an organization in South Africa that mobilized local communities to overcome social challenges. I was glad to see Swapna excited about her trip.

On another visit to Nizamabad a few months later, I met Swapna again. She had just returned from South Africa with a marvellous new self-confidence. She seemed to have gained even greater strength to break the shackles that tradition had clamped on her. I was immensely hopeful. King's College had pointed out that English language skills would be the only requirement for Swapna because she had the remaining qualifications. I made arrangements to improve her English. Rajvi helped me by organizing English language classes for Swapna in Hyderabad.

The date of Swapna's departure for London was approaching and I was trying to raise funds for her living expenses and travel. London is an expensive city to live in, and I wanted Swapna to be financially comfortable so that she could get the most out of the experience.

The following month, I returned once again to Nizamabad for a few days to oversee our anganwadi projects.

'I've heard Swapna is not going to London,' one of the women at the local dispensary told me while I was making my usual rounds in the community.

'Who told you that?' I asked.

'That's what people around here are saying. In our tradition, Devadasis don't leave the temple,' she replied.

Later in the day, Rajvi called me. She sounded panicked.

'Maa, I tried to convince Swapna but she does not want to go,' she told me.

'Did you ask her why?'

'She is not telling me. I think she has a boyfriend here in Nizamabad, and he is telling her not to go!' said Rajvi, distressed.

The next day, a few others told me that the community had threatened Swapna and told her not to leave. I decided to speak to her.

'I cannot go to London, madamji,' Swapna told me.

'Is that a choice that *you* have made?' I asked her.

Swapna did not answer.

Swapna did not tell me why she declined the offer to study at King's College, and I chose to neither probe further, nor convince her. *She* had the right to decide for herself, irrespective of what decision *I* thought would be appropriate for her.

Consequently, I will never know the real reason why she declined. In many ways, I have always felt that Swapna's refusal was my failure. Should I have met her more often? Perhaps I should have engaged more with her mother. What else could I have done to bring her community on board? Making choices for individuals seemed to be the prerogative of the community in Nizamabad.

If the preservation of tradition could lead to progress, or if tradition and modernity could walk hand in hand—as our Constitution intended—I would celebrate that. But this is not always the case in India. The dogmatic observance of archaic rules of community, jati and caste supersedes individual volition and freedom. By no means am I opposing tradition, but my point is that if either 'modernity' or tradition hinders individual free will, that cannot be progress.

I was elated to be making myself useful in resolving some of the most critical issues in the world through my job at the World Economic Forum. But working with my tiny NGO in India also convinced me that firstly, I needed to return to India to be aware of the ground reality; and secondly, I needed to find a platform in India so that I could make an impact on a larger scale. The scope and outreach of my NGO was too small and the challenges in India were far too many and too large.

Another reason I felt I needed to return was that while we had brilliant development economists who had written on India, often based out of other countries, they rarely chose to be full-time practitioners in implementing the required changes. For instance, some environmentalists in India have been actively and vociferously engaged in protecting rivers and opposing large construction projects that damage the environment, but there are not many similar 'practising' economists at significant positions. Raghuram Rajan, the former governor of the Reserve Bank of India, broke this trend, but he left the role in 2016 after a stint of three years.[19] India's Planning Commission was replaced by the government's policy think tank, NITI Aayog, in 2015, and economist Arvind Panagariya from Columbia University in New York was brought in to head it, but he too left within two years. A number of other economists did not live in India, and their assessments of the challenges here were often made from universities and research institutes at a distance from the action in India. As a result, these assessments—however astute they may

---

[19] *Hindu Business Line* 2016.

be—were often based only on secondary reports, sample groups, and at times their consultancy experience with the non-academic world, there being no actual engagement. So I wondered how they could reveal an accurate picture of India's development.

While working at the World Economic Forum, I therefore searched various avenues for almost a year to find the best platform through which I could combine impact and scale to contribute. There were opportunities and offers that came my way from time to time, but I turned them down, mostly because they did not have the scale I was looking for.

On the afternoon of 26 February 2014, I had an exchange of phone messages:

'How are you doing?' wrote Naveen Jindal, a member of Parliament, and the owner of one of India's largest business conglomerates, Jindal Steel and Power, and a friend of mine.

'Doing well. Still trying to find a way to return and make myself useful to India,' I replied.

'Why don't you join me in politics here?'

'No, not politics.'

'Oh.'

'How about joining our company?' he inquired after a few minutes.

'I have been thinking about that.'

A week later, I flew to New Delhi to meet the chief executive officer of Naveen's company. Together, we carved out a new position for me—chief sustainability officer. I would be responsible for ensuring that the growth of Naveen's $3.6 billion company included the commensurate improvement of the lives of its employees and the well-being of local communities around their plants and factories. This included ascertaining that the surrounding air and water resources had not been polluted, and contributing to the development of our country in various other creative ways.

Three months later, I had started work at the Jindal Group's headquarters in New Delhi, moving to India after fourteen years of being abroad.

The company's production facilities were concentrated in the states of Odisha, Chhattisgarh and Jharkhand—which had large tribal populations. I spent the larger part of each month living in these areas, touring the forests and surrounding villages and our factory premises. Some of the tribes, such as the Birhor tribe of Jharkhand, were so primitive that they were on the verge of extinction.

To establish mines and plants, private companies had to acquire land belonging to the Adivasis, with their consent and at times accompanied with various development programmes such as those offering free education and skilled jobs for the landowners and their families. These are all well-intentioned attempts at modernization. The Birhor tribals, for instance, are traditionally expert rope makers, skilled in tying knots and making traps for hunting.[20] The Jindal Group provided them with industrial waste sacks—free of cost—from which they could extract jute to make ropes. Saranda was an Adivasi zone in Jharkhand where private companies had provided animal husbandry training to the Adivasi population. In the neighbouring Godda area, the Jindal Group had set up a formidable vocational college in which 60 per cent of all students were Adivasi; they had been enrolled in a specially designed programme to develop skills such as carpentry, welding, electrical goods repair. Their tuition, boarding, meals, study materials, and clothes were fully sponsored by the company.

However, all these efforts seemed fairly ironic because in reality the Adivasis had little use for the interference of private companies in their lives. They were reluctant to participate in the skills training

---

[20] Kumar and Kumar 2017.

programmes and take up jobs. Even the building of a road in the
Adivasi area made them apprehensive, for roads brought with them
external influences. The Adivasis I met were self-sufficient and
content with the resources they had, isolated from the tumult of the
modern-day world. Their path of progress, I felt, was not necessarily
the same as the one that we in urban pockets considered desirable.
I wondered, what gave us private companies the legitimacy to
'develop' the Adivasis? What gave us the right to believe that the
Adivasis did not know what was good for them? If their well-being
was our primary intention, why were we imposing on them a system
that *we* felt must be appropriate for them?

To make matters worse, the Adivasis were threatened by violent
insurgent groups—or Maoists—which claimed they were trying
to 'protect' them from modern developmental attempts. In an
essay titled 'Adivasis, Naxalites and Indian Democracy', published
in the *Economic and Political Weekly*, the historian Ramachandra
Guha has explained the failure of the formal political system in
India that has created a space for Maoist revolutionaries to occupy.
He writes:

> . . . there is a double tragedy at work in tribal India. The first
> tragedy is that the state has treated its Adivasi citizens with
> contempt and condescension. The second tragedy is that
> their presumed protectors, the Naxalites, offer no long-term
> solution either.[21]

The Maoists' primary aim, I gathered, was to capture power in
New Delhi, and they were using the Adivasis as a stepping stone
in this larger endeavour. Over the past few decades, the Maoists
had been living with tribal populations as the hills and forests of

---

[21] Guha 2007, 3305.

central India were well suited to their methods of roaming guerrilla warfare. Their violent actions had indeed occasionally protected and helped the Adivasis survive—for instance, the Maoists had procured for the Adivasis higher wages for labour in a landlord's field, and higher rates for the collection of forest produce. However, their involvement in the Adivasis' habitat and affairs has not been consensual. The Adivasis have suffered during Maoist attacks on the government,[22] being caught in the crossfire,[23] for instance, when security forces poured into the state of Chhattisgarh to restore the primacy of the Indian state against the Maoists.[24]

Apart from the corporates, the Maoists and the police, Christian and Hindu missionaries have also intervened in many Adivasi areas with schools and hospitals.[25] The Christian missionaries have been around since the fourteenth century,[26] while the Hindu missionaries have been active for a while as well.[27] They have been fairly successful in providing education to the Adivasis as well as in converting some of them to their own respective religious philosophies.

Modernization—just as much as tradition—is welcome only if it results in social progress. In India, however, despite all the modernization interventions, the Adivasis seem to have gained the least and lost the most. Let us compare the progress made by the Adivasis to some of the other backward classes in India. The literacy rate of Adivasis is only 59 per cent,[28] even lower than the Dalit literacy rate of 66 per cent.[29] Nearly 55 per

[22] Ganguly 2012.
[23] *Hindustan Times* 2017.
[24] *Al Jazeera* 2017.
[25] Hardiman 2008, 423–25.
[26] Neill 1986.
[27] Guha 2008.
[28] Firstpost 2015.
[29] Jaffrelot 2016.

cent of Adivasi schoolchildren drop out by the time they reach the upper primary level, which is more than the 40.8 per cent among India's total population. In addition, 70.9 per cent of Adivasi children drop out by the time they reach the secondary level,[30] a higher rate than the 56.1 per cent recorded among Scheduled Caste children. According to the World Bank, over 43 per cent of the Adivasi population in 2016 in rural India was poor,[31] while this was recorded as 29 per cent in the Scheduled Caste population.

I will point towards an aspect of the desperate state of Adivasis that I consider strikingly crucial for progress—their abject lack of freedom of choice. Hardly any of the interventions—by the government, private companies, Maoist groups or religious missionaries—has been the choice of the Adivasis. In the name of modernization and development, which the Adivasis have rarely asked for, others have often caused mayhem in their once-peaceful habitat. So what progress are we talking about here? There can be no progress without freedom. By imposing our version of modernity on them, we have robbed the Adivasis of even the freedom to chart their own destiny.

Choice can be achieved through various channels of democracy. In this context too, Dalits and lower castes have been more successful than the Adivasis. The former have managed to establish themselves as major interest groups on the national stage, while the Adivasis have not. Dalits and Scheduled Castes are evenly distributed across India and are important vote banks for politicians so as to sway the outcome of state and national elections. Dalits also have successful political parties such as the Bahujan Samaj Party, which has been in power in India's

---

[30] Statistics of School Education 2010–11.
[31] World Bank 2017.

largest state, Uttar Pradesh. They have an efficient second rung of activists who know how to build political networks nationwide.

On the other hand, the Adivasis, demographically concentrated in India's densest forests, do not constitute a vote bank large enough to be considered significant. We have never had an Adivasi Ambedkar, a leader of pan-Indian significance, who could be a role model. In the past five decades, the Adivasis have sometimes expressed their public and collective discontent with the policies and programmes of the state, but their protests—in Bastar in 1966, in Jharkhand in the late 1970s, among others—have been led by traditional Adivasi leaders who were largely irrelevant at the national level. Only in some cases, such as in the Narmada Bachao Andolan, have Adivasis been mobilized by non-Adivasi social activists from an urban background.

About seventy million of these Adivasis live in the heart of India, across the states of Gujarat, Rajasthan, Maharashtra, Madhya Pradesh, Chhattisgarh, Jharkhand, Andhra Pradesh, Telangana, Odisha, Bihar and West Bengal.[32] However, another 10.2 million or so tribals live in the north-east of India.[33] I shall not include these tribes in this particular argument because they differ from their tribal counterparts in the peninsula in terms of socio-economic progress for at least two crucial reasons. One, the chances of their absorption into the Indian (or even global) economy is higher, thanks mostly to their English language skills and higher literacy rate. And so they have gained a large share in the Scheduled Tribes quota in government and civil services jobs, reserved seats in universities, as well as jobs in private companies that need communication skills. Two, they have been largely

---

[32] Guha 2007, 3305.
[33] Fernandes 2007, 1.

exempt from the trauma caused by land dispossession because of their location in a corner of the country.

I will now take up the goriest example that relates to another socio-economically disadvantaged group in India.

The partition of the Indian subcontinent into Hindu-majority India and Muslim-majority Pakistan in August 1947 led to one of the deadliest migrations in human history. In a blatant violation of freedom of choice, Muslims in India were forced to trek to West and East Pakistan (the latter is now known as Bangladesh), and the Hindu inhabitants of those regions were forced to move to India. In the process, more than fifteen million people were uprooted, and between one and two million died.[34] Most Muslims who live in India today—making up 14.23 per cent of India's population[35]—are those remaining from that great migration to Pakistan. Either out of choice or compulsion, they did not leave. Ever since, they have had to bear the consequences of history.

Hindus can never seem to forget the million-odd Hindus who were killed during Partition, but they do forget that a nearly equal number of Muslims were also killed by Hindus.[36] They also hold against Muslims the earlier military invasions and conquests of the Mughals from the north, which took place hundreds of years ago.

Even today, it is only to a certain extent that Indian Muslims have benefited from democracy. For instance, there is not a single state government till date that employs Muslims in proportion to

---

[34] Dalrymple 2015.

[35] According to the most recent census in 2011, 79.8 per cent of the Indian population is Hindu, while 20 per cent of Indians follow other religions, of which 14.23 per cent—India's largest minority population—are Muslim, and the rest are Sikh, Christian, Parsi, Buddhist or Jain.

[36] Dalrymple 2015.

their share in the state's population. The number of Muslims in government jobs has indeed risen from 5 per cent a decade ago to 8.5 per cent in 2014–15,[37] but this is still abysmally below their proportion in India's population.

There are, however, Muslims who have risen to become prominent political leaders, including Dr Zakir Hussain and Dr A.P.J. Abdul Kalam, former Presidents of India. The presence of Muslim leaders in high-level politics dates back to the Indian National Congress. As Guha wrote in his book *Democrats and Dissenters*: 'Even before Gandhi assumed its leadership, the Congress had to face the charge that it was essentially an upper-caste Hindu party. To combat this criticism it had to reach out to Muslims and lower castes.' This practice of presenting a pro-Muslim image and agenda and putting up Muslim political representatives continues in most national and regional political parties. Since Muslims represent a large percentage of the population in India, politicians have indeed needed to be attentive to their votes, but much of that may be mere lip service. In Muslim-dominated parts of Delhi, the local politicians are often Muslims as well, yet the areas they are responsible for often remain underdeveloped. In most other parts of our country too, the economically depressed condition of Indian Muslims is testimony to the fact that democracy has not helped the community much.

The rate of Muslim literacy is far less than that of other sections of society. The current gross enrolment rate of Muslims in higher education is 13.8 per cent, much lower than the pan-Indian figure of 23.6 per cent.[38] The literacy rate among Muslim adult males is 81 per cent, compared to 91 per cent among Hindus, 94 per cent among Christians and 84 per cent among Sikhs, according

---

[37] Haq 2016.
[38] Bahri 2016.

to a report of the National Sample Survey Organization.[39]
The literacy rate of Muslims has, however, risen from 59.1 per
cent in 2001 to 68.5 per cent in 2011, even though the rate of
their work participation continues to be the lowest among all
minorities.[40]

Muslims have, at times, even sought low-quality but free
education in government schools as well as in religious schools
or madrasas. Some of India's greatest historians and educationists
have been Muslims. Sir Syed Ahmad Khan, the founder of the
Aligarh Muslim University, and the historian Irfan Habib are
just a few examples. They are not only learned but also resilient,
succeeding despite the extraordinary forces pulling them down,
and they have helped the members of their community to learn,
earn and rise.

I first met Bano and Adnan Farooqui[41] in 1998 at Jawaharlal
Nehru University (JNU) in New Delhi, where Adnan was a
professor at the Centre for the Study of Regional Development
(CSRD). Bano and Adnan had been married thirty years, and
they had a daughter and two sons. I first met the family because of
the younger son, with whom I would go on to live as a domestic
partner across seven countries over a span of eight years—more on
that some other time. But this is how I joined him in calling his
mother Bano 'Ammi' (mother) and father Adnan 'Abbu' (father).
A large part of my understanding of the Muslim population in
India comes from this experience.

Living in India's capital city, New Delhi, my educated and
otherwise rational parents had prohibited me from interacting

---

[39] Haq 2016.
[40] Ministry of Minority Affairs 2016; Phadnis 2016.
[41] Identity withheld.

with the son of the Farooquis. At age nineteen, I was grounded and prohibited from attending university for several days until it was confirmed that I would have nothing more to do with a Muslim boy.

My family's is a point of view from among the educated lot in India's capital city. The condition is more sinister in small towns and rural India, where people may be more strongly bound to historical animosity. In cities as well as villages, many cases of murder over religious animosity go unreported.

On the other hand, I remember Ammi as smashing every stereotype. She was a soft-spoken, graceful, traditionally dressed Muslim woman, but more modern in the mind than anyone else I knew. She fiercely supported me all along, recognizing the societal challenges that any educated, independent-minded girl would face. Abbu was more involved in my academic research than my parents, perhaps because he too had struggled for an education.

Abbu hailed from Kanpur in central India, and he was brought up in a low-income Muslim family of seven siblings. Born a few years before India's independence, he was the only one among the seven to get a basic education. He moved to New Delhi in his early twenties, initially to work as a laboratory assistant for statistics under the guidance of Professor Moonis Raza, the founding chairman of CSRD at JNU. Raza was also Muslim. Alongside his job, under Raza's mentorship, Abbu went on to pursue a PhD on the statistical methods deployed in geographical studies.

Raza himself was a luminary. During the course of his academic career, he was chairman of the Indian Council of Social Science Research, president and vice chancellor of Delhi University, rector of JNU, and director of the National

Institute of Educational Planning and Administration. Abbu often spoke fondly of Raza and the liberal ethos and open-minded culture he had established at JNU.

Abbu kept himself above conflict. It was as if the ugly communal reality outside the gates of the campus where he and his family lived could never touch him. He was a practical and plain-speaking man who would rarely ever display any great emotional crests and troughs. His colleagues and students were equal in his eyes, irrespective of religion.

Even then, upon Abbu's retirement from the university—which meant he would have to relinquish the elegant campus accommodation—he and Ammi chose, without much deliberation, to move to an area in Delhi that was known to be a Muslim ghetto.

Shaheen Bagh, located in the eastern part of Delhi, has a predominantly Muslim, uneducated populace working in tiny shops along narrow, garbage-strewn roads. The entire area was a winding maze—I do not remember a single time that I had been able to find my way to the new Farooqui home without an SOS phone call to them for help with directions. The local municipality councillor and the member of the Legislative Assembly at that time were both Muslim; yet the development of the area had been grossly neglected. For many years, the only other large construction in the area, besides the Farooqui family's home, had been the local mosque, while the rest were shops akin to holes in the wall.

The Farooqui family felt that Shaheen Bagh would serve as a safety net for them. Ensconced within the protection of their own community, they would be unharmed if any anti-Muslim riots broke out. They felt safest among other Muslims. Many of Abbu's Muslim colleagues had also moved there after retirement for the same reason.

The feeling of persecution and the threat of impending poverty are two of the biggest issues weighing on the minds of the deprived sections of society in India. More than the average population, Muslims tend to have jobs in the informal sector, which are usually without a written contract or a regular salary.[42] At the time of writing, not even one of India's top twenty largest businesses has been founded, or is run, by a Muslim. According to the 2011 Census, 24.9 per cent of the 370,000 beggars and homeless people in India are Muslim, which is disproportionately high given that Muslims make up 14.23 per cent of India's total population. Meanwhile, Hindus make up 79.8 per cent of the population, and have a share of 72.22 per cent (268,000) in the total beggar population. On the other hand, Christians, representing 2.3 per cent of India's population, make up 0.88 per cent of India's beggars, and Sikhs, who are 1.72 per cent of India's population, constitute 0.45 per cent.[43]

Democracy has, therefore, not served to expand freedom of choice for India's poor.

By the time I returned to India to take up my role at the Jindal Group, I was no longer in touch with the Farooquis. But I had heard that the family had left their sprawling home in Shaheen Bagh to move to a much smaller apartment in a more culturally diverse colony in west Delhi. Poverty and crime were on the rise in Shaheen Bagh, and some of the roads had gradually become so narrow that even a bicycle could hardly make its way through. For the same reasons, their other Muslim peers from academia had also been forced to make the same move.

---

[42] Social, Economic and Educational Status of the Muslim Community of India 2006.

[43] Census of India 2011.

The journey of socio-economic progress for various groups in politically free India has been different. Democracy has been a game of snakes and ladders for different sections of Indians to improve their social and economic conditions. In this game, some have gained and some have lost. Then there are those who have found that while caste is not negotiable, economic status is. They have worked hard to change the destiny that they were born with. India is a tough place to live—the opportunities are few, the level playing fields fewer, and many people are seeking the same goal.

One factor in the success stories is the renewed respect for hard work in India. For the first time in our history, the new millionaires are looked up to with pride and reverence, in contrast to an earlier era when the newly rich were objects of scorn and derision. Earlier, the 'old bourgeoisie' with inherited wealth and families even remotely connected to royalty would look down upon the toil and enterprise of farmers and labourers. They felt that those who worked hard were ideologically barren, without any social class or manners. However, those with a rags-to-riches story are now considered role models who have proved the success of hard work and merit. We have plenty of success stories such as those of Dhirubhai Ambani, Sunil Mittal and Om Prakash Jindal who hailed from modest backgrounds but built massive business empires. Indians marvel that even though Dhirubhai Ambani's first trading office was so small that it could not accommodate more than four people, when he died in July 2002, his business empire was worth over $12 billion.

It is the ability to make and implement an informed choice that ultimately plays a vital role in shaping who we want to be and the life we seek. Choice is a rational decision that determines change. But only when a free and informed choice can be made will we be deemed to have made progress. The meaning and path (or the lack of it) of progress (or the lack of it) have been unique and different for each of the backward communities in India. For some, it has meant gaining political power. For others, it has meant improving their financial conditions, while for many others, it has meant just leading a more dignified life. The realization of progress has invariably depended upon the ability of members of a backward community to also implement their choice of how to lead their lives, without the constraints of tradition, the forces of modernization, and the limitation of the surroundings. That choice could be anything—to continue one's life in the forest or to get a job at a factory; to live in a Muslim neighbourhood or not; whether or not to be bound by community traditions; to get an education or not; to start a business and make it grow.

In India, we do not all have equal freedom of choice. We also have different levels of resources granted to us to implement that choice. A man enjoys a larger set of options for earning his living than a young woman, as she is under greater pressure from society to abide by age-old clichés and stereotypes. A wealthy man who openly declares his homosexuality has a greater chance of acceptance than a common man, who might be immediately targeted by the society for being gay. Even though the caste system—of pursuing an occupation according to one's varna or jati—has been dismantled to a large extent, the 'caste identity' persists and influences every sphere of life, be it politics, marriage, or societal relations. A person of a higher caste, say a Brahmin, benefits from having many more choices than a man belonging to the Shudra caste, who might be disadvantaged in job interviews, on social networks and even in romance and love because of his family name, heritage, and upbringing. And so I have often wondered if Swapna could simultaneously ever have the choice in India to be—or not to be—a sexually independent woman and free to get an education anywhere while also being a member of the Devadasi community?

Education offers us a chance to know and understand the choices available to us, but in India, education does not always empower us enough to implement these choices. Progress is made only when an individual can make an informed choice and is able to implement that choice freely. Until our most backward communities are able to do this, we cannot say that India is progressing.

References

Adiga, Aravind. 2008. *The White Tiger* (Noida: HarperCollins India).

Al Jazeera. 2017. India's Maoist rebels: An explainer. 26 April.

Bahri, Charu. 2016. Muslims at bottom of higher-education ladder, alongside backward tribes. Indiaspend, 22 July.

Bhaduri, Amit. 2009. *The Face You Were Afraid to See: Essays on the Indian Economy* ((New Delhi: Penguin Books India).

Bock, K.E. 1955. Darwin and social theory. *Philosophy of Science* 22, pp. 123–34.

Bongaarts, John, and Christophe Z. Guilmoto. 2015. How many more missing women? Excess female mortality and prenatal sex selection, 1970–2050, *Population and Development Review* 41.2, pp. 241–69.

Census of India 2011. http://censusindia.gov.in.

Colundalur, Nash. 2011. Devadasis are a cursed community. *Guardian,* 21 January.

Dalrymple, William. 2008. Serving the goddess: The dangerous life of a sacred sex worker. *New Yorker,* 4 August.

Dalrymple, William. 2015. The great divide: The violent legacy of the Indian partition. *New Yorker,* 29 June.

Das, Gurcharan. 2002. *India Unbound,* first edition (New York: Anchor Books).

Economist (US). 2017. The war on baby girls winds down. 21 January.

Fernandes, Walter. 2007. The Indian indigenous peoples for sixty years. *North Eastern Social Research Centre,* p. 1.

Firstpost. 2015. Literacy rates of scheduled tribes far below national average, says Parliamentary panel. 15 March.

Ganguly, Meenakshi. 2012. Between two sets of guns. *Human Rights Watch*, 6 July.

Guha, Ramachandra. 2007. Adivasis, Naxalites and Indian democracy. *Economic and Political Weekly*, vol. 42, no. 32, pp. 3305–3312.

Guha, Ramachandra. 2008. Lost in the woods. *Hindustan Times*, October 23.

Hardiman, David. 2008. *Missionaries and Their Medicine: A Christian Modernity for Tribal India* (Manchester and New York: Manchester University Press).

Haq, Zia. 2016. Untouched by economic growth: One in 4 beggars in India a Muslim, reveals census. *Hindustan Times*, 30 July.

Hindu Business Line. 2016. Raghuram Rajan to quit after term ends. 18 June.

Hindustan Times. 2017. Sukma ambush in response to gang-rapes, murders by security forces: Maoist statement. 28 April.

Jaffrelot, Christophe. 2016. Dalits still left out. *Indian Express*, 18 February.

Kaminsky, Arnold P., and Roger D. Long. 2011. *India Today: An Encyclopedia of Life in the Republic* (Santa Barbara: ABC-CLIO).

Kumar, Jai, and Rajni Kant Kumar. 2017. Assessment of development plan and protection for Birhor community of Duru Kasmar village, Mandu, Jharkhand. *IOSR Journal of Humanities and Social Science* 22.05, pp. 77–82.

Ministry of Minority Affairs, Press Information Bureau, Government of India 2016. http://pib.nic.in/newsite/mbErel.aspx?relid=147450.

Neill, Stephen. 1986. *A History of Christian Missions* (Penguin Books).

Phadnis, Aditi. 2016. Story In numbers: Muslim literacy rates rising faster than work participation. *Business Standard*, August 1.

Pylee, Moolamattom Varkey. 2003. *Constitutional Government in India* (New Delhi: S. Chand Publishing).

Rana, Preetika, and Joanna Sugden. 2013. India's record since Independence. *Wall Street Journal*, 15 August. https://blogs.wsj.com/indiarealtime/2013/08/15/indias-record-since-independence.

S., Rukmini. 2017. Five charts that tell sad and surprising stories about suicides in India. Huffington Post India, 3 January.

Social, Economic and Educational Status of the Muslim Community of India. 2006. http://mhrd.gov.in/sites/upload_files/mhrd/files/sachar_comm.pdf.

Socio-economic Caste Census. 2011. http://secc.gov.in/reportlistContent.

Spencer, Herbert. 1860. The social organism. *Westminster review* 17.

Statistics of School Education. 2010. http://mhrd.gov.in/sites/upload_files/mhrd/files/SES-School_201011_0.pdf.

Tewari, Saumya. 2015. 75 percent of rural India survives on Rs 33 per day. *India Today*, 13 July.

Water.org. 2017. India water crisis: Clean water scarcity In India. https://water.org/our-impact/india.

World Health Organization. http://www.who.int/countries/ind/en.

World Bank. 2017. https://data.worldbank.org/indicator/SE.ADT.LITR.ZS.

3

Exploration

We have made it incredibly difficult for ourselves to roam freely.

The last time I landed at the Lahore airport in the summer of 2013, I was greeted by a man in a Western-style suit without a tie, wearing a badge with his name and holding up a placard with my name on it. I was visiting to conduct meetings on behalf of the World Economic Forum with our stakeholders in Pakistan, and so I presumed that he had been sent by my official hosts in the country. He completed all my immigration formalities, picked up my bags, and put me in a taxi to the Pearl Continental hotel. The next four days were filled with meetings with various political and business leaders in Lahore and Islamabad. I also got to experience the warm, generous hospitality of the friends I made among my professional acquaintances. It was time for me to head to the airport again, this time to take my late-night flight back to Geneva. At the penultimate check, the immigration officer held me back.

'You cannot board this plane,' he said.

'Why not?' I asked.

'You are Indian. Indians are supposed to report to the local police station in the city and register themselves there. You have not done so.'

'But I did not know . . .' I started to explain.

'Here, take her inside.' The immigration officer beckoned to a colleague standing close by, and pointed to a room on the other side of the immigration hall.

The room turned out to be the Lahore airport police station.

'Should we let her go?' one cop asked the other in what I thought was Punjabi.

'No . . . let's keep her,' the other chuckled, looking at me seated across the desk.

I was allowed to pick up my luggage as I was offloaded from the aircraft.

'I am so sorry . . . The citizens of both countries are friendly, it is just that the military and politics keep us apart,' said a Pakistani man as I turned my suitcase around to drag it back to the airport police cell, accompanied by a few policemen.

After a few phone calls to my hosts in the city, at around dawn the following day, the police let me go and I returned to my hotel in Lahore. I didn't sleep a wink as I waited for my worried hosts to visit me at the hotel.

'I did not know I had to register with the police upon arrival,' I told them.

'Did they give you any such instructions when you were at immigration while entering the country?' they asked.

'I wouldn't know—the man you had sent to the airport . . . he did my immigration procedures,' I said.

'Which man?'

'The man wearing a badge, standing at the gate holding a placard with my name, the one you sent.'

'But we sent nobody!'

After a few more visits to the police, I was finally able to fly out of Lahore the following day. Only later did I find out that the man assisting me at the airport had been sent by Pakistan's Inter-Services Intelligence, and that he had gathered all the information from my passport and probably also covertly followed me to my meetings in the country.

The following year, when the World Economic Forum again applied for a visa for me at the Pakistani consulate in Geneva, all it received were weeks of silence and inaction. Despite follow-up inquiries made at the ministerial level in Pakistan, there was no news. Until one morning when, while on my way to work, I received a phone call.

'I am calling from the Pakistani consulate,' a man announced at the other end.

'Thanks for this call. I had applied for a visa for my work trip to Lahore, which is in two days!' I exclaimed, delighted to finally hear from the consulate.

'I am calling to tell you that there is no visa application from you,' he said.

'What do you mean?'

'I mean that your application never existed. Even if you get whomsoever in Pakistan to help, you will still not get a visa,' he explained in an icy voice.

'Why not?'

'Diplomatic reciprocity, beti,' he said coldly, and disconnected the call.

This is an example of the difficulties faced in exploring India's contentious neighbourhood. Migrants who travel to more distant countries to live there for long periods, sometimes permanently, must face even greater challenges. How ironic it is that we ourselves have cut up the planet with political borders, such that we need to take great pains to now cross them. Diplomatic relations, immigration policies, visas, national and international laws, work permits—these are all structures and procedures of our own making, intended to secure our borders in order to protect us, yet they restrict the free movement and exploration that our species was once naturally meant for.

I therefore find it admirable that in each of the eight countries—France, Germany, Belgium, the US, the UK, Egypt, China and Switzerland—I lived in over fourteen years, there has been a sizeable Indian migrant community. In Europe, where I lived for ten years, I noticed that people of particular communities in India did specific jobs in different cities to overcome the challenges of immigrant life. This was essentially the consequence of a grand chain reaction of learning from and following in the footsteps of those who had arrived earlier. In Paris, Indians worked in restaurants, set up shops selling cheap international phone calling cards and sold roses to tourists on the streets. In Berlin, a large number of Indians were nurses or medical doctors from Kerala.

To ease the hardship of living in a new country, the Indian community often live concentrated in one area, which is usually the outskirts of a city. They support each other by working together in the same area, thus creating a bustling quarter alive with Indian restaurants, the sound of loud cricket commentary, and colourful pirated Bollywood DVD stalls.

I conducted about three thousand interviews with these Indian migrants in Europe for my PhD research. I found many stories of how they courageously and painstakingly established themselves in a new country.

And so upon my return to India in 2014, I wondered more than ever why the large number of immigrants I met had made such valiant efforts to move *out* of the country to which I had just returned.

Our international diaspora is sixteen-million-strong, the largest in the world.[1] And even within India, four out of ten Indians—the combined population of the US, Germany and Canada—are migrants.[2] It seems that more than any other people in the world, we are ready to pack our bags and leave. Why?

I found all this bewildering because, first, looking at it sociologically, in a society where joint families are still the norm, a family member's immigration to another city or country has many socio-economic consequences. Second, from a religious point of view, the *Manusmriti*[3], the *Baudhayana Dharma Sutra*[4] and other religious scriptures at times specifically dissuade Brahmins from sea travel and impose penalties and penances on those doing so. Third, historically, the Indian subcontinent has been invaded several times, but we have rarely gone looking for new regions beyond the Himalayas to conquer.[5] Author Gurcharan Das[6] mentions the 'know-it-all Indian attitude' in his book *India Unbound*, which traveller Al-Biruni[7] has also described in his

---

[1] Menozzi 2016; Sims 2016.

[2] Saha 2016.

[3] Buhler 1886, 333; Olivelle ed. 1999, 134.

[4] Callahan 2013.

[5] The empire of Emperor Ashoka (268–232 BC) extended beyond Kandahar in the north, but did not go beyond Karnataka in the south, and did not encompass what is today north-east India (Alikuzai 2013, 64). Among the Guptas, Samudragupta (AD 336–80) did have an empire slightly beyond present-day Gujarat and Rajasthan. The Khiljis, under Alauddin Khilji (AD 1296–1316) ruled almost until Kandahar, once again. In the south, the Cholas, under Rajendra Chola I (AD 1014–44), controlled Sri Lanka.

[6] Das 2002, 10.

[7] Al-Biruni (AD 973–1048) was an Iranian scholar, mathematician, polyglot, and traveller who came to India around AD 1000, and wrote of it in his travelogue *Tahqiq ma li-l-hind min maqulah maqbulah fi al-aql aw mardhulah*.

writings on ancient India. I wondered then, if we are so bound
by political boundaries, visas, society, religion, geography, or—as
Das and Al-Biruni suggested—if Indians are simply not curious
enough, how is it that so many Indians now migrate to other
locations within the country and outside of it?

In fact, a great deal of scientific research has been done on
the psychology of curiosity that challenges Das's and Al-Biruni's
suggestions. Some absolutely fascinating research on curiosity was
conducted in two 'waves' of intense academic activity amongst
psychologists. The first wave, in the 1960s, focused on curiosity's
underlying cause. Psychologists speculated about why people
voluntarily sought curiosity-inducing situations such as mysteries
and puzzles. Some interpreted curiosity as a primordial drive and
viewed it as aversive, predicting that people would want to minimize
curiosity rather than seek it out. A few others—a limited number
of researchers in fact—examined the situational determinants
of curiosity. The first wave of curiosity research subsided before
the situationalist revolution in psychology could even take off.
The second wave began in the mid-1970s and concentrated on
the problem of measuring curiosity.[8] Can we correlate levels of
curiosity with individual characteristics such as age, gender, origin
and IQ? The researchers of the second wave conducted several
experiments, but every attempt to cross-validate the curiosity
scale with an individual's other traits failed. This means we cannot
determine if specific profiles of people are more or less curious than
those of others. We cannot say that people of a certain age group
are more curious than others, or that all women are curious while
men are not. We cannot, therefore, make the sweeping statement
that *all* Indians are disinterested, incurious and have a 'know-it-all
attitude'.

---

[8] Loewenstein 1994, 79; Langevin 1971.

There are, of course, several other approaches to curiosity studies, but they all seem to point to the same conclusion—that the adage 'curious by nature' cannot be true. For instance, another commonly studied aspect of curiosity is the dichotomy between state and trait curiosity. 'State curiosity', in academic literature, refers to the curiosity aroused by a particular situation. 'Trait curiosity' refers to the general capacity or propensity of a person to experience curiosity.[9] At the core of this discussion is the question: do situations make people curious or are some individuals just more curious than others? Does the situation in the pre-migration country of potential migrants make them curious about living in a new country, or is it just their 'innately curious nature'? After experiments, it was concluded once again that there was no curiosity trait per se in people—it was the environment that people lived in that made them curious. For example, an environment of mental stimulation at school can make a child curious about the world. The condition of slavery can evoke curiosity about freedom. A state of deprivation, say, in a dictatorship, can catalyse a revolution based on citizens' fascination for what they do not have. A country in which life is full of great hardship can make its citizens curious about what lies beyond and perhaps cause them to leave.

Why did I leave India many years ago?

When I was all of nineteen, my parents found their daughter's groom-to-be via a newspaper advertisement and a few photographs. I had met the boy twice.

The first time was at a dinner that my parents pleaded with me to attend. I found my parents' dream boy to be soft-spoken, and I noticed how he combed his hair with a neat parting on the side. He embodied the very definition of an ideal match in India—

---

[9] Ibid.

Bengali like me; Brahmin by caste, like me; an engineer from the Indian Institute of Technology (IIT), India's premier engineering school; a management graduate from IIM, another great Indian institution. And as if this seemingly made-to-order curriculum vitae for marriage was not good enough, I was told that he worked in a large global investment bank, and lived in Tokyo.

He was really lovely, and so, when our parents left us to talk in private for a few minutes, I told him I was not interested in marrying him, or anyone else, for that matter. I also told him I had a boyfriend who was Muslim, and that my parents were enormously paranoid about the outcome of that relationship. I explained to him that a few months ago, they had kept me locked up at home for days and prohibited me from going to university until I agreed to never meet my Muslim boyfriend again. But of course we continued to. The boy nodded his head at what I told him, and we returned to join our families at the dinner table. Pleased with myself for having closed this case, I never gave that evening another thought. The entire incident had just seemed very bizarre to me and I felt it was best forgotten.

A year later, I met the same boy for the second time due to the persistence of my father, who paid me a surprise visit at JNU, picked me up and dropped me off at a restaurant, where I found that the boy was waiting to meet me. Five minutes into the conversation, this boy gathered that I had not been told the news. So he gently informed me about our engagement which was to take place that evening. Rushing out of the restaurant, I took an autorickshaw to go home.

Robert Butler, in his book *Curiosity in Monkeys*, writes that monkeys kept in a colourless, shielded cage learnt to discriminate the colour of the window that would afford them a glimpse of what lay outside.[10] He compares this trait to that of humans who,

---

[10] Butler 1954.

like most animals, can be powerfully motivated by the situation they are in to explore outside that realm.

On my way from the restaurant that afternoon, I too felt trapped. Images from when I was six years old flashed in front of my eyes, of a priest who spoke in a language I did not understand, of my dismay at finding out that even my parents did not, and how nobody was interested in explaining to anybody the reason or meaning of the rituals. Ever since then, I had managed to find a way to not participate in religious rituals.

I remembered how, at fifteen, I had withstood the pressure to be an engineer simply because I did not want to become one. At seventeen, I remembered how I quit my first job within a week— which, to my father's delight, would send home a chauffeur-driven car to pick me up—because I did not want my precious hours spent on anything that lay outside my area of interest. I liked to eat nutritious food, dress well, buy plenty of books, go to a health club, play sports—to pay for all this, I worked on all kinds of odd jobs, from translating documents to being an usher at public exhibitions in the city for a few days each month. Despite my father's insistence, and much to his chagrin, I did not wish my middle-class family to take care of this extra expenditure, and would pay my expenses myself.

Sitting in the back seat of the autorickshaw, the wind hitting my face, I remembered how I would find our Bengali family weddings outlandish with their superficial display of wealth and chants no one understood. I remembered how I had hardly ever accompanied my parents to any of those weddings. I remembered how my parents had thus given up on me, proclaiming that I was just trying to be different from the rest.

Upon reaching home, I found that the news about my engagement was indeed true. Without saying much, I packed a few pieces of clothing into a sling bag and left home to live with two friends in the boarding facility of my university. I slept on the floor for six months before I got a room of my own, which I shared with another student. Between classes, I worked as a junior editor at a nearby magazine so that I could pay for my education. With no means of transport, I would walk to work and back to class several times a day.

A year later, I completed my degree with the best grades in my university. I enrolled in a master's degree course and returned home. But within days of my return, I discovered, hidden in a cupboard, a stack of continuing correspondence between my parents and their chosen groom for me—the same Bengali boy living in Tokyo. My parents had not given up.

This was the situation that motivated me to leave India. I was curious about the world, but my curiosity was not a strong enough factor to make me want to leave home. Instead, it was the situation that I felt trapped in that pushed me towards the decision.

Like Robert Butler's monkey in a cage, I immediately recognized a window of opportunity when it opened up.

One morning, a professor at my university called me to his office to say he would like to recommend my name for an academic fellowship to study for a year in Paris at Sciences Po, France's premier university. He asked me if I would be comfortable with that. After a brief conversation, I agreed. After a few months, I managed to win a monthly student stipend of €624 from the French government. The only challenge was my air ticket to Paris. It cost €1000, and I did not wish to burden my parents with this amount. My younger brother was bright and my parents were spending a fortune on his coaching classes so that he could make it through the IIT entrance exams. They had taken several loans for his studies already and worked overtime to make ends meet at home.

I wrote to thirty organizations—private companies, foundations, government agencies—to sponsor my air ticket to

France. None responded, except one non-profit firm located in south Delhi. Its founder was an Indian woman who lived in the United States but was briefly visiting Delhi. I was asked to meet her at the organization's office.

The office turned out to be an apartment in a residential complex. It was run by three staff members, one of whom accompanied me to the lounge. A few minutes later, a woman who appeared to be in her fifties entered the room dressed in pants and a floral chiffon shirt. She was smiling, her eyes twinkling. Seating herself across me, she introduced herself as the founder, and then, even without much of a chat, she took a chequebook out from her bag and flipped through its pages.

Holding a signed cheque for Rs 50,000 in her hand, she told me, 'Here, you get this cheque for your air ticket on three conditions. One, you will forget this ever happened [I try but I obviously have not]; two, you will never, ever get in touch with us, three, you will do this for another girl if you ever can later in your life.'

This was how I moved out of India to an unknown country 6500 kilometers away.

My story is one of hundreds of millions. Every migrant who moves to another city or country has a compelling situation that motivates them to leave, and a few enabling factors or people that help them make the move. Each era in history has had 'push factors'—situations that compel a person to leave their place of origin—and pull factors which are aspects of the host location that attract a person to live there. For these reasons and more, each migrant has a unique story and journey.

During the course of my academic research on migration, I met migrants across Paris, Berlin, Brussels, Rome, London, New York, Geneva, Cairo, Dubai, Nairobi, Beijing, Lahore, Islamabad and Dhaka. At university, I learnt migration theories and history from books, but my real learning came from the streets. The journey of every migrant I met has been unique, often linked to their specific situation in India. Yet, among the thousands of stories I heard, the most fascinating ones, and indeed the most heartbreaking, were the ones that emerged out of the subcontinent's history of war and strife. I came across entire families that were forced to move every few years across unexpected routes—one of them through Uganda and Rwanda, before ending up in Dubai! I found that until 1948, the majority of Indians migrated to other countries neither because of curiosity, nor even by consent. For a better explanation, let us look at three major migration waves of Indians moving to live overseas. In doing so, my objective is to point out how much of it was out of free will and how much was not.

The first wave of forced migration occurred in the colonial era. From the 1830s onwards, international migration from British-colonized India comprised largely unskilled workers from the poorer socio-economic groups who went to other colonized countries. Even in faraway Australia, a small number of Indians arrived as convicts and later as labourers, transported by the British colonial government in India. Between 1834 and 1937, nearly thirty million people were forced to leave India for other British colonies, of which nearly four-fifths managed to return.[11] Those who stayed back in other colonies often became 'twice-migrants' when they again moved to the UK or other colonies. Many would embrace the new culture and never return to India.

My second example is the migration that occurred from the early twentieth century onwards, during the independence struggle. As compared to the first wave, this was a smaller but still significant migration. While the Indian subcontinent fought for freedom, there were several Indians who voluntarily left to study at universities, often in the UK and other parts of Europe. While

[11] Tinker 1974; Davis 1968, 99.

in Europe, many members of this overseas Indian intelligentsia were actively involved in covert activities that they felt contributed to the fight for independence in their motherland. Berlin, Paris, Vienna and Zurich, at various times, became offshore hubs of India's freedom movement. Freedom fighters such as Subhash Chandra Bose mobilized hundreds of Indians in Berlin to help in the struggle. Bhikaji Cama founded the magazine *Vande Mataram*, publishing it out of a basement in Paris, for the readership of these Indian revolutionaries in Europe. Covert meetings were organized in the attics of Indians residing in Europe each time an Indian freedom fighter visited their city from the homeland.

It is fairly well known that many Indians, including India's first prime minister, Pandit Jawaharlal Nehru, and business leaders such as Jehangir Ratanji Tata, studied in Europe and then returned to India. But we often forget that there were many others who could never return. They stayed back because of the crackdowns that took place across Europe, instigated by British authorities. Homes were searched and any Indian suspected of carrying out activities related to the freedom struggle in the Indian subcontinent was taken into custody. Thousands of Indians were forcibly detained and many more went undercover, fleeing from the authorities. Much against their will, they could never board a ship back to India.

The third wave came in 1947 with the greatest migration of humans ever recorded in the history of the world. Millions of Muslims were forced to move from India to West and East Pakistan while an equal number of Hindus and Sikhs headed in the opposite direction. Hundreds of thousands never made it and died on the way.[12] The memories of this catastrophic episode still weigh on the Indian psyche.

---

[12] Dalrymple 2015.

Meanwhile, after Independence, the nation's leaders went about establishing educational institutions and developing industries. Prime Minister Nehru was a passionate believer in industrialization as much as he was in the socialist model of developing it. The country, under Nehru's leadership, took the unusual path of becoming a democracy without capitalism, and building industries without a free market. One of the consequences of this was the lack of a level playing field for Indians. Restrictive state controls and red tape hindered entrepreneurship. The elites, who were favoured by the state, benefited from the system, whereas the much larger majority who were poor and anonymous became even poorer. The need to earn a living, combined with the poor environment for entrepreneurship, drove people towards education and jobs that were available only in specific cities. Opportunities for prosperity were few and not uniformly distributed across the country. And so a few cities became more crowded than others as Indians flocked to them for education and jobs. This trend of moving to the cities for jobs continues even today.

Yet, interestingly, Indians have migrated within India mostly for the purpose of marriage. It is difficult to find exact data on this, but several sources indicate that close to 90 per cent of marriages in India are arranged by families of the groom and the bride, who usually do not know each other prior to the match.[13] It is common for the two to be living in different cities or villages, oblivious to each another's existence till they are brought together. These marriages are often arranged across cities between those belonging to the same caste and regional origin or linguistic group. According to the census, a total of 454 million Indians living in India were domestic migrants in 2011, and 49 per cent of these Indians, or

---

[13] CNN 2012; Statistic Brain 2016.

224 million people, migrated for marriage. Just as a comparison, only about 10 per cent moved because of work or employment in the same year.[14]

After a wedding, it is customary for the bride to move to the husband's house, wherever that might be. The most recent census data reveals that 97 per cent of the 224 million Indians who migrated after marriage are women.[15] Moreover, 78 per cent of rural women who migrated in 2011 did so for marriage as compared to 46 per cent of urban women who moved for the same reason.[16]

The reasons for Indians living abroad are not too different from those of our domestic migrants who leave their homes.[17] Many have migrated abroad for jobs. Approximately half of the total migrants are women who have followed such men after marriage, which is often arranged with a boy of the parents' choice, just like mine nearly was. Indian migrants have moved to high-income countries, and, as of 2015, they are concentrated the most in the UAE, which is inhabited by around 3.5 million Indians, and in the US, where around two million Indians live.

Overall, it is in search of a better life—emotionally, socially, financially—that we leave. The fact that India produces the largest number of migrants in the world, but hosts only about 5.2 million international migrants[18] is an indicator of where migrants perceive the environment is conducive for a better life. The Middle East has

---

[14] Varma 2016.

[15] *Business Standard* 2016.

[16] Ibid.

[17] The number of migrants who migrated rose by 18 per cent in 2015 from 8.5 million in 2010. Pew Research 2017.

[18] Connor 2017.

offered migrants jobs, the United States has beckoned to them with
its universities, and they've been attracted to the quality of life in
Europe, Singapore and Hong Kong. But in the future, a change of
political or economic scenarios in these countries could alter the
factors that attract migrants to them. We are witnessing this already
in Indian migration to the US, where President Donald Trump's
anti-immigration policies have resulted in Indian migrants hesitating
to go to the United States since January 2017,[19] and a larger number
of Indians now seeming more likely to choose to live in Europe.[20] In
the medium to long term, the overall number of Indians moving out

---

[19] President Donald Trump's election campaign prior to his formal
inauguration on 20 January 2017 promised to reduce illegal and legal
migration into the United States. Accordingly, the RAISE Bill, an
acronym for Reforming American Immigration for a Strong Economy,
introduced as a bill in the United States Senate in 2017 (not yet passed as
an Act till 2017), proposes to cut by half the number of legal immigrants
accepted into the US each year. This bill would do three things: First,
limit the number of foreign nationals who are able to get green cards to
reunite with their families already in the US. Second, cut the number of
refugees in half. Third, eliminate the diversity visa lottery—a programme
that gives visas to countries with low rates of immigration to the United
States. Another executive order under consideration will reduce the
number of H1B visas awarded each year to employed migrants in the
United States. Companies will have to show proof for why they chose
an immigrant over a citizen for a job that paid up to a certain amount,
which used to be $60,000 annually but which will now be revised to
$100,000 annually.

In no proven correlation to President Trump's actions, according to a
survey of more than 250 American colleges and universities conducted
by six top American higher education groups, students from India in the
fall semester of 2017 registered a 26 per cent decline in undergraduate
applications while a 15 per cent decline has been reported in graduate
applications (*Times of India* 2017).

[20] Anand 2017.

of India will not drastically reduce if the environment offered by the destination country is no longer attractive; they will find another destination. It will reduce only if the living conditions for Indians in India improve. Unless the fundamental reasons and situations—often exacerbated by economic and social inequality—that drive us out of India change, we will continue to find new destinations to move to.

Also, a more equitable society for the boys and the girls of this land, and the rich and the poor, irrespective of caste and ethnicity, will offer a meritocratic platform for us to strengthen our roots here in India. The strength of our roots will determine our commitment and attachment to being an important stakeholder in India's future. It will not matter then whether we leave or stay, because strong roots do not mean that the tree cannot have branches that reach out to the sky. Quite the contrary. Exploration and attachment are related, and in fact, the latter is a prerequisite for the former.

About five decades ago, researchers[21] observed fifty infants in a situation that was new and not too frightening. In some cases, the infant's mother was present, in others, she had left, and in yet others, she was replaced by a stranger. They found that exploration was greatest when the mother was present. Observation of young apes and monkeys and other studies of human infants in similar experiments since then have all supported the view that successful exploration takes place, ironically, when there is secure attachment.

The establishment of attachment is an instinctual priority. When it is absent, the need for attachment is dominant and we engage in attachment-searching behaviour similar to that of a baby, who is likely to cry or seek its mother. When we are attached to our city or country of origin, attachment can be taken for granted. In this case, just as an infant would feel free to move

---

[21] Ainsworth and Bell 1970, 49.

out of its crib knowing the mother is always present, we feel more secure in leaving our home base to explore the new and often frightening world. Exploring other lands clearly does not just mean physically living elsewhere. It means being curious about and getting emotionally involved in those places.

Strong roots in our home base liberate us to explore or engage more meaningfully with the world. Lacking this, we will move in large numbers but spend less time exploring, instead seeking the missing mother (land) anxiously in a place where she does not exist.

References

Ainsworth, Mary D. Salter, and Silvia M. Bell. 1970. Attachment, exploration, and separation: Illustrated by the behaviour of one-year-olds in a strange situation. *Child Development* 41.1, pp. 49-67.

Alikuzai, Hamid Wahed. 2013. *A Concise History of Afghanistan in 25 Volumes*, vol. 1 (Bloomington: Trafford Publishing).

Anand, Geeta. 2017. For Indians, Trump's America is a land of lost opportunity. *New York Times*, 23 April.

Buhler, George, trans. 1886. *The Laws of Manu* (Oxford: Clarendon Press).

Business Standard. 2016. 97 per cent of Indians migrating for marriage are female. 15 December.

Butler, Robert A. 1954. Curiosity in monkeys. *Scientific American*, pp. 70–75.

Callahan, Sharon Henderson. 2013. *Religious Leadership: A Reference Handbook* (California: Sage Publications).

CNN. 2012. The Freedom Project. http://edition.cnn.com/specials/world/freedom-project.

Connor, Phillip. 2017. India is a top source and destination for world's migrants. *Pew Research Center*, 3 March, http://www.pewresearch.org/fact-tank/2017/03/03/india-is-a-top-source-and-destination-for-worlds-migrants/.

Dalrymple, William. 2015. The great divide: The violent legacy of the Indian partition. *New Yorker*, 29 June.

Das, Gurcharan. 2002. *India Unbound,* first edition (New York: Anchor Books).

Davis, Kingsley. 1968. *The Population of India and Pakistan* (New York: Russell & Russell).

Langevin, R. 1971. Is curiosity a unitary construct? *Canadian Journal of Psychology* 25.4, p. 360.

Loewenstein, George. 1994. The psychology of curiosity: A review and reinterpretation. *Psychological Bulletin*, 116.1, pp. 75–98.

Menozzi, Clare. 2016. *International Migration Report 2015*, United Nations, New York.

Olivelle, Patrick, ed. 1999. *The Dharmasutras: The Law Codes of Ancient India* (Oxford: Oxford University Press).

Rana, Preetika, and Joanna Sugden. 2013. India's record since independence. *Wall Street Journal*, 15 August.

Sims, Alexandra. 2016. India has the largest diaspora population in the world, says UN report. *Independent*, 14 January.

Saha, Devanik. 2016. 97 per cent of Indians migrating for marriage are female. Indiaspend, 5 August.

Statistic Brain. 2016. Arranged marriage statistics. https://www.statisticbrain. com/arranged-marriage-statistics.

Times of India. 2017. US universities register drop in Indian student applications. 27 March.

Tinker, Hugh. 1974. *A New System of Slavery: The Export of Indian Labour Overseas, 1830–1920* (Oxford: Oxford University Press).

Varma, Subodh. 2016. 4 of 10 Indians are migrants, most move for marriage: survey. *Times of India*, 2 December.

4

Procreation

Sex is a dirty word in India, but our population numbers are still booming. In the land of the Kamasutra, most Indians deem it inappropriate to teach children about sex at home or at school. In a country where family, the government and various institutions have stifled the subject, we continue to make babies and are all set to overtake China by 2030 to become the most populous country in the world.[1]

The list of ironies around our attitude to sex is long and extremely baffling. Here are some more. We are shy about discussing sex with our spouses, but we worship with gusto the lingam, which is God's phallus. We expect our women to produce babies but often do not offer them pleasurable sex—only 32 per cent of Indian women achieve orgasm, which is half as many as the men who said they do.[2]

---

[1] World Population Prospects 2017.

[2] According to a survey in 2008 by the contraceptive company Durex, while 60 per cent of Indians claimed sex is 'fun, enjoyable, and a vital part of life', only 44 per cent were fully satisfied with their sex lives (Trivedi 2014, 70; News 18 2008).

In fact, we have been hypocrites on this topic for a while, because a part of India's sexual history is not very different from the present. The Rig Veda says that the vaginal blood from the bride's deflowering is highly dangerous. If clothes are stained with this blood, they must be given away to a priest, or anybody who touches them will be destroyed. The *Arthashastra* provides guidelines on what must be done if a girl loses her virginity, and it also declares that a marriage is invalid if the girl is not a virgin. The girl is not a virgin, according to the *Arthashastra*, if blood is not seen on the sheets after the wedding night. The *Manusmriti*, an ancient legal text, imposes large fines on men who destroy the virginity of a girl outside marriage.[3] An entire book written in India around 2000 years ago, as part of the seven-volume Kamasutra—otherwise a fascinating source of progressive erotic commentary—is devoted to the *kanya* or the virgin. This book also mentions, or rather assumes, that a girl is a virgin on her wedding night and so the man must make her content, or he will ensure the girl's marital life is unhappy.[4]

Due to this age-old emphasis on chastity, a woman is not allowed to experience sexual pleasure until she marries, and when she does, she is only allowed to have sex with one man and bear his children. Unfortunately, these extreme views on sex in Indian history are the only ones that have survived, and the more liberal ones—which I will elaborate upon in this essay—have been erased. This has led to lies and deceit in millions of relationships and marriages in India, which could otherwise have been healthy and transparent. Young girls, unable to seek guidance from their parents, get abortions done under dangerous conditions on the sly, even though abortions before twelve weeks of pregnancy have

---

[3] Ibid, 41.

[4] Ibid.

been legal in India since 1972.[5] And devastatingly, we implant guilt, contradictions, timidity, and shame in the minds of millions of our women for their sexuality.

The earliest lesson at my home was when I turned thirteen and was told that being in a temple while menstruating was sacrilegious. It was an invasion of my newly acquired sense of sexual privacy to have it whispered within the family that I was menstruating and therefore prohibited to enter the temple we had at home—not that I wished to enter it anyway.

As I grappled with irregular menstrual cycles and discomfort every month, I would also feel I was doing something wrong. It sowed the seeds of the notion that my sexuality was unholy and 'bad'. I had understood correctly, just as every little girl does in India, that everything related to sex is profane. I later discovered that millions of those who mistrust anything sexual worship the Goddess's vagina at the temple of Kamakhya in Guwahati, Assam, which is considered one of the most sacred sites in India. I found it even more incongruous that the holiest time at the Kamakhya temple is the four-day annual festival when Kamakhya Devi, the Goddess, is believed to be menstruating.

Manusmriti, the discourse of Svayambhuva, the spiritual son of Brahma, was written around the third century AD, and it is merely one among the many Hindu *dharmashastra*s. Today, however, it is considered an important text governing Hindu culture, including marriage, relationships and sex. This text receives as much reverence as criticism. Many consider it to have sounded the death knell for the liberal world of the Vedic age, while others respect it as the ultimate guide to one's rights and duties. Dr B.R. Ambedkar held the *Manusmriti* responsible for

---

[5] The Medical Termination of Pregnancy Act, 1971. The Act came into effect on 1 April 1972.

the caste system in India.[6] Mahatma Gandhi, however, opposed Ambedkar's view. Gandhi recommended that one must read the entire text of the *Manusmriti*, accept those parts that are consistent with truth and non-violence, and reject the other parts.[7]

However, before the primacy of the *Manusmriti*, it was the Kamasutra, written by Vatsyayana in Sanskrit, which dictated human sexual behaviour in India. Kama, meaning desire, is one of the four goals of Hindu life, the other three being dharma (duty), *artha* (purpose) and moksha (freedom). *Sutra* means a thread that holds things together. The Kamasutra presents itself as a guide to living gracefully, and discusses the nature of love, family life and other aspects pertaining to the faculty of pleasure. It discusses the philosophy and theory of love, what triggers desire and what to do to sustain it. The Kamasutra was passed on in the oral tradition for over 2000 years, subject to many interpretations, until around the second century AD when Vatsyayana, a lesser-known philosopher of the Vedic tradition, wrote it out, largely in prose, with a few verses of poetry inserted.

Vatsyayana's and Manu's attitudes to sex were in some ways polar opposites. Manu saw sex as a strictly procreative, monogamous activity, as opposed to the pleasure-giving experience Vatsyayana wrote about. The Kamasutra emphasizes that a woman who is not pleasured might hate her man and leave him for another, while Manu's laws say that 'a virtuous wife should constantly serve her husband like a god, even if he behaves badly, freely indulges his lust, and is devoid of any good qualities'.

The Kamasutra has an entire chapter on 'Other Men's Wives', whereas the *Manusmriti* warns that 'if men persist in seeking intimate contact with other men's wives, the king should brand

---

[6] Keer 1954, 106; Mishra 2010, 243.
[7] Gandhi 2013 reprint, 129.

them with punishments that inspire terror, and banish them'. Vatsyayana saw adultery as a means of providing pleasure, while Manu worried about the violation of the caste system should a woman bear a child with an unknown man of the wrong caste.[8]

There were also other texts that opposed the erotic perspective of the Kamasutra. The Bhagavad Gita, which is believed to have been composed before the Kamasutra, also denounced our indulgence in the senses. It admonished that doing so is evil. Incidentally, the Bhagavad Gita was a discourse given by the grown-up Krishna, who once romanced the cowgirls of Vrindavan for pleasure.

Even though Islam has had its ups and downs as far as its attitude towards sex and sexuality is concerned, during most periods of the Mughal rule from 1526 to 1857 in India, sex was not frowned upon. The Mughal period showed a playful sensuality in its explicit art and a more balanced view on sex and sexuality than the era that had preceded it.

India's rich sexual history has, therefore, been chequered. From the time of the Rig Veda to the age of the Kamasutra, and then at the courts of the Mughal emperors much later, sex—most of the time—was not a bad thing. It was discussed openly in literature, conversation and art. Many Hindu gods and goddesses, as well as apsaras or heavenly nymphs, were depicted romantically in ancient Indian temples such as in Khajuraho in Madhya Pradesh, and in the cave drawings of Ajanta and Ellora in Maharashtra.

However, of all the diverse phases and texts in India's sexual history, it was the *Manusmriti* that stuck with the British. One reason was perhaps that Manu's prudish values resonated with the Victorian culture of that time. Secondly, the *Manusmriti* was one of the first Sanskrit texts studied and translated into English by the

---

[8] Trivedi 2014, 27.

British, and so they hastily borrowed from it to create the legal and administrative systems for India. The rest of the texts—the more liberal parts of the Rig Veda and the Kamasutra—were largely ignored. Manu, for the British, became the ultimate authority on India's societal structure.

Manu's laws, however, have several confusing contradictions related to women's rights. Verses 9.72–9.81 allow the man as well as the woman to get out of a fraudulent or abusive marriage and remarry. They even provide legal sanction for a woman to remarry when her husband has been missing or has abandoned her. But it is also restrictive for women in verses 3.13–3.14, opposing her marriage to someone outside her own social class. It preaches chastity to widows, such as in verses 5.158–5.160. In verses 5.147–5.148, the *Manusmriti* declares that 'a woman must never seek to live independently'. In other verses, such as 2.67–2.69 and 5.148–5.155, the *Manusmriti* preaches that a girl should obey and seek the protection of her father, a young woman must do the same of her husband, and a widow must do so of her son. While it states that a woman should always worship her husband as a god, in verses 3.55–3.56, the *Manusmriti* also insists that 'women must be honoured and adorned', and that 'where women are revered, there the gods rejoice, but where they are not, no sacred rite bears fruit'.

The *Manusmriti* is a complex commentary from a women's rights perspective, but the British merely picked and emphasized certain aspects that seemed appropriate to them for codifying women's rights for Hindus in India, while ignoring the other sections.

And so the parts of the *Manusmriti* that sharply restricted women's freedom, regulated their behaviour, and reduced their access to social and political power, besides establishing a highly conservative stand on sex in a society that was once fairly liberal, became the values that the British propagated in the subcontinent during their rule.

Actually, it was not the British alone. They were joined by the enthusiastic anglicized Indian elite, who were somewhere between the British and the Indians in their ways, and at times preached the same prudish values to the middle class in the subcontinent.

Here is an example. The Brahmo Samaj was an institution that propagated a new kind of Hinduism, inspired by the Hindu Vedanta, Islamic Sufism and Christian Unitarianism. Its founder, Raja Ram Mohan Roy, had two houses in Kolkata—one was his 'Bengali house' and the other his 'European house'. In the Bengali house, he lived with his wife and children in the traditional Indian way. The European house, on the other hand, was tastefully done up, with English furniture, and was used to entertain his European friends. Someone teased him by saying that everything in the Bengali house was Bengali except for Ram Mohan Roy, and everything in the European house was European except for Ram Mohan Roy! While celebrated for being an eminent reformer and uplifting women with his anti-sati and anti-child-marriage movements, Roy also had a puritan, British-influenced condemnation of non-Brahminical sexual and gender relations.[9]

Mahatma Gandhi also had a conflicted attitude to sex, which is apparent in his memoirs.[10] On the one hand, he declares that he was tormented by sexual passions, which he described as uncontrollable, while on the other hand, he took a vow of chastity at the age of thirty-six and passionately preached chastity to everyone. He said women were the embodiment of sacrifice and non-violence, as also the keepers of purity. During his time in South Africa, when Mahatma Gandhi saw a young man harassing

---

[9] Das 2002, 283.
[10] Gandhi 1940; Adams 2010.

his female followers, instead of confronting the man, he personally cut off the girl's hair.[11]

The great saint Swami Vivekananda had a paradoxical view of sex as well. He revered their maternal instinct, but disliked the erotic.[12]

He preached that the highest love is the love that is sexless— that is perfect unity, while sex differentiates bodies.[13] He confided to his disciple Sarat Chandra Chakravarty that 'the American sluts and buggers used to be sexually aroused' after hearing his lectures.[14]

At a lecture in Chennai in 1897, he asserted, 'The women of India must grow and develop in the footprints of Sita, and that is the only way.'[15] In the Indian epic Ramayana, Sita, the wife of Ram, is chastity incarnate.

Adding to the confusion created by the hypocritical attitude to sex in India is the matter of role models. Radha is Krishna's love, Sita is Ram's wife. Radha and Sita, both mythological figures, are worshipped in India. Radha is sensual, older than Krishna by many years, and some texts say she is married to another man while romancing Krishna. In almost all interpretations of the Radha– Krishna story, their relationship is clandestine. While Sita is an example of a woman in a monogamous, legitimate relationship, Radha is remembered and revered for loving Krishna despite his other flirtations. Sita is a queen, Radha an ordinary village girl focused on her relationship with her lover.

In line with Swami Vivekananda's counsel, Indians have indeed accepted Sita as the role model for a woman. Sita sets the

---

[11] Connellan 2010.
[12] Sil 1995.
[13] Vivekananda 1915.
[14] Sil 1995.
[15] Vivekananda 1897, 20.

standard high: A woman must be chaste and monogamous, a romantic relationship must be validated by marriage, husbands must be expected to fight and overcome challenges to be worthy, and the couple must make sacrifices for the sake of society, even if that means forsaking a personal relationship.

But Radha is a role model too—at the opposite end of the moral spectrum from Sita. While Sita is the loyal and chaste wife, Radha is the passionate and adulterous lover. Sita is a public figure due to her political stature as queen, while Radha is the subject of thousands of paintings and statues, and has been established as a goddess in many temples across India. She has also influenced movements in poetry, art and literature, many of which are well known. Who can ignore the fervour of the Bhakti movement and the devotional poems and songs, inspired by Radha and Krishna, written by Mirabai, the legendary princess from Rajasthan?

Ira Trivedi, in her fantastic book *India in Love*,[16] has presented several reasons why Radha and Krishna might not have married. One, she says, Radha was already married and so a second marriage was tough. Two, Krishna's love was spiritual and had nothing to do with marriage. Third, Radha needed to be Krishna's lover because it was not possible to have the same degree of passion in a marriage.[17]

The third hypothesis is particularly remarkable, rather ridiculously indicating that a marriage need not have passion.

The dark side of the social taboo on sexual relationships between unmarried couples, and the many passionless marriages, are the pregnancies that occur out of wedlock, and the babies that are then abandoned. In Nizamabad, where my not-for-profit organization operated a few years ago, there were children being

---

[16] Trivedi 2014.
[17] Ibid, 20.

raised on the streets or by other families without any legal adoption procedures. Besides, there were at least two dozen orphanages in that district alone. These orphanages, located in the economically backward slum areas of the district, were frugally managed, funded by international organizations and charities.

'The medicines for the kids have stopped coming in,' explained the manager of one such orphanage to Rajvi, the vice principal of the college in Nizamabad, and me as we sat across from him in his damp office.

'Some new project officer working at our funders' comes in, and this person just decides that the funding to our organization should stop, and that's it . . . It is the children who ultimately suffer, because now we have no money to continue their treatment,' he continued in an exasperated tone, pointing to a child who had just come in and was coyly watching us from the door of the manager's office.

Rajvi had told me that a large number of orphans in Nizamabad were born HIV-positive, but the local community considered this a matter of great shame and did not want any outside interference.

'What will you do now?' I asked.

'The treatment for AIDS is slow and expensive, but the locals here will not let me go out and get help for these children,' he replied. 'They feel that this will reveal the community's secrets to outsiders.'

On our way out of the manager's office, a crowd of children ran towards us. As they came closer, they seemed to me to be in the age range of four to ten, and particularly exuberant, perhaps because they were seeing us in their 'home'. Their hair was oiled, the girls' mostly in two plaits, and their eyes twinkled. They were thin, but did not seem ill. They stood all around Rajvi and me, and some of them jumped to give me a high-five—copying one child who had done it. Some of them said hello, and a few others at the back waved shyly. Like most children anywhere in the world, they were full of questions. 'What is your name?', 'Where do you live?', 'Do you know America?', 'When will you come back again?'

Leaving the orphanage, I too had a question, for Rajvi. 'Why are there so many orphans here in Nizamabad?' I asked.

'The community elders don't like to talk about this,' she replied, 'but what else can our women do if their men have gone off to Dubai?'

Nizamabad, I learnt, was the home of a large number of immigrants working in the Gulf countries as plumbers, electricians and general labour. One immigrant would tell an aspirant living in Nizamabad about the tricks and procedures to get a job in the Gulf. They would share contacts of agents and employers with each other, leading to a great chain migration of menial labour that had occurred over the last decade or so to the UAE, Bahrain and Oman. The salary was the main, and often only, attraction, because the living conditions were not. The money would be enough to pay for a cramped shared dormitory in the new country, and the remaining cash would be sent off to the wife left behind in Nizamabad. These jobs hardly came with the luxury of a spouse visa.

As is the practice, upon arrival in the new country, the employer would take away the immigrant's passport for a year or more, depending on the work contract. Usually, for multiple-year contracts, an annual leave of a few weeks was permitted, but the labourers would hardly have enough savings for a return air ticket to home and back. This meant that they were forced to be away from their families at home in Nizamabad for extended periods.

'The wives left behind by their husbands get lonely,' explained Rajvi.

'What do you mean?' I asked.

'They feel deprived of sexual pleasure because their husbands are away in the Gulf for one or two years at a stretch,' she said, 'and so they seek it from other men in the locality.'

'And then they have unwanted pregnancies?' I checked.

'Exactly. These men and women do not practise safe sex; they are not aware of contraception measures. Many of them are uneducated, but then there is no concept of sex education at schools anyway. Also, the women cannot be seen buying condoms at the pharmacy, especially if their husbands are away!' Rajvi said.

'Getting an abortion is not easy either, maa,' Rajvi continued. 'The women do not have the money for abortions, and we have very poor medical services here in Nizamabad and the surrounding areas.'

'So they deliver the baby, and then give it away?'

'Yes, and worse. The women have several sexual partners, and since people here do not have protected sex, HIV/AIDS spreads easily. So many innocent children are born with AIDS. What is the fault of these children, maa? They are dumped in the orphanages here.'

I understood that in this way, the social sanctity of these long-distance marriages remained intact, whereas the sexual relations among the locals became secrets buried deep within the community. Indeed, their innocent children were the ones who bore the burden of shame and paid the price of it all.

This high social pressure of keeping up the Ram–Sita image in public has created double standards in our attitude to sex. Chastity before marriage is assumed to be the norm and divorce rates in India are very low—0.3 per cent, as compared to 50 per cent in the US as of 2015.[18] Yet, a conservative estimate of the number of sex

---

[18] India's 0.3 per cent divorce rate is calculated based on Census 2011. However, data on the divorce rate in India varies across sources from 0.11 per cent to 1.3 per cent (Dutt 2015).

workers in India is around five million,[19] which is almost as large as the entire population of Switzerland! Who is giving sex workers business in India—an unmarried Indian who is expected to be a virgin, or the married one who is supposedly monogamous?

To find answers to these questions, I took a friend who was also visiting Kolkata at that time along with me to meet the 10,000 and more sex workers of Sonagachi, an area in north Kolkata, and Asia's largest red-light area, beating even the Kamathipura red-light area in Mumbai. I was curious to meet the ladies of Sonagachi. Where did they come from? What was their life like? Who were their clients—bored husbands, unlucky singles, sexually experimental folks? What was the attitude of their clients towards them? Were the clients obnoxious? I found it incredibly ironic that red-light areas of such a gigantic size would thrive in a country that is prudish about sex.

It can be slightly tricky to find the mouth of the narrow lane that leads into the maze of brothels in Sonagachi. My friend and I were told that it was right off the main road, but so tiny that we would probably miss it. Around the area, we rolled down the window of our taxi to ask the two men standing at the bend of the road for directions. We wanted to go to a brothel called Neel Kanth, we told them.

The two men, almost identically dressed in checked lungis and white cotton vests, stared hard at our faces, as if in doubt or suspicion. Our taxi driver honked, impatient to be done with the ride. Then one of the men limped forward towards us, mumbling that a couple does not come seeking a sex worker in Sonagachi. The friend accompanying me was a man. I had deliberately picked him to accompany me in my 'sting operation' at Sonagachi, so that he could pose as a client in the brothels. But the men in the lungis were still suspicious.

---

[19] Trivedi 2014, 117.

We ignored the comment and instead asked the man our question again. Standing very close by now and peering into our taxi window, his eyes fixed on me, he told us to get off the taxi there, which we did.

He pointed to a lane behind us, which he said would take us to Sonagachi. There would be plenty of people in that area to help us around, he said, and take us to Neel Kanth.

In the research for my trip to Sonagachi, I had read that the brothel Neel Kanth was something of a mystery. One person who wrote about Neel Kanth mentioned that it was 'hidden' and extremely difficult to locate. Another wrote of it as an elusive brothel that housed the Agrawalis (girls from Agra), who were apparently descendants of the courtesans in the Mughal courts. The Agrawalis were the wealthiest and most influential community in Sonagachi, we had heard. Their community had a norm that barred male members from earning a living. Men would be supported by their sisters. One particular person had written passionately about the beauty of the Agrawalis, especially their white skin, in a blog. In fact, we had also read a contradicting report that said only a lucky few had seen the Agrawalis as they did not step out of Neel Kanth and were picky about customers.

We set off on our search. It was a wet, muddy road—even though it had not rained—lit up with the lights in the six-storey buildings sticking to each other on both sides of the narrow lane. With each step we took, pebbles and small stones turned over and made a crackling sound, which was drowned out by the music floating out of shops and the general cacophony. Every few metres, women stood in groups of three or four.

'Are you here to work?' one of them asked me in Bengali.

'I am here just accompanying him,' I replied, pointing to my friend.

'Why accompanying?' she giggled. 'Does he want to try me out? Ask him. I am around for a few more hours.' She had guessed by then that my friend did not comprehend the language of our conversation.

'Where will you go after that?' I asked.

'Home.'

'You don't stay here?'

'No, no, this is my day job. I go back to my husband. I have two children at home.'

'Ah, okay. Would you know where the Agrawalis are?'

'They live in expensive flats around here,' she said, pointing to the buildings.

Her answer did not help at all. The road ahead curved to the right and then branched off into several narrower streets. We randomly took a turn into a street where there were only residential buildings, with women and men sitting on plastic chairs and charpoys outside, but the ambience did not seem very familial. Hardly had we stepped into this street when a small, feeble man dressed in a crushed white cotton dhoti and a cream-coloured old, half-sleeved kurta came hobbling towards us. He was bald and the skin on his face was dark brown and wrinkled.

'What type are you looking for?' he asked my friend, his beady eyes searching his face.

'We are looking for a girl to do a threesome with us,' my friend replied, putting his arm around my shoulder.

'All types available,' the man continued, without pausing to comprehend what my friend had just said. 'High class, low class, Marwari, Nepali, Rajasthani, Baangali, Agrawali . . .'

'Can you take us to Neel Kanth?' I asked, ecstatic that he had mentioned the Agrawalis in his offer.

'Yes, Neel Kanth is right here. Come, follow me,' said the man to us.

He took us through dark, dingy, nameless, criss-crossing lanes with buildings. Each building seemed to have a winding staircase, and was made up of small single rooms only, partitioned by curtains. It was intriguing and disturbing at the same time because of the questions they raised about the abundance of sexuality in India and the disrespect for it. How much violence and abuse will take place when the curtains are drawn, thanks to the centuries of sexual repression? As we walked, I looked at the men and women around me and wondered how many had lied at home and come here looking to get or to give sexual pleasure? How many were sex workers under the legal age of eighteen? Were they duped and forced to work here? The exchange of sexual services for money in India is legal for adults, although soliciting in a public place, owning or managing a brothel and child prostitution are crimes. Also, it is legal only if sexual services are provided in a private residence, but many brothels thrive illegally in India, and pimps, such as the man leading us, do business.

'This building here has Marwari girls,' our pimp told us, pointing at the building next to us. 'And this one here has Nepali girls,' he continued excitedly, pointing at another one.

'Okay, let us take a look at the Marwari one,' I said.

We met more than fifty sex workers at the Marwari, Nepali and Bengali buildings during the course of the evening as we walked to Neel Kanth. Among these, I could speak in detail to only about two dozen women. I asked them where they came from, why they were here, and the attitude of their customers. Most of the others wanted us to get to the point and agree on a price.

The diversity at Sonagachi, I found, was as astonishingly and perversely stratified as in the rest of India. Class and community ranking here underpinned even the common objective of sexual pleasure. Girls belonging to the same caste, class or regional community lived in the same building, separated from the rest who lived in similarly culturally homogeneous groups. Sex workers hailing from different regions in India moved to live with their community here because it gave them a greater sense of comfort and community support. Some of them were brought here by deceit, but slowly, they adjusted. Consequently, the residents of different buildings in Sonagachi spoke languages that were each distinct from the other. Every building reflected the native culture of its inhabitants. The ghetto effect in the area reinforced community stereotypes. Each girl in the business was acutely aware of not only her professional but also her cultural, linguistic and regional identity, and used these different strands according to the profile and taste of a potential customer to earn her living. If the customer spoke her language she would speak to him in it. If he had a fetish for women from her region, then she would accentuate her cultural affiliations, they told me. There were no inhibitions among them to be exhibitive of cultural and ethnic origins, or to use those as a differentiating factor from the rest for profit.

They were not poor any more, but they all had once been so. Customers of all backgrounds came to Sonagachi. The girls labelled 'high class' had higher rates and offered better rooms, whereas 'low class' girls meant a budget score on a straw mat. Many of these customers were married, the girls told me. A few had peculiar sexual fantasies while others were violent. There were cases of abuse and some of the girls said they had been beaten. The majority of the customers did not like protected sex. Business on most days was lucrative, and so, they told me, they did not care about the occasional violence or the dangers of catching a deadly virus. Money was the only factor that drove them to become sex workers. As we spoke, the children of some of the girls I met peeped into the bedrooms.

India's rapid but unequal economic growth has had a profound and mixed impact on the personal lives of millions. It has all happened too quickly in India, and in uneven patches of extreme wealth and heartbreaking poverty that connect with each other in spaces such as Sonagachi. The great urban migration has meant that the lower layers of India's stratified society are forced to mix with the rich, but the discrepancies and inequalities remain. Those with new wealth but old patriarchal thought processes are pitted against a vulnerable and impoverished mass of people in locations such as Sonagachi.

Yet, they have ready access to sexualized content on television or the Internet. The search volume index for the word 'porn' on Google has doubled in India between 2010 and 2012,[20] one in five mobile users in India wants adult content on their 3G-enabled phones, and there is an increased consumption of affordable and accessible pornography among men and women such that seven Indian cities rank among the top ten in the world for online porn traffic.[21] Most of these Indians watch porn secretly to quench their sexual curiosity. All this chaos and confusion inevitably lead to sexual frustration.

Violence, especially of a sexual nature, is often an extreme expression of this frustration and weakness of Indian men. Look at the role models they have—in contemporary culture, sadly, it is the aggressive and obsessive Bollywood hero, refusing to take no for an answer, who influences the values of these young people. Moreover, if large numbers of India's youth remain unemployed, and labour trends continue to show young people withdrawing from the workforce, violence, including sexual violence, will continue to thrive.

---

[20] Trivedi 2014, 47.
[21] Ibid, 48.

While the perpetuators of sexual violence clearly use unacceptable outlets for their frustrations, the sex workers in Sonagachi tolerate it in return for money. Sex is one of the oldest professions of the world, but in India, because of inequalities and inherent social hierarchies, it is sexual violence, including rape, that is rampant on the streets and even more so in the brothels.

Poverty breeds overpopulation and overpopulation again breeds poverty and ignorance. The poor have a lack of awareness about family planning, and also need more hands to earn or at least help out at home. So they often give birth to more babies than they have the resources for, making the whole situation worse. The other three main reasons for our population growth, besides poverty, are the high fertility rate of women, the decline in the mortality rate, and the lack of other sources of entertainment such as television (or even electricity) among India's poor.

We have, in the past, tried various contraceptive measures. The intrauterine contraceptive devices in the 1960s allegedly failed, and the backlash against Sanjay Gandhi's disastrous experiment of compulsory sterilization in the 1970s brought down the Indira Gandhi government and set back the country's family planning efforts by decades. The mainstay of India's family planning policy currently is to reduce women's fertility—not solely by devices and female sterilization, but also by improving health, education and literacy. However, the baffling results of India's National Family Health Survey 2015–16 show that the use of contraception did not correlate with the increased literacy rates in those regions.[22] For example, the report showed that between 2008 and 2016, in Kerala, the state that has the highest total literacy rate, condom use plunged by 42 per cent but the usage of condoms in the same period doubled, and the use of oral pills rose four times in Bihar,

---

[22] National Family Health Survey 2015–16.

which has the lowest total literacy rate in India. This is perhaps because sex education is not part of the school curriculum in India, and so literacy levels do not correspond to the awareness of the topic. In terms of education at home, Indian parents also usually avoid any conversation related to sex, including advice on the use of condoms or guidance on oral birth control pills.

It is no wonder that the report shows that over the eight years from 2008 to 2016, as India's population surged, the use of contraceptives declined by almost 35 per cent, while abortions and the consumption of emergency pills—both having hazardous side effects—doubled. Worryingly, our men are becoming more reluctant than ever to use contraceptives—the use of condoms has declined 52 per cent, and vasectomies have fallen by 73 per cent during this period. Meanwhile, women remain largely unaware of the benefits of regular oral contraceptive pills. Even the meagre usage of oral birth control pills fell 30 per cent between 2008 and 2016, further surrendering the control of family planning to the men, who, as we know, are not keen on using condoms.[23]

We are yet to successfully introduce the simplest of contraceptives, female condoms, in India. During my time at the Jindal Group, I tried to do so. In partnership with Hindustan Latex Family Planning and Parenthood Trust—a public sector enterprise known for its odd and long acronym, HLFPPT, and for being the largest condom distributor in India—I designed, and got manufactured, sleek, strong condom-vending machines with our own company-manufactured steel. I had learnt that all past attempts by the government to place condom-vending machines in

---

[23] India's National Family Health Survey 2015–16 shows that although 660 million condoms were distributed nationwide in 2008-09, that figure fell by more than half to 320 million in 2015–16. Andhra Pradesh and Madhya Pradesh recorded the highest falls, 83 per cent and 79 per cent.

public had failed on account of two main reasons: one, vandalism of the earlier flimsy vending machines that were made of tin, and two, people's reluctance to buy condoms in public. Moreover, all these condom-vending machines only sold male condoms. But what about women? Why do women need to depend on the good sense of their male partners to avoid getting pregnant? I managed to convince HLFPPT to sell female condoms in India at a heavily subsidized rate, which still turned out to be around three times the price of the male condom. Together, we placed our first few tough, steel vending machines in private corners of public spaces (including men's and women's toilets and near ATM machines) in New Delhi.

The consequences were striking—more female condoms than male condoms were purchased by men and women over the first three months. A subsequent anonymous survey revealed that much of that was because of the initial curiosity about what a female condom looked like, since no one had ever seen it. Two, the women eventually felt it inappropriate to have such a product sold in a public space. One morning, a group of women decided to cover the vending machines placed near the ATMs with tape and chart paper. Ultimately, the women, not the men, lobbied to remove the machines altogether.

How can India's population stabilization programme get anywhere without shedding its double standards and inhibitions about sex? I disagree with anyone who says that the attitude to sex is changing, because it is not changing fast enough or widely enough. I am not just talking about cities, but also about villages and small towns like Nizamabad, and slums such as Sonagachi. Overall, in India, we do not talk about sex; ironically, we have the largest population among all countries except China.

The dichotomy, hypocrisy, irony—call it what you want—around sex has been in India's past (as we have seen earlier in this essay), and continues to flourish in the present. Historically, it's been a mixed bag of some progressive and a few extremely conservative views on sex, and sadly, the latter have survived, to the detriment of our physical and mental health. Abortion has been legal in India for over forty years now, yet unsafe abortions persist. Masturbation, which most sexologists consider to be healthy elsewhere, is considered by most in contemporary India to be obnoxious, if not an illness. Sexually liberal societies do not tolerate rape, violence against women, child molestation and sexual harassment, which are all rampant in India. The chaste man and the virgin woman are considered the gold standard. These definitions of 'bad' and 'good' stem from a deep sexual repression and mistrust of anything and everything sexual.

As we continued on our journey through Sonagachi, guided by our untiring pimp, we met children playing on the roads or sitting outside the rooms where their mothers were working. There was another group with kites in their hands and one more bunch singing Hindi songs on the pavement. The children looked as if they could belong to any of the hundreds of other unfortunate slums in our country, but the truth was that in a society with such double standards towards anything sexual, they were, unfortunately, growing up in the lowest and most despised levels of existence in India. Their abnormal upbringing had been worsened by skewed representations of them on television and films. One of the sex workers had told me earlier in the day that there were *angrez* filmmakers who had come to Sonagachi and represented the children in a way that was not true.[24]

What will these children grow up to be like? Will they be politically astute citizens and decisionmakers in policies that concern and affect them? Or will they be obliged to take up prostitution in order to repay the community for bringing them up? Do they have alternative choices? Some children are

---

[24] Brisk and Kauffman 2004.

not aware of their mothers' profession, while some young girls are being prepared to join the same line of work. Growing up in an environment where double standards, superstition, and frustration meet poverty and desperation, the opportunity to grab on to something that gives you identity and purpose is a dream.

Leaving the children behind, we walked to a three-storey building a hundred metres away. It was crowned with a faded yellow cement moulding and had paint peeling off its turquoise blue walls. It was located next to a wide open gutter that was overflowing with black fluid and floating plastic.

'The famed Neel Kanth,' announced our pimp, pointing proudly at the dilapidated building.

References

Adams, Jad. 2010. *Gandhi: Naked Ambition* (London: Quercus Books).

Brisk, Zana, and Ross Kauffman. 2004. Born into brothels: Calcutta's red light kids. https://www.youtube.com/watch?v=WfWSRRRUIJY.

Connellan, Michael. 2010. Women suffer from Gandhi's legacy. *Guardian*, 27 January.

Das, Gurcharan. 2002. *India Unbound*, first edition (New York: Anchor Books).

Dutt, Apoorva. 2015. How and why number of young Indian couples getting divorced has risen sharply. *Hindustan Times*, 4 January.

Gandhi, Mohandas K. 1940. *An Autobiography: The Story of My Experiments With Truth* (Boston: Beacon Press).

Gandhi, Mohandas K. 1948. *An Autobiography: The Story of My Experiments With Truth* (Courier Corporation).

Gandhi, Mohandas K. 2013 reprint. *Hinduism According to Gandhi* (New Delhi: Orient Paperbacks).

Keer, Dhananjay. 1954. *Dr. Ambedkar: Life and Mission* (A.V. Keer).

Mishra, S.N., ed. 2010. *Socio-economic and Political Vision of Dr. B.R. Ambedkar* (New Delhi: Concept Publishing).

National Family Health Survey. 2016. http://rchiips.org/NFHS/factsheet_NFHS-4.shtml.

News 18. 2008. 'Durex Survey: Indians Not Sexually Satisfied, *News 18*, 30 April.

Sil, Narasingha P. 1995. Swami Vivekananda's concept of woman. *Bengal Studies Conference, University of Chicago,* https://www.lib.uchicago.edu/e/su/southasia/TESTold/Narasingha.1.html.

Trivedi, Ira. 2014. *India In Love* (New Delhi: Aleph).

Vivekananda, Swami. 1915. *The Complete Works of Swami Vivekananda* (Kolkata: Advaita Ashrama).

Vivekananda, Swami. 1897. The Sages of India lecture at Victoria Public Hall, Madras. 11 February.

World Population Prospects: The 2017 Revision, UNDESA Population division, New York. http://www.prb.org/pdf07/07WPDS_Eng.pdf.

Part II

ANCHORS

5

Love

More than anywhere else in the world, today in India we are experiencing many unforeseen and fast-changing socio-economic forces that are shaping and changing our destinies. We are catching up with capitalism, experimenting with our version of democracy, and constantly receiving information about the world that we may (or may not) interpret within our own differing local contexts. The unparalleled diversity of India ensures that the changes that take place here are never the same in two different regions of our country, and have varying levels of impact across economically and culturally different groups.

Evidently, as individuals and as a culture, our chances of survival depend on our ability to deal with these rapid and incalculable changes.

The amorphous nature of the ambiguity and chaos surrounding us makes it hard to deploy only our intellect as a compass to chart through life. I would argue that we also need to be in touch with our emotions to intuitively wade through unpredictable waters.

Drawing deductions from the information gathered by all our sensory organs and from memories buried in our subconscious mind, our emotions gauge the situation we are in. They tell us how we feel about it. We roar with laughter; smile broadly; have feelings of love, affection, sympathy, anger, envy; shed tears of joy and sorrow and so on, thus physiologically reacting to the emotions swelling within us.

Of course, the deductions that we make are biased, coloured by our experience of the various elements found in the situation. They are, after all, our perception of reality—a judgement made by the various faculties of our body. But so is the case with our intellect, reason and all the other deductive activity of the 'conscious' mind. These are also based on our own perception of what goes on around us. So, in fact, there is no objective reality. Emotions and intellect are both biased.

Emotions and intellect have their distinct roles in ensuring human survival and evolution, yet they are far from being divorced from each other. Both emotions and intellect are functions of our mental faculty. It is our brain that triggers feelings of pleasure and pain, falsifying the popular adage 'Think from the head, not the heart!' When we are equipped with intellect as well as emotional bandwidth, we can fully explore the human experience.

Just as we develop our intellectual capabilities, our emotional well-being also lies in allowing our body to explore the freedom to grasp clues from the environment to deduce how we truly feel. Do we permit ourselves to freely scan a situation and tell our brain how we really feel? Or are we trapped within our own biases? Are we limited by societal norms about feelings we must not acknowledge? While there is societal legitimacy in most places in the world for developing our intellectual capabilities, there are varying proportions of significance given by different societies to our emotional health.

In contemporary India we are often told to be wary of our softer emotions. If in love, we must deny it. If we are passionate, we must be 'sensible' and overcome it. If distressed or clinically depressed, we should not acknowledge it. It is common for a married man to be perceived as not manly enough if he is publicly devoted to his wife. Homosexuality is a contentious legal issue. Even a public display of heterosexual affection is socially taboo. We are hard on ourselves.

I have wondered if we hold a peculiar negative bias against the feeling and expression of love towards one another in India. Is love popular in the fantasy world we create in our cinema precisely because in our real world it is a threat? We fantasize about love in 'reel life' perhaps because we do not permit ourselves to experience it in reality. In our movies, a man can fight all societal pressures and court his woman incessantly until love wins against society, which is a dream for many in the audience. This popular storyline, as well as the unrealistic storytelling form of our movies, in which we break into song and dance at the slightest pretext, are both fantasy. In reality, neither do we in contemporary India break into a jig just like that, nor do we fight for love. In many societies, popular cinema is a mirror of reality, but that is not the case in ours. Instead, it seems to me that with over one billion of us scrambling for scant resources, we are prone to considering love—an emotion that it is as physiologically important and necessary to develop as our mental faculties of reason and intellect—as an unnecessary encumbrance at best.

On the banks of the river Ganga in Benares, in December 1952, Jiddu Krishnamurti—perhaps India's greatest contemporary philosopher—spoke to boys and girls aged between nine and twenty. His ninth address to them began with these words, 'You remember, yesterday morning we were discussing the complex problem of love? I do not think we shall understand it until we understand an equally complex problem which we call the mind.'[1]

---

[1] Krishnamurti 1952.

He asked the children, 'Why do we have to have love? Why should there be love? Can we do without it? What would happen if you did not have this so-called love?'

Indeed, why do we love? The question has intrigued philosophers, scientists, poets, historians and lovers all over the world, across all eras. The amount of attention given to this powerful emotion is befitting because it has so many variations—love between friends and family, the bond of love forged by soldiers who fight side by side in a war, flirtation, love for one's own self, a larger love for humanity, sexual passion and desire. It can be blind, one-sided, unreciprocated, misguided or unconditional. Love can be long-lasting, with commitment, goodwill and understanding, or fickle if passion and lust die early. It is a matter of popular debate whether only a long-lasting romantic relationship is considered love, whether all other forms of giving and receiving love are not 'love'. If one loves and lets it go, is it not really love? Without the commitment, is it mere infatuation? Without the passion, is it just dedication?

From an evolutionary perspective, all variations of love—short-lived or not—are a survival tool for our species. In any relationship involving love, individuals learn and grow from the experience. What love is depends on where we are in relation to it. In some instances, love might torment us or even emotionally destroy us for a while, but from this experience too, we learn about ourselves and about the other person. In that state, we desperately draw strength from all resources to survive, and grow as a person.

Love in all its delightful forms is an evolutionary mechanism to promote social relationships, support and feelings of safety and security. Whether long-lasting or short-lived, love provides an anchor. Even when love breaks, it leaves behind many lessons about managing the self in relation to others. There can be no mistakes in love, nothing right or wrong, as every instance of it leads to a greater understanding of humankind. There is therefore no reason to be fearful about love as there are only lessons of personal and collective growth and evolution to be gained from it.

Krishnamurti explains love's evolutionary role to his young audience thus:

> If your parents began to think out why they love you, you might not be here. They think they love you; therefore they want to protect you . . . Fortunately, there is this feeling of love . . . otherwise, you and I would not have been educated, would not exist.
>
> The real thing is to understand yourself . . . you will find out that the more you know about yourself physically as well as psychologically . . . the more you will find out the truth . . . It is that truth that will help you to be free.

I have found it perplexing that in India these days, while anger is permissible—and even sometimes perceived as courage and manliness—love is not. 'First comes marriage, then love!' is how we do it in India. It is difficult to find data on the number of arranged marriages in India, but various sources indicate that around 90 per cent of Indian marriages are not borne out of love.[2] Instead, they are arranged by families in the hope that love will blossom later. The alternative, where a couple falls in love first, literally called a 'love marriage', is a dirty thing. Nowhere else in the world does the term 'love marriage' exist, because most marriages now by default are preceded by love. But here, it is not so. In India, parents dread that their daughter's innocence will be lost in a love affair, and the careers of their sons ruined if they waste their time courting a girl. Any romance before

---

[2] I have written more about this in Chapter 3 titled 'Exploration'.

marriage must be covert, and affairs are likely to be dropped sooner or later anyway for a marriage arranged with a spouse chosen by the family.

In this regard, we have a peculiar sense of modernity, where many families consider themselves modern in giving their sons and daughters the worst lessons of hypocrisy. They tell their progeny that they are free to court the opposite sex for fun (not love!), but not marry them. Young ones are admonished against falling in love: 'Have fun, but do not fall in love!' For ultimately, when the time comes to marry a partner of the family's choice, breaking an attachment to someone else will only cause pain. Moreover, love makes us, quite literally, weak in the knees and vulnerable—and most of us in India are taught all our lives that it is not appropriate to be so. We are told that we must not let the bothersome animal encumbrance of our emotions take over.

Take a look at our epics. In the Ramayana and the Mahabharata, there have been great tales of love, such as that between Ram and Sita, which I have written about earlier in this book.[3] The nature of this relationship is, till date, held up as an example for today's generation. It is not uncommon to hear the compliment 'Ram aur Sita jaisi jodi hai' (the couple is like Ram and Sita). Even in this ancient epic, love developed in these relationships only after marriage. Ram won Sita over in a svayamvara ceremony—one of the seven permitted ways to choose a groom in the Vedic age— organized by Sita's father. Ram and Sita were married, and only thereafter came the love between them. On the other hand, in the Mahabharata, the great love affair between Radha and Krishna was never formalized as marriage. We also never hear a compliment likening a contemporary couple to the lovers Radha and Krishna.

---

[3] See Chapter 4 titled 'Procreation'.

The 700-verse Bhagavad Gita, set in a narrative framework of a dialogue between Krishna and Arjuna in the Mahabharata during the war against the Kauravas, warns that we must stay away from love. It defines love in the context of desire. It says that if we have a continuous desire for someone, it generates imagination (*bhavana*) about that person, which slows down our thought processes. The Gita further explains that such a state first leads to attachment (kama) and then to anger (*krodha*), which leads to infatuation (*sammoh*), then to the confusion of memory (*smritivibhrama*), thereafter to the loss of reason (*buddhinasha*), and ultimately to total ruin (*pranasha*).[4]

In an even earlier era, the Nyaya-Vaisheshika philosophy of the Vedic age considered love, and in fact all other emotions, to be a defect (*dosha*) or an impurity (*upadha*). Nyaya and Vaisheshika were two separate schools of thought, both belonging to the Vedic school of philosophy, but over time, they became so intertwined with each other that the two came to be referred to as one. The Nyaya-Vaisheshika philosophy explains that these 'defects' are the result of ignorance (*mithyajnana*) and they give rise to actions that lead to the feeling of pleasure or pain. It classifies the defects into three groups: attraction (*raga*), aversion (*dvesha*) and illusion (*moha*). In the first group, we find love, selfishness and greed. The second group includes anger, jealousy, envy, malice and resentment. The third group encompasses error, suspicion, pride and negligence. So according to this philosophy, there are no positive emotions. Even love was deemed a defect, ultimately, because all emotions lead to attachment and error.

Narada Muni, the great Vedic sage, travelling musician and witty and wise storyteller, who miraculously makes an appearance across several eras in the Mahabharata, the Ramayana, as well as in the mythologies of the earlier Puranas, has similar wisdom to

---

[4] Chidbhavananda 1965.

impart about love. This omnipresent sage has explained that an emotional state of attachment to someone can lead to five types of behaviour. One, if we consider the other superior to us, the attachment is called devotion (bhakti). Two, if we consider the other inferior to us, then the attachment is called infatuation (*vatsalya*). Three, if we consider the other equal, the attachment is called friendship (*maitri*). These three are relevant when a person is attached to another individual. If the attachment is to an object, he says, it is called craving (kama). Only when these four types of attachment are combined is it called love (*rati*). Narada explains that once someone is in love, that person becomes fully satisfied and does not think of or try for anything else—and therefore loses momentum!

The Brahmachari tradition in India is based on the principle of living a chaste life. Various yogic traditions also advise abstinence from attachment. On the other hand, the Kamasutra, written sometime between 400 BC and 200 AD, as well as various sculptures, paintings and literature, openly treats the themes of making love, erotica, sexual union and techniques of achieving pleasure. In an earlier essay in this book, I have written about the problematic relationship Indians have with sex. Now, I would argue that while we may be conflicted about our physical expression of attraction, desire, passion or lust, we have a clear bias against the emotional component—love.

Our bias against love is especially baffling when compared to the acceptance and, indeed, admiration we have in India for those who express love towards the divine. While love for a human being is considered the source for 'total ruin' by the Bhagavad Gita and indeed by large sections of contemporary Indian society, love and devotion towards God have been considered righteous, respectable and admirable in all eras. For instance, we have never had a large-scale 'Indian renaissance' that has attempted to place science above religion, nor have we ever had a social movement questioning the utility of devotees dedicating their lives to the love of God.

Instead, in India, losing oneself in immense love for the divine, to the extent of being able to think of nothing else, is held in high regard. The Bhakti Movement that originated in the south of India (but gained prevalence in the north from the fifteenth century onwards), revolved precisely around a person's immense love of God. Mirabai's devotional songs for Lord Krishna are well known. Besides, many of our gods come in pairs. The mythological stories of Vishnu–Lakshmi, Shiva–Parvati and Brahma–Saraswati (in the Hindu trinity) are full of tales of romantic love. In the south of India, both the wife and the lover of Lord Balaji are revered. Lovers Radha and Krishna are both worshipped.

This list of examples of the emotion of love mixing with divinity in India can go on and on, and most of them fall into three categories: first, the idea of God as the lover (Radha and Sita), second, love for God or the divine (love as worship), and third, the idea of the wife and husband as gods (the wife as Lakshmi and the husband as *pati-parameshvar*, or the worship of the husband through Shiv puja, *karva chauth* and so on).

It all leads one to wonder: Can love in India only have divine sanction? If, according to our ancient teachings, intense love towards humans and towards God has the same effect on our behaviour, how is love in both cases not admired equally by society?

There was no better place for me to find my answers than the city with maddening crowds and a striking culture, in which a sea of abject poverty ironically basks in the splendour of the Goddess of strength.

Kolkata, the city that Rudyard Kipling wrote about as having 'poverty and pride—side by side', had inspired V.S. Naipaul to draw a hellish literary image, despite its eccentric buildings resplendent with old-world charm. This city was home to the deceased Mother Teresa or 'saint of the gutters', a title that was as paradoxical as her city.

The day was drawing to an end, but sitting in my rusty Ambassador taxi, these thoughts had kept me alert. Watching me through his rear-view mirror, my taxi driver decided to entertain me. He inquired about the well-being of all members of my family. Was I married? Why not? Why was I in Kolkata? Ah! I was Bengali too! He was so pleased.

The closer we got to our destination, the more difficult it became to hear him speak above the roaring diesel engine on the increasingly bumpy ride. I stuck my head out of the window while the driver continued to list out all the spots in Kolkata that the local Bengalis flocked to.

'But they don't come here,' he added, as the vehicle made a definitive halt at a point where adults and children, clad in rags, lay sprawled in front of me—so many that the old Ambassador could proceed no further.

'Why don't they?' I asked, stepping out and passing him the Rs 50 taxi fare through the open window of his driver's seat.

'Who wants to see dying people, baba?' he replied, pushed his leather-sandal-shod foot on the dusty accelerator, and drove off.

I walked a few steps up the street, through the filth and the pairs and trios of starving people and dogs. On my left was a building once painted blue, with a prominent board announcing it as the Kalighat Municipal Corporation. At the turn on my right was a double-storey temple structure that displayed, at its entrance, a small signage that read 'Home For The Dying—Nirmal Hriday'. I entered it, climbing up a few steps that immediately led into an enormous hall that I estimated to be about 50 feet in length. It was lined with beds on two sides, on which lay those who had been abandoned by their families, brought here by volunteers to die with more dignity.

The sounds of pain and lament from the occupants of the beds mixed into one unholy humming sound that resounded in the hall.

I walked down the hall. The most fragile men that I had ever seen in my life lay on both sides of me on the plastic-covered mattresses of their beds. Some of them were wailing in a high-pitched voice, their eyes closed, fists clenched. A few intently watched me from atop their bed, their eyes following my moves. I walked over and sat by their side for a while. Some had been served a frugal meal of rice and lentils that they were hastily eating with their hands. There was very little medical support. Volunteers in casual clothes sat beside a few patients, a finger on the pulse of their patient's wrist, or holding their palms out with tablets on them.

'My son left me here to die,' one of the patients screamed at me from his bed. I went over and held his hand.

Stepping out of the hall, I stood at the base of the stairway that led to the nuns' quarters on the first floor, and the women's hall in an adjoining wing on that floor.

I felt a sudden tight grip on my ankle.

Looking down, I saw a man huddled in a blanket, sitting on the floor, gasping for breath and holding on to my feet with his hands.

'Are you a doctor?' he asked.

'No, I am not.'

'I need a doctor. Help me,' he pleaded, his eyes gleaming as if with anger.

I wondered if these would be his last words.

I quickly looked around for a volunteer, and saw a dozen of them in the hall busy helping the men breathing their last. I realized rather uncomfortably that I could not see a single Indian among them. Why were my fellow billion Indians not here to help? I walked over to a volunteer, who looked Scandinavian, and handed him a piece of paper with the numbers of a few local general practitioners I had scribbled on it.

I headed to the women's hall on the first floor. In the hall Just at the end of the stairway, I came across a group of Korean volunteers sitting around a large wooden dining table drawing up charts, along with an Indian resident missionary who introduced herself to me as Sister Rukmini.[5]

'I took a train from Bhopal twenty-two years ago to come here and meet Mother (Teresa),' she said.

'Why did you want to meet her?' I asked.

'I had wanted to dedicate my life to working for the needy. Mother was doing that and I joined her.'

'That's great. And what are they doing here?' I asked, pointing towards the group of Koreans at the dining table.

'They are drawing up a timetable which we will put up in the halls,' explained Sister Rukmini.

'But why do I not see any Indian volunteers around?' I probed.

She paused for a few seconds, and then slowly said, 'The Kalighat Municipal Corporation donated this temple to Mother Teresa. This is where Mother started her work in India, creating the Missionaries of Charity, out of love and compassion for the most needy. We are grateful to the municipality, but besides that, there has been little support from the locals,' she replied.

'Come, look here.' Sister Rukmini pulled me by my hand to the terrace outside. 'All these hundreds of people here, they stay away from Nirmal Hriday.'

She pointed, in the dim light of the setting sun, at the mile-long stretch below.

As a stark contrast to the atmosphere where we were, I saw a sea of animated people on the street downstairs. The street was lined with tightly packed shacks occupied with street

---

[5] Identity withheld.

hawkers energetically selling, to thousands of devotees, items to worship and adore the Goddess Kali's idol in the adjoining temple.

I hastily ran down the stairway and out on to the street.

'What are these garlands for?' I asked a woman, probably in her forties, a rose garland in one hand, a ten-rupee note in the other, who was elbowing her way through the crowd in front of her to the seller sitting in the shack.

'To offer to Maa Kali, what else for?'

'Why don't you visit there?' I asked, pointing to Nirmal Hriday, located about 50 metres away. 'That building, there.'

'I do not know what that building is,' she screamed, turning to look back at me from her spot, now at the front of the crowd. 'A temple?'

I asked a young man on the road, 'Do you know about Mother Teresa's home?'

'Yes, right here,' he replied, pointing with his chin towards Nirmal Hriday, which stood on our left.

'Have you ever been there?'

'No . . .'

'Why not?'

'Because I'll catch some deadly virus in there! God knows what kind of people they bring there and the diseases they have!' he said, alarmed.

A newly married couple was buying a set of utensils made of mud, each piece filled with a special offering to the Goddess. They stood in front of the shop, considering their final selection.

'Have you ever been to Mother Teresa's home for the dying?' I asked as they made their payment to the seller.

'No,' replied the man. 'It is bad luck to be near the dying.'

'But they are human beings like you. What bad luck can befall you if you offer them your support when they need it?'

'They are dirty people. I don't know who they are,' he said with a scowl.

'Why do you say they are dirty?' I insisted.

'Beggars, poor people, they are brought off the roads . . . who knows what work they did and where they lived?' he said, shrugging his shoulders as he walked off with his wife, holding their newly purchased offerings for God.

I spent the evening speaking to at least sixty more locals along the street. As night fell, the crowds got thicker. I persisted in seeking their attention.

'But she has got so much funding!' someone told me. 'Mother Teresa got money from everywhere in the world . . . her work doesn't need us.'

'No, I have never been there. I cannot touch strange people . . . I would feel weird doing that,' confessed another person.

'I have my own worries in life to tend to, baba!' said one man.

'Those are poor and sick people,' another man declared with repugnance.

The contrast was startling—revulsion towards humankind and exuberance towards the Goddess. I could accept that the locals kept away from Nirmal Hriday out of the fear of catching a disease, but I found it baffling that they considered poverty and homelessness 'dirty'. To be dirty is the physical state of being polluted. Poverty and homelessness, however, are socio-economic conditions. Evidently, here they were conflating an individual's socio-economic condition with his physical status!

I chose to write about our notion of dirt in India in the context of love because of our peculiar inability to embrace it. Our love for our fellow Indian citizens, or, for that matter, for humanity in general, is often carefully directed only towards those we do not consider 'dirty'. In the past, status in India was prescriptive, a consequence of one's birth. The lower castes were perceived as 'dirty'. Today, status in India can be acquired by other means such as wealth, lifestyle and political power. But this has clearly not made people more egalitarian in their outlook. The definitions have just been reworked—of who the 'dirty' people' are—and incorporated into society's new pecking order.

Poor people, the homeless, homosexuals, even women, are apparently on the low end of society's pecking order today. And by habit, we feel that these 'dirty' people are undeserving of love and compassion. These sections of our society, in turn, often make do with receiving less of these emotions. There is evidence from behavioural science and economics, the work of Mullainathan and Shafir, which shows that scarcity creates a psychological ability in everyone struggling to manage with less than they need.[6]

I found this trait to be linked to an evolutionary mechanism. We have a primordial ability to nurture and take care of those we do not consider 'different' from our own selves, and in that sense, consider part of our group. It is this instinct to protect one's clan that has helped preserve several animal species, even humans. And so, in a stratified society such as India, we only consider those who are at our 'level' to be part of our group. Earlier, this was defined by caste, and now, it is increasingly by socio-economic status. Those who are at a socio-economic level below ours are not part of our group and we cannot care for them.

We cannot even perceive the pain of those 'below' us in status, because we are unable to empathize with them. We can argue that empathy in the human species is also born out of a survival instinct. It originates from the perception abilities of animal groups that need to be able to interpret the appearance of other animals to predict their behaviour, so that they can take appropriate action such as attacking, hiding or playing dead. While empathy is valuable for

---

[6] Shafir and Mullainathan 2013.

survival, an important precondition for it is that we must consider the subject of our empathy to be like our own selves. We typically have empathy for those in whom we see our own selves in some way. But when we consider someone inferior to us (or even superior), we find it difficult to empathize with them.

In India, inequality permeates several aspects of our personal life. Often, arranged marriages in India are also based on the principle of inequality, and not love. Large parts of India have a patriarchal society. Here, the groom and his family are superior in status to the bride. They may ask for many gifts (dowry) from the bride's family, and impose rules upon her against her wishes. According to media reports, in 2010 alone, grooms and their families have been reported to have burnt alive 8391 brides on pretexts such as disobedience and lack of dowry. A decade before that, in 2000, there were 6995 such cases.[7] In the majority of arranged marriages, however, since they have the same cultural background and family support, the couple adjusts to each other. Many of these marriages are stable because both do not have equal power, and therefore do not step on each other's toes. In a couple that comes together based first on love, they form certain said and unsaid rules by which both are equally bound. In contrast, in an arranged marriage, it is only one (in most cases the husband) who leads the way, and the spouse follows. This is one of the several reasons for India's low divorce rates—0.3 per cent in 2011 as compared to about 50 per cent in the United States.[8] The 'arrangement' of arranged marriages seems to last and last.

This is why, in comparison to the topsy-turvy emotional route that love takes us through, Indian society prefers the stability

---

[7] Varma 2012.

[8] According to the Census of India 2011, there were 4,225,940 divorces for a population of 1,247,000,000. On this subject, see Dutt 2015. I have also discussed this in Chapter 4 titled 'Procreation'.

induced by the inequality of an arranged marriage. No wonder our epics, ancient scriptures and sages warn us to be wary of emotions. Marriage, not love, has become the anchor for family, community and society in India while love here is for the movies and for God—both not easily reachable for ordinary mortals.

References

Chidbhavananda, Swami, ed. 1965. *The Bhagavad Gita: Original Stanzas* (Tamil Nadu: Tapovanam Publishing House).

Dutt, Apoorva. 2015. How and why number of young Indian couples getting divorced has risen sharply. *Hindustan Times,* 4 January.

Krishnamurti, Jiddu. 1952. Ninth talk to boys and girls at Rajghat, 19 December. http://jiddu-krishnamurti.net/en/1952/1952-12-19-jiddu-krishnamurti-9th-talk-to-boys-and-girls.

Shafir, Eldar, and Sendhil Mullainathan. 2013. *Scarcity: Why Having Too Little Means So Much* (London: Macmillan Publishers).

Varma, Subodh. 2012. Dowry death: One bride burnt every hour. *Times of India,* 27 January.

6

Parenting

A visit to the city of Kota reveals a million real stories about parental pressure on children in India.

Kota is India's capital city when it comes to test preparation, which has spawned a $400 million exam industry here.[1] Aspiring students come to Kota and study in the city's 'test preparation schools' for as long as three months to several years—an essential rite of passage for many seeking admission to India's top colleges. They dream of winning admission to the exclusive IITs, the sixteen public colleges whose graduates are recruited immediately by global companies offering large salaries. Graduating from one of the IITs, considered the Ivy League of engineering education in India, is a ticket to an elevated social status and a guaranteed job in India or Silicon Valley in the US.

Every year, about 1.5 million students take the IIT entrance exam, but less than 10,000 are accepted into the institutes. In 2016, about 160,000 students from across India flocked to Kota's schools, but only a few were successful. In the meantime,

---

[1] Lakshmi 2016.

twenty-nine of the students in Kota who failed the entrance exam committed suicide.[2]

One of the suicide notes read, 'I am responsible for my suicide. I cannot fulfil papa's dream.'

Another boy wrote, 'Daddy, I hate maths. I am a good-for-nothing son,' ending his suicide note with a frowny face.[3]

These juvenile suicides, committed under the burden of ambition, are not uncommon in India, and we must ask whose ambition it is that they are burdened with. At the age of fifteen or less, it is not likely that all of them have such an intense ambition in them to clear an exam.

It is also not uncommon to hear of Indian parents goading their children to study hard for a stable job—regardless of what stability means in an increasingly unstable world. If we look at data on this subject, a recent survey conducted by a global bank found that 'career success' turned out to be the most popular goal Indian parents have for their children, outranking that of a 'happy life'.[4] The same survey indicated that Indian and Mexican parents were the keenest in the world that their children be successful in their careers. And more parents in India than anywhere else believed that a postgraduate degree was necessary for their children to achieve their life goals.

Whether it is love, money, education, status, freedom, friends, affection or time, a real or perceived deprivation in any of these aspects of life could leave us all (parents or not) reacting in ways different from the normal. We could be thinking obsessively of nothing else other than that specific pressing need. It might develop in us a keener sense of the value of the resource we lack, or it might be

---

[2] Ibid.

[3] Ibid.

[4] Malhotra 2015.

so debilitating that it could shrink our mental horizons and narrow our perspective. Indeed, in the country with the largest number of malnourished children on the planet, there are several situations that induce a sense of deprivation. It is then these reactionary behaviours by parents that severely affect the context in which children in India grow up. Parents indeed want the best for their children, and when they have been deprived of something themselves, they would often be keen to ensure their children aren't.

Many parents, frustrated with their own condition, search for avenues of social justice in the schools of Kota. The test preparation schools here, and plenty others elsewhere in India, promise to catapult families out of their state of deprivation. Kota is rife with stories of how children of railway station baggage handlers, truck drivers and cycle rickshaw pullers study and make it to IIT and other prestigious colleges, changing the fortunes of the entire family. Bringing up a child in India involves the same intensely nurturing emotions as anywhere else in the world, yet parenting here holds a mirror to the dark, dubious side of a fast and unequally developing economy.

I would argue that for children in any country, it is not the GDP of a nation per se, but the quality of economic growth in areas such as health, the crime rate, income distribution and so on that matters more. A healthy mother is more likely to give birth to a healthy child. A society with a low crime rate will be a more nurturing environment for the child to grow up in, with safety and freedom. On the other hand, if there is inequality in the economy—no matter how fast it is growing—there will be parents who will live their entire lives feeling a lack of resources. And these parents would be bringing up their children in a different way from what they would have done otherwise.

In India, not only is there a severe lack of health and nutrition interventions, which inhibits a child's developmental potential, but also an abnormally skewed pattern of education opportunities. On the one hand, there is a vast illiterate population, and on the other a privileged few are likely to get the best education resources to become even better. Increasingly, boys and girls are equally likely to be enrolled in school, but boys are more likely to be attending private schools and to have more money spent on their education.[5] We do not have enough primary schools—and even fewer schools where teachers are not missing from class—but we have world-class higher education institutions.

However, while we hear the success stories of a few sacrificing parents who train the 'first-bench boys' of our country, the majority, whose children occupy the middle and last benches, are invisible. The pressure exerted on children in this category is terribly damaging. The consequent cases of juvenile suicide are often ignored, because every success in India is supposed to herald the birth of a thousand dreams, whereas every failure anonymously fades away.

I had been spared, but my brother, nine years my junior, was at the receiving end of my parent's life project. They aspired to make him an IIT success. My brother was an average student, a keen cricket player, and an excellent debater. When he was in middle school, I wrote his debate speeches, my mother would sit up with him all night to make him learn by rote what I had written, and he would go on to deliver a spectacular performance to bring home the prize.

By the time my brother reached senior school, we had moved to live in New Delhi as my father had retired from the Indian Air Force. After a lifetime of service to the country, he had been awarded a pension which was barely enough to cover our family's

---

[5] Boyden and Dercon 2012, 1.

monthly bills. My mother worked as a teacher at a local school, and in the evenings, she would teach at home to help our family make ends meet. I did odd jobs, such as working as an usher at exhibitions to cover my university fee and all living expenses. My brother studied in the school in which my mother taught, and so his school fee was waived. However, three years before his IIT entrance exam, my parents decided to shift him to another school that was reputed for having the maximum number of students qualify for IIT. There would be no more sports and co-curricular activities for him. In the evenings, after school, my father would drop him off at an IIT coaching centre in south Delhi, where he, along with some five hundred young children, would be trained in a cramped, windowless room for a test that was three years away.

My father took loans and worked at jobs far beneath his calibre as an aeroplane pilot. Unable to cope with either the corruption or the callous attitude in the 'civilian world', as we call it, he would quit each time. We would all be relieved when this happened as none of us liked seeing him struggle. To make up for the loss of income, my mother would increase the number of students who came home every evening for tuitions. At night, my father would pick up my brother from his coaching class, so that he could study from another remote-learning coaching package he had been enrolled in, complete the homework prescribed by the teachers at his new school, and prepare for his frequent assignments and exams. Bafflingly, the curriculum for the IIT entrance exam is different from the curriculum at school. On his fifteenth birthday, I had bought him a basketball and hoop, which he immediately put up in the courtyard of our home. For three years, the only physical activity he did was shoot the ball in the basket a few times during study breaks.

At the end of three years, my brother's school marks dipped because of his focus on the IIT entrance exam. He was unrecognizable in appearance and spirit—he had fattened up and was irritable most of the time. He was demanding with my mother, who would sit up with him at nights, helping him learn by rote lessons in organic chemistry, a subject she had herself never studied. There was one picture of the monkey god Hanuman on his study table and one inside his books. My parents became more devout than ever before. There were always more books to be bought for my brother, and we sold our family home to continue his coaching classes and get him all the study material he needed.

Finally, the time came for the IIT exam. My brother's scores did not make for the top percentile, which was required to study at IIT. This meant he had failed. Moreover, his moderate performance in school got him a seat in a relatively low-ranked college in Delhi. I will never forget the reaction—my family remained unfazed by his results. My brother decided to forsake his seat in college, take the year off from any formal education, and instead prepare again for the IIT entrance test the following year. My parents supported him wholeheartedly. By then, I had moved out of India to pursue my own university education in Paris on a full scholarship. I worried for my parents in New Delhi, working as a team to support my brother, who did nothing else but sit at home and prepare for the fourth straight year to make it through to IIT.

The following year, he succeeded in clearing the IIT entrance. It was as if an unsurmountable weight had been lifted off our family's shoulders. We could laugh and make plans again. With the savings from my scholarship money, I organized tightly budgeted holidays for my parents in Europe. When I started working, I would get my brother to live with me in Paris during his summer vacations and send him off with a camera I'd gifted him to Amsterdam, Madrid, Rotterdam. I would hook him up as an intern at local companies in Paris, and take him out to bars. All those years of preparing for one ghastly test had to be undone.

My brother eventually regained his social skills and physique, as well as his humour. He completed a master's degree in the human computer interface degree at Carnegie Mellon University in the US, and after a year of work in Washington DC, he joined Google's headquarters in San Francisco. I was not sure whose dream it was—his or my parents'—that had come true. Perhaps my parents' dreams had become my brother's. I was only glad that things turned out the way they did instead of going wrong as they do for so many people.

I have often talked to my parents about those gruelling years they chose to put my brother through. We reminisce about the shared experience of the struggle, and the pride it ultimately brought us. My parents—much to mine and my brother's frustration and admiration—have insisted on living their lives in exactly the same manner as before. They do not accept financial support from us. Indeed, the story of each child and each parent is different. However, after returning to India as an adult and a soon-to-be-parent myself, I feel I am better able to understand the sense of perennial deprivation that frames the context for this behaviour.

First, there is an overarching sentiment among adults in India that nothing ever works here. It is not just the 21.9 per cent of Indians living below the poverty line who feel the lack of resources.[6] The colossal size of our population, combined with pathetic distribution systems of food, money and health services,

---

[6] World Bank 2013.

leaves hundreds of millions wanting more. We are habituated to expect that due resources will either not reach us at all or not be received in their entirety, and certainly not on time. Adults, no matter how wealthy, are frustrated, and do not wish this life for their children.

Second, most of our educational institutions were established in the decade or so after Independence, by the elite who focused on higher education as that was what they themselves desired the most. They ignored the needs of the masses, who still lack primary education. Since then, education, and Macaulay's gift of the English language, has at times become more of a divisive force than one that could unite Indians—there are many who shame those who are uneducated in English and speakers of vernacular languages. The generation that does not speak English wants their child to do so. Education is an asset that has changed fortunes— parents who have not had any know its value, and push their children towards it.

Third, the social stratification of the caste system, fortified by class hierarchy based on wealth and societal status, bestows a feeling of relative deprivation on anyone who is not top of the pecking order. A wealthy businessman might feel he lacks the influence of a major politician. A working-class woman could feel she deserves a better job. A street beggar might feel that education could have got him money and more dignity. There are many social ladders of hierarchy in India—far more in number and rungs than any other country—and most of us are simultaneously positioned at different levels on several ladders. As a result, we are lower than someone else on one ladder or another. Often, we see the continuation of our own lives in our children, and the climb up these ladders continues through them.

An entire book can be written on the number of reasons Indians feel constantly deprived of resources. The approach to parenting in India has been severely affected by this, with parents hoping that their children will make up for what they lack, in terms of the evolution of social and/or economic status. We ask ourselves as parents: How can I ensure that my child has what I do not have? Can my child improve my own condition?

While the first question seems altruistic, the second question is considered selfish and unspeakable. A parent who sacrifices many years of his life to further the career of their child, and does not work hard enough towards their own, is regarded as morally superior to the parent who works at achieving his own personal ambition. This is odd, because by this logic, an industrialist who toils to produce a fortune and a man who robs a bank can be regarded as equally immoral, since they both have sought wealth for their selfish benefit. There is a demonization of selfishness that has created double standards and contradictions in relationships, including that between a parent and a child.

Working mothers suffer from the guilt and social stigma of being too selfish to not be with their children all day. In India the forces that make them feel so are at work even before a child is born.

Around the time I began writing this essay, I discovered I was pregnant. Elated at the news, I immediately went to a gynaecologist at a well-known clinic in the posh Khan Market area of central Delhi. The doctor was a pleasant, middle-aged woman dressed in a pastel cotton salwar kameez. Swinging out of her chair behind the desk, she briskly walked over to her ultrasound machine and asked me to lie down on the bed next to it. A quick check later, it was confirmed that a child was indeed in the making. Thereafter, she was chatty, obviously accustomed to naive first-time mothers-to-be like myself, and was ready to offer ample advice.

'You must now restrict yourself to the bed. Just lie still and avoid movement,' she said.

'Lie in bed for the next seven months?!' I asked, aghast. 'What about travel? I have to be in Dubai and Paris for work next month!'

'No, no, avoid air travel. No exercise. No sex. Eat bland food,' she admonished. 'Make these sacrifices for your baby.'

I sat there staring at her, devastated at the pronouncement and the prospect of the next few months. A few moments later, I felt even worse, guilty that I was thinking about lifestyle and work commitments instead of the well-being of my unborn child. But I had erroneously presumed that an experienced doctor's advice must be based on scientific facts.

'Do not eat papaya and pineapple,' the doctor continued with her advice.

A few months later, at a jazz bar in one of Delhi's luxury boutique hotels, I was stopped by a bouncer at the door.

'Madam, no. You cannot enter,' he said.

'Why not?'

'You are pregnant.'

'Yes, so?' I asked, surprised. 'I have a few months to go before I deliver!'

'Sorry, we can't let you in—hotel policy,' he said, holding me by my elbow and taking me aside.

'Which law is this hotel policy based on?' I asked. By now, the man had been joined by his colleague, both dressed in black pant suits with walkie-talkies in hand.

'No, no policy, there is just loud music and a lot of movement inside. People are walking around, it is not safe for pregnant women,' the second man said.

'And who are you to decide what is safe for me?' I asked. 'A pregnant woman is capable of using her own judgement about what is best for her.'

'I have heard pregnant women should not go to bars,' said the first man. 'You cannot enter, madam.'

Another two months later, in the last trimester of my pregnancy, I began to wonder and plan how I could best manage all the changes that would come with the baby. I decided to work till the end of my pregnancy, until the delivery, and thereafter take about three months of maternity leave. The Government of India had recently and generously extended the duration of paid maternity leave from three months to six. I wanted to be active, productive and financially secure as well as a good mother, and give my utmost to my firstborn. In all the previous organizations I worked at—none of them in India—I came across women who were pregnant, yet living a healthy, active and efficient work and social life until the last day of their pregnancy. That was how I had always aspired to be. Moreover, since age seventeen, I had earned my living and I wanted to continue doing that to fend for myself and ensure my baby's comfort. I had checked that I was medically healthy enough to do so.

'You must keep your priorities straight,' a top human resources executive once told me.[7]

'And which are?'

'Your priority is your baby. In the last two months before your delivery, you should stop working. There is nothing much to do at work anyway. Budgets have been squeezed as well.'

'Of course not. I am in good health, and I will work till the end of my pregnancy.'

'No, it will not be possible for us to allow that. I have consulted all our colleagues and we think it is best for you to rest and return only after six months or so.'

---

[7] Identity withheld.

'Six months! That is for me to decide, isn't it?' I asked, rolling my eyes at this judgement passed by the company's all-male top management. 'What about maternity? Will these six months be paid?'

'No. You can avail the medical insurance provided by the company. We have a very good insurance package that will cover a lot of the medical costs,' he said.

The beginning of the journey of parenthood is often scarred by stereotypes based on the personal beliefs of doctors, entertainment providers and employers, who would usually be expected to abide by science, fact and law. But in India, this is not always the case. For example, I later discovered that my gynaecologist had mixed old granny tales of abstinence from papaya and pineapple into her medical beliefs. Regular exercise and a healthy sex life, I later learnt, are beneficial during pregnancy. My unborn baby and I travelled to six countries and there was no problem. All this makes me wonder how many pregnant women in India are grounded by the agents of society, their health ruined by lack of activity, spirits dampened by clichés, and their careers written off by narrow-minded employers who wrongly undermine their capabilities. If they do not give in to these pressures, they are made to feel terribly guilty about being bad parents.

The demonization of selfishness continues to be inflicted on parents even after their baby is born. Parents who cannot afford to provide the best material facilities for their child are made to feel that they have been egoistic and not sacrificed enough. On the other hand, young couples who are both working hard to earn a livelihood in the 24/7 corporate work culture in India are shamed for being 'absent parents'.

Divorced parents face the social stigma of choosing their own happiness over that of their children, who are assumed to derive a benefit from the presence of quarrelling parents. In contrast, as I pointed out earlier, parents who make great sacrifices of their own happiness, for the education or careers or well-being of their children, are considered by society to be morally superior to those who have not done so. Often, this is despite the tendency of the sacrificing parent to suffer a deep sense of resentment. Such a parent might hope that the child would make sacrifices for the parent's benefit as well, making it akin to a burden.

These ethical parenting conflicts are common in India's urban pockets as well as in the sixteen-million-strong Indian diaspora, where parents struggle to build a life in a new environment as well as raise a family. The majority of Indians—68 per cent of our population, or 833 million people—who live in villages, have other additional issues.

In rural India, a farmer who needs more male hands for farm work might have his infant daughter killed as she is perceived as useless while he seeks to pursue the economic stability of the family. Female infanticide has been banned since 1870[8] in parts of the subcontinent, but it persists in many corners of our country even today. One of the major reasons it occurs is the uneven allocation of resources (not always the lack of them).[9] Limited resources are often distributed unevenly, and so within poor households, the least-advantaged person, often the girl child, is likely to suffer the most from shortfalls and incomplete protection. And so, even if she is allowed to live, the daughter is still likely to be treated as a burden because her eventual marriage will involve dowry and gifts demanded by the groom's family. She is not considered much help on the work front anyway.

---

[8] The Female Infanticide Prevention Act, 1870.
[9] Poddar 2013.

Meanwhile, it is common to hear in public conversations among the educated lot in India that a daughter is a great liability for the parents, which ends only when the daughter gets married. The socio-economic context is such that this is said without hesitation, and often as a gesture of parental love for daughters. This attitude is ultimately echoed in contemporary Indian films, popular television shows and literature. It is a dangerous chicken-and-egg situation that produces a highly regressive attitude towards the girl child who is perceived to have little to do in improving her own condition or that of her parents, and is therefore considered better off married and gone.

The attitude is so pervasive that girls are married off dangerously young across the country. Currently, 320,000 girls below the age of fifteen in India are married, and have already given birth to two children—an alarming increase of 88 per cent from 2001. Further, 280,000 married girls in the age group of fifteen to nineteen have already given birth to four children, which is also an increase of 65 per cent from 170,000 in 2001.[10]

This trend is not symptomatic of only parental neglect or aversion—it is also a consequence of the persistently degrading socio-economic scenario in India. While the GDP was soaring, 82 per cent of rural India still lacked basic amenities in 2010, and 240 million Indians do not have access to basic electricity even in 2017.[11] Moreover, the presence of television and other media have made them aware of what they are not privileged enough to possess. Therefore, if undue parental pressure, female infanticide, regarding a daughter's education inferior to a son's[12] and early marriage are considered actions taken by desperate

---

[10] Saha 2016.

[11] Singh 2010; Singh and Sundria 2017.

[12] Kingdon 2005.

parents to improve their socio-economic condition, we can agree that the only way to put an end to these practices is ensuring more equitable economic growth.

The state of parenting in India, when seen through this lens of resource deprivation, shows us the darkest side of unequal economic growth. In a fast developing economy that lacks equality, the risks for the most vulnerable sections are cumulative. The greatest burdens fall on those who are disadvantaged to begin with, and the greatest threat is to the development of young children in families who feel pressured and disadvantaged.

Children are influenced by their experiences, actions and interactions, as well as by broader environmental influences, including the values and feelings of their parents, which in turn are coloured by the condition they grow up in.[13] If parents feel pressured by societal expectations and financial constraints, their angst is reflected in the upbringing of their children. The quality of children's social, emotional and moral development, especially their sense of identity and self-worth, is shaped by how they understand this, and their interpretation of their role in causing pain to their parents. This is how children gradually gauge their relative social position, competence and access to opportunities for personal, social and economic advancement. And so, growing up in an atmosphere of the parents' real or perceived resource deprivation has adverse influences on a child.

For India's economic growth to benefit our children, we need equitable access to jobs, effective fiscal regimes, and policies to support families, especially those that have been consistently

---

[13] Engle and Black 2008; Rogoff 2003; Sameroff 2010; Wachs and Rahman 2013.

excluded till date. We need growth that promotes good health, a safe environment, law-abiding employers, and a strong social security net, provided by the government and the private sector, which eliminates absolute poverty and reduces feelings of relative deprivation.

References

Boyden, Jo, and Stefan Dercon. 2012. Child development and economic development: Lessons and future challenges. UNICEF, p. 1.

Census of India 2011. http://censusindia.gov.in.

Engle, Patrice L., and Maureen M. Black. 2008. The effect of poverty on child development and educational outcomes. *Annals of the New York Academy of Sciences* 1136.1, pp. 243–56.

Kingdon, Geeta Gandhi. 2005. Where has all the bias gone? Detecting gender bias in the intra-household allocation of educational expenditure in rural India. *Economic Development and Cultural change*, 53.2, pp. 409–52.

Lakshmi, Rama. 2016. A spate of suicides highlights the pressures on students in India. *Washington Post*, 23 January.

Malhotra, Aditi. 2015. What Indian parents want most for their children. *Wall Street Journal*, 13 August.

Poddar, Namrata. 2013. Female infanticide—India's unspoken evil. Huffington Post UK, 26 April.

Rogoff, Barbara. 2003. *The Cultural Nature of Human Development*. (Oxford: Oxford University Press).

Saha, Devanik. 2016. Nineteen million women in India have given birth to seven or more children. Wire, 10 May.

Sameroff, Arnold. 2010. A unified theory of development: A dialectic integration of nature and nurture. *Child Development* 81.1 pp. 6–22.

Singh, Mahendra Kumar. 2010. 82% rural India still lacks basic amenities. *Times of India*, 16 November.

Singh, Rakesh Kumar, and Saket Sundria. 2017. Living in the dark: 240 million Indians have no electricity. Bloomberg, 24 January.

Wachs, Theodore D., and Atif Rahman. 2013. The nature and impact of risk and protective influences on children's development in low-income countries. *Handbook of Early Childhood Development Research and its Impact on Global Policy,* pp. 85–122.

World Bank. 2013. Poverty and Equity, http://povertydata.worldbank.org/poverty/country/IND.

7

Values

Over and above linguistic, religious and other diversities, we Indians also belong to more than a thousand caste-based communities. We can further be affiliated to various other groups based on kinship, political beliefs, love for a sport, personal wealth, shared interest in spotting Martians on Earth, and so on. An Indian could typically be part of more groups at once than anyone else in the world.

In light of this, the place for individuality in India is therefore supremely interesting. How do we manoeuvre between societal and individual values and beliefs? If we do manage to balance the two, where does that balancing act lead us? Ultimately, what are our values? These are the main questions I will investigate in this essay.

As individuals, a particular value might be very significant to you, but unimportant to me, and there might be some values that are crucial to the entire group that you and I both belong to. Further, you might have a certain value that you are—often not consciously—obstinate about, whereas about others you might be more flexible. This creates your own hierarchy of values; it's as if they are stacked right at the top of your head, and the most important ones make you react with feeling as soon as they are activated.

For example, if freedom is an important value for you, you will fight when it is threatened, feel despair when you are helpless to protect it, and be ecstatic when you can enjoy it. If you value freedom less, you will be less affected by its presence or absence. This hierarchical structure of values ascertains which beliefs we consider more or less important. And the group that you and I both belong to could demonstrate a completely different hierarchy of values than yours or mine. Ultimately, your actions depend on the strength of your own individual beliefs as well as the flexibility the group practises in allowing individual members' values to dominate the group's values.

This manoeuvring between individual and group values is significantly more so in India, where we put a great deal of effort into retaining our relations with kin and clan. More than people in most other parts of the world, an Indian will be likely to place greater faith in his personal ties with family and community than in the state or other institutions in general. Why?

First, in India, there are no state-level policies offering significant unemployment dole or health insurance to all. The government does not provide us any substantial social security. And so when the chips are down, we have few options besides relying on kith and kin.

Second, the implementation of labour laws across all sectors in India is alarmingly weak, and even corporate employers have poor employee protection mechanisms. In the absence of governmental social protection and with the high attrition rates at corporations, private insurance companies in India shy away from offering products such as redundancy insurance, intended to protect an individual from job loss. This is a fairly common insurance product offered by companies in many parts of the world. In case of a loss of employment, it is the family and community that come to the rescue in India.

Third, politicians gathering votes during election campaigns in India have placed a premium on appeasing the various groups we belong to, and not the needs of individuals. Thereafter, the policy emphasis of the politician in power has also been on communities more than on individuals. The individual is not the focus of the state, and the citizen knows this so well that it adds to the growing deficit of trust in the state among the masses.

Fourth, this deficit of trust between the state and citizens is further increased by the fact that influential Indians often manage to successfully leverage state resources, police protection, government projects and so on for their own benefit, while the masses are left high and dry.

There is, therefore, hardly any alternative for Indians but to keep relations with family and traditional community groups strong, so they can be used as fallback options during periods of crisis. The retention of these community ties then becomes a sort of social insurance or a safety network.

European sociologists have often emphasized that the flourishing of what they call 'traditional' community ties, with kith, kin and clan, for instance, is not a characteristic of a 'modern' society. According to the French sociologist Émile Durkheim, in such traditional cultures, there is little individuation.[1] He explained that as a society becomes more complex and modern, individuals play more specialized roles and become more dissimilar in their experiences, interests and values. However, as we know, Indian society is distinctly reliant on community bonds and affiliations. In India, we do not operate alone. By this token, then, are we pre-modern?

---

[1] Durkheim 1893.

I find it extremely problematic to assess Indians' 'modernity' on the basis of a Western framework of analysis. This was what was done by orientalist British writers such as William Jones, Henry Colebrooke, Nathaniel Halhead, Charles Wilkins, and philosophers such as John Stuart Mill. This is problematic because the context of European thinkers such as Durkheim, a century and a half ago was characterized by the advent in western Europe of industrialization and the birth of capitalism, with no democracy. Modernity in Europe, therefore, primarily meant technological progress, individual specializations and profit, sans the feeling of shared nationhood. In India, on the contrary, we fought against the British, and established democracy fifty years before we began to embrace capitalism. There was no place for individual entrepreneurship in India for almost fifty years after we won our political freedom. The free market did not exist and, till the 1990s, we were not thinking much about things like beating the competition and making individual headway for profit. The inversion of the sequence of events regarding democracy and capitalism in India, vis-à-vis Europe, has altered the trajectory of social evolution here.

Today we have Indians who, in their writings, also measure India from the Western perspective of modernity. Many contemporary Indian writers in English cater to the international interest in the 'darker side of India'. In a study on contemporary orientalist writings in India, Lisa Lau and Om Prakash Dwivedi write:

> The production and consumption of Indian writing in English takes place within a distinctly postcolonial framework, and clearly re-Orientalism and Orientalism permeate this industry at all levels, and in no insignificant degrees.[2]

---

[2] Lau and Dwivedi 2014, 118.

But to understand India and its values, we need to look at India from an Indian perspective. We need to inspect our own social history in cities and villages. Without boxing ourselves into separate tranches of 'modernity' and 'tradition', we must assess, in the Indian context, what our affiliations to communities means to us. Even if we agree that traditional clans and culturally determined communities wield substantial influence on how we think and act, this cannot make us 'pre-modern' by Europe's standards. Rather, let us then find out what those influences are that our family and communities wield on us. In what way does the society around us influence our individual values and beliefs?

There are several villages located around the Jindal Steel and Power Group factories in the Raigarh district of Chhattisgarh in central India. About two years ago, at dawn, a stroll along the main roads encircling the villages offered me a view of at least a hundred bare buttocks in a row. Men, women and children sat on their haunches with their backs turned towards me, defecating. Walking further, I discovered that the local waterbody—essentially the reservoir of a small dam—was spotted even more profusely with naked bodies performing intimate ablutions. The same water, I knew, was used for drinking and cooking.

This was as saddening as it was baffling, because, according to the district administration, this specific village was covered in the government's Open Defecation Free States programme. Under this scheme, families had been granted Rs 12,000 each by the local municipal authorities, with which they were to construct toilets in their homes.[3]

'Why are you not using the toilet at home?' I asked a four-year-old who was on his way home after finishing the big job.

'My mother told me to go outside,' he replied shyly.

---

[3] *Indian Express* 2016.

I followed the little boy to identify his home, and then returned later the same day to speak to the boy's family.

A woman in a brightly coloured sari, perhaps in her late twenties, opened the door I knocked on. I introduced myself meekly as an employee of the Jindal Group, not knowing how she would react to my sudden visit. I added that I wanted to speak to her for her opinion on a sanitation project we wanted to do in her village.

She said her name was Dhoopwati[4] and welcomed me into her brick house, offering me a seat in a living room whose walls had been plastered with mud painted a bright shade of pink. She left me to fetch a glass of water. Looking around, I saw that the house had a similar layout to the others I had visited on earlier occasions— the entrance was small and led to a narrow corridor, where shoes and slippers were removed before entering the rest of the house. A few rooms were located on both sides of the corridor, including the small living room where I sat. The kitchen was large, occupying the most prominent part of the house next to an open courtyard.

As I sat waiting for Dhoopwati to return, I noticed a 2-foot wide chamber constructed of sheets of asbestos across the courtyard.

After some polite talk about the village and her well-being, I pointed to the asbestos contraption and asked, 'What is that?'

'It is a toilet,' she said.

'Can I go and see it?' I asked, to which she nodded her head in agreement.

Four narrow cement steps led to a door clasped with a rope to the rest of the structure. Inside the chamber, there was a hole in the floor.

'Where is the flush?' I asked.

---

4 Identity withheld.

'What is a flush?'

'How does everything get drained out?'

'Oh, we don't use this,' Dhoopwati explained. 'The government told us to make this, and gave us some money,' she went on. 'But in our culture, we cannot have toilets in the house. So we do not use this.'

'Why can you not have a toilet in the house?'

'*Chhi chhi,* it is dirty. It has to be far away from the house. Here we cook food that we eat,' she said, pointing to the large, majestic kitchen of her home.

Over the next few weeks, I visited thirty more families in Dhoopwati's village, and another fifty families in the surrounding five villages. Each time, I made the highly unusual request of investigating their toilets, if they had one at home. Maintaining a photo diary of the toilets I visited, I compared my list to the government records for toilets built under the Open Defecation Free States scheme. Many of the toilets I saw were just shanties built over a hole in the ground. I discovered several addresses mentioned in the official records that did not actually exist in the village. And in most cases, I observed, the villagers still went out of their homes to urinate and defecate. I also visited a public toilet that had to be unlocked for me, as it had not been used since its construction several years ago.

In one village, the local sarpanch, a lady, had taken an iron-fisted approach. She had laid down the rule that anyone who saw another villager defecating in the open would whistle aloud in public, and report the case in the weekly village council meetings. The offender would be fined Rs 1000. The sarpanch explained to me angrily that the non-usage of toilets at home was not so much a matter of discomfort as of culture.

By this time, I had started evaluating the benefits of using the resources of the Jindal Group to build toilets in these villages. At the time of my investigation, 45.3 per cent of rural households in India did not have toilets.[5] It was indeed important to build them, but I realized that the hygiene challenge was not one of infrastructure alone.

I asked villagers their reasons for defecating in the open, and heard many stories about their perspective on hygiene and 'dirt'. Bodily excreta, including hair and spit, was considered so dirty that it needed to be removed to a place outside the house. This place could even be just outside the house, but never inside. There were specific people assigned to deal with the 'dirt'—barbers who performed tonsures and disposed of the hair somewhere far away, sweepers who cleaned the house, only to dump the waste on the street outside. How could they defecate *inside* the house?

I found that they applied the same principle of 'dirt' to people as well. Certain classes of people were considered too dirty to be in physical proximity to oneself. Each community, no matter how 'low' in status it was relative to other groups, found another community or person to be even lower and hence dirtier. These classifications were also reflective of a deep bias: that people of different castes and communities were 'naturally' different because they were made of different substances. One's body needed to be protected from the inferior substances.

It occurred to me that even today, in urban settings, it is common for elite and even middle-class households to have separate vessels from which cleaners and maids eat and drink, and large homes definitely have a separate maid's toilet. In many parts of India, different communities and castes eat separately. Inter-caste marriage is definitely a big taboo almost all over the

---

[5] National Sample Survey 2016.

country. Why? Because in all these cases, the 'inferior' person's bodily substances—saliva, remains of excrement, semen—must not enter our body and 'pollute' us.

Eventually, the Jindal Group did start to construct toilets in Chhattisgarh, and they also conducted a large number of workshops with women so that they would take responsibility for their maintenance and use. Women, we found, were the agents of change in the families and if we put them in charge of improving hygiene and influencing beliefs, we would stand a greater chance of success in our endeavour.

Meanwhile, my observations in these villages reminded me of conversations I had had about fifteen years ago with the formidable Indian sociologist Dipankar Gupta.[6]

I got the chance to spend a few days with Gupta when he was visiting Paris, where I was studying at that time. Gupta and I were both residing at the Maison de l'Inde in Cite Universitaire, an area in the south of Paris dedicated to lodgings for students and academics. We took many memorable strolls in the campus. Gupta's primary research had been about social stratification in India and at that time he had just released a book on India's 'mistaken modernity'.

Gupta said that he felt that there was a general confusion among people between 'contemporaneity' and 'modernity'. Consequently, those who argued in favour of 'multiple modernity' even considered Taliban-like forces modern because they were contemporaneous and used sophisticated machines. He thought that true modernity must be measured by people's values towards equality in society. According to him, modernity was about

---

[6] Dipankar Gupta is a sociologist and former professor at Jawaharlal Nehru University's Centre for the Study of Social Systems. He is best known for his research on the Indian caste system and social stratifications.

how people related to other people. And he felt that the caste system—even though it has been largely dismantled[7]—had left its legacy of extreme inequality embedded in us. He showed me what he had written in his book:

> The caste theory of personhood is extremely biological . . . It holds that substances routinely expelled from a person's body are polluting and dirty, even to the person concerned . . . There is some similarity between this and racism, but . . . in a racist society, there is no stricture that forbids a white person from engaging a black cook.[8]

Indeed, because the basis of the stratification of Hindu society (about 80 per cent of the Indian population today) as illustrated by the caste system was so biological that the remnants of it have percolated down to the core belief systems that exist even today. Now, they are manifested in our attitude towards 'dirt' and all those we consider 'dirty'. It is worth mentioning here that the list of people we Indians consider dirty is stupefying: menstruating women, sick persons, widows, sweepers, people who have been assigned a lower caste at birth and so on. I have written in an earlier chapter of this book about our practice of equating socio-economic inferiority with the physical state of being 'dirty'.[9]

The toilets in the Chhattisgarh villages I visited were perhaps an extension of the notions of 'pure' and 'dirty' in the caste system, which is also manifest in our values. We consider ourselves 'pure',

---

[7] I have written more on how the caste system has been dismantled, yet how caste identities persist, in Chapter 2 titled 'Evolution'.

[8] Gupta 2000, 35.

[9] See Chapter 5 titled 'Love'.

and there is always someone from a different community, or a person perceived as being lower down the social or economic hierarchy who is considered 'dirty'. And from this inferior or dirty person we must keep a physical distance. As Gupta noted, such a physical separation among people based on perceived biological inequality is unique to India.

'In traditional India, "high" castes could demand services from "low" castes because of their superior material and physical resources. This exploitation is explained in Hindu texts as being ordained by the gods,'[10] wrote Gupta.

Today, there are a number of reasons for a large chunk of India's population to uphold rather than abolish the inequalities in our society.

First, for an individual to be perceived as 'higher' in the social hierarchy, many others must be perceived to be 'below' this individual. And so, instead of acquiring social respect through accomplishments, it is easier to gain a high social status by merely allowing the existing system of abject inequality to continue.

Second, the profitability of businesses in India often depends on accessing cheap labour from the poor, and the high spending power of the wealthy. I will write about this in greater detail in a later essay in this book, but for now, it suffices to point out that business too flourishes in India if inequality continues.[11]

Third, inequality works to maintain the family structure in India. As I wrote earlier, typical arranged marriages last in India

---

[10] Gupta 2000, 122.

[11] I have written more on the arbitrage practices of businesses with regard to availability of cheap labour and high spending capacity in Chapter 12 titled 'Money'.

often because they are based on the principle of inequality. The bride-taker is considered superior to the bride-giver, and so the groom (and his family) can drive the marital relationship mostly unilaterally.[12] Once the all-important ceremony of *kanyadaan*, which literally means 'donating the bride', is completed by the father of the bride, the groom and his family can take charge of the couple's life. Thereafter, a woman is considered to be abounding with 'good values' when she unquestioningly subjugates herself to her husband. Why should subjugation to the groom and his family be a sign of good values? This is so firstly because this means that the bride relinquishes her individual beliefs to those of the new family's—not because of love or influence or habit (she barely knows the groom or his family yet), but because she knows that she is supposed to uphold group values, whatever those may be, over her own. Secondly, subjugation would mean that the bride will not rebel against the groom and his family's wishes, which is indicative of stability in the marriage.

Fourth, democracy and elections give the impression of providing a fair representation of people in Parliament and in the government, but both politics and governance here are riddled with nepotism. The poor in urban and rural India have neither the voice nor the will to oppose the drops of patronage coming their way, which, as I mentioned earlier, in the absence of any social security in the country, are a life support to many.

So, who would want to change the current ethos of inequality in India? For reasons like status, self-esteem, stability, profitability and power, Indians are dependent on those considered socio-economically inferior. Many middle-class and elite Indians therefore have hardly any incentive to dismantle the inequality in relations among people in India today. Our politicians cannot win

---

[12] See Chapter 5 titled 'Love'.

elections without wielding power over their minions. Businesses need the poor for increasing profits. On the other hand, the absence of social security provided by the government means the poor need to preserve at least the lifeline of their 'superior' benefactors. Even the family unit is held up by marriages based on inequality.

All this has led to a society in India that is riding on the steam of inequality.

The deep rifts between the various socio-economic strata have created an aggressive environment for all of us to live in. 'Modern'-looking technologically savvy hospitals treat patients from poor backgrounds contemptuously. Our police forces do not feel the need to speak respectfully to a person from a humble background. Companies invest in the most modern production machines, but ill-treat their employees. In fact, so ingrained is the value of inequality in our society that the current social, economic and political systems cannot do without it.

This is why I argue that inequality is the most dominant influence on individual beliefs.

This does not mean that individuals in India do not have their own personal moral compass. In the face of the unequal environment, there are many who squirm with discomfort, in far larger numbers than they did before. But the important question is whether individuals are able to support their own individual values against the force of society's interest in keeping inequality alive.

In order for an individual to be ethical, it is important that they have an ethical and just environment around them. Else, there are high chances that an environment that has a general interest in continuing with corrupt practices will bring this individual down. For instance, an entrepreneur needs an ecosystem that allows him to ethically get legal permits, make payments to vendors and so on in an ethical way. If the ecosystem has unsaid rules that bribes must be paid or payments are to be done illegally only, the entrepreneur will find it difficult to get by without submitting to these rules. If a young girl values honesty but lives in a community that would harm her if they discover that she is pursuing an education, a love affair, or a salaried job, she would have two choices: to be dishonest and pursue her ambitions, or to give up on them. In both cases, the environment would have influenced her individual values.

Some people use communities to get results in their individual favour for financial or political gains. For instance, while some Indians will not marry, or even eat or drink from the same vessel as someone of a lower caste, the same individuals will lend other castes support by forming a political alliance to gain power or money (or both) as a merged group, if they see their own individual benefit in such an alliance. Political alliances, such as the Kshatriya–Harijan–Ahir–Muslim and the Ahir–Jat–Gujar–Rajput[13] groups, have been driven by the ambitions of a few to garner political power and win elections. Even as the caste system is slowly dissolving in India, caste identities persist and individuals correlate their caste identity with personal ambitions for political and financial gain.

With the trickle-down effect—however painfully slow it is at the moment—of a more equitable economic growth pattern in India, there are chances that there will be greater homogeneity in education, spending power, choices and aesthetics among different communities separated by history,

---

[13] Varma 2005, 51.

culture, prejudice or social and economic factors. In a society where every individual has equal power to understand, procure and implement action from the same set of choices, the political class will not be able to manipulate ignorance or socio-economic differences, because there will hardly be any. The elite will need to rise on their own merit, not by bullying the rest. It will be a somewhat level playing field for everyone to offer more opportunities as much as to gain, and so the mad scramble to win might abate.

Only equality among individuals can generate empathy among people who do not have any kin, clan or ethnic connections. With empathy, individuals will understand the dilemmas and challenges of the other. They will connect with others on the basis of shared individual values, and not because of the values of a group they were deemed to be part of since birth. Gradually, people will begin to trust those beyond family and community as well.

If this happens in India, those on an equal footing will come together in new groups based on the shared individual values of their members. They will each still be part of several communities, but these will be communities in which members have not identified with each other only due to affiliations by birth. And there is nothing pre-modern about that.

References

Durkheim, Émile. 1893. *The Division of Labor in Society* (Paris: Presses Universitaires de France).

Gupta, Dipankar. 2000. *Mistaken Modernity: India Between Worlds* (Noida: HarperCollins India).

Indian Express. 2016. Chhattisgarh: 8,582 villages become open defecation free. 16 December.

Lau, Lisa, and Om Prakash Dwivedi. 2014. *Re-Orientalism and Indian Writing in English* (New York: Palgrave MacMillan).

National Sample Survey Report. 2016. Most of rural India still opts for open defecation. *The Hindu*, 21 April.

Varma, Pavan K. 2005. *Being Indian: The Truth about Why the Twenty-first Century Will be India's.* (New Delhi: Penguin Books India).

8

Nationalism

There is a large and influential consensus about the timing of the birth of nationalism in India. Almost every nationalist historian in India has said that nationalism here was born at the time of India's awakening for freedom from the British. Subalternists Sumit Sarkar and Ranajit Guha too have deliberately focused on the period of the freedom struggle, emphasizing the role of the masses instead of the elites in developing India's nationalism.[1] Some historians say that nationalism began precisely

---

[1] The subalternist approach can be explained as writing history inclusive of voices that are traditionally marginalized or ignored. Subalternists distinguish between the social and economic hegemonic classes, or 'the elite', and the subaltern masses or 'non-elite' domain of Indian nationalism. The subaltern school within historiography in India started in 1982, when historian Ranajit Guha and others formed a collective called the Subaltern Studies Group, and published a series of studies of Indian history. The focus for Guha was the subaltern—the peasant, the worker, etc.—and their place within the larger historiography of Indian nationalism.

in 1885 with the formation of the Indian National Congress.[2] And others have largely believed that Indian nationalism was conceived and formed by various other political events in India's freedom struggle, over the period from the last two decades of the nineteenth century right up to 15 August 1947.

There has been another consensus—not just among intellectuals in India but also the world over—about the origin of nationalism. They mostly agree that nationalism arrived in the colonies from Europe.[3] Starting with the French Revolution, a wave of nationalism or devotion to one's country, along with the creation of national symbols, national slogans or values, and citizen rights, spread in Europe in the eighteenth and nineteenth centuries. Countries such as Germany, Italy and Romania were being formed by uniting regional states under a common national identity, whereas others such as Greece, Switzerland, Poland and Bulgaria emerged after uprisings against the Ottoman Empire and Russia. A European import, this brand of nationalism was supposedly bequeathed by former colonial powers to the lands they had once ruled over. It is often believed that nationalism was one of Europe's most useful gifts to the rest of the world.

Not just India, but other erstwhile European colonies such as Vietnam, Indonesia, Algeria struggled to establish their own nationhood. As their people laid down their lives to become free, they stole the limelight from Europe by building various 'modern' political and economic institutions in the 1950s and 1960s. Europe was still regarded as the vanguard,[4] but gradually, nationalism began to be associated more with these victorious anti-colonial struggles in Asia and Africa.

---

[2] Singh 1996.
[3] Anderson 1991.
[4] Chatterjee 2014.

Within a few years, many leaders of the African anti-colonial struggles became drunk on their newly acquired power. Leaders of countries such as Libya, Egypt and Tunisia became corrupt and established brutal regimes. In some other countries like Germany, South Africa, and later in Serbia and elsewhere, nationalism became a matter of ethnic politics and the reason for people killing each other. Nationalism started to get a bad name. So much so that by the end of the twentieth century, there was hardly any legacy of nationalism left in the world that would make Europe feel good about it.

The Irish political scientist and polyglot Benedict Anderson's views have perhaps been the most influential on ideas about nationalism in contemporary times. He said that nations in Europe, and everywhere else in the world, were in fact 'imagined' into existence.[5] This, Anderson explained, meant that nations were not the determinate products of given sociological conditions, such as language or race or religion, but instead communities that came together to acquire tangible shape by establishing major institutional forms. He then went on to say that the historical experience of nationalism in western Europe, the Americas and Russia supplied a set of modular institutional forms, and that communities from Asia and Africa had chosen their own forms from that set.

I have one problem with Anderson's argument. If, as Anderson posited, the rest of the world has to choose from 'modular forms' of nationalism supplied by Europe, America and Russia, how much is left for these communities to 'imagine'? Is there no indigenous form of nationalism that can be established by people in the rest of the world?

Building on that same 'problem', I would also argue that amid all the thought that has gone into decrypting nationalism, there

---

[5] Anderson 1998.

are at least two important assumptions that I believe might not always hold true. First, that nationalism has a political meaning; two, that there is a gallery of set 'models' of nationalism—ethnic nationalism, civic nationalism, religious nationalism and so on—that is doing the rounds internationally and from which countries deploy one model or the other.

On the first assumption, I concede to Anderson that communities come together on the basis of their imagination of what their country must look like. I would add that as they do so, they collectively feel a range of emotions towards their country—love, pride, a feeling of security or insecurity, inclusivity (or not), rebellion, nostalgia, responsibility—that constitute their nationalism. A country is made by the coming together of ordinary people who experience these or similar emotions towards it, and not only by those who are involved in political activities. Instead, in India, when we talk of the birth of nationalism, we refer to freedom fighters and the words and actions of contemporary politicians. Perhaps we have taken the meaning of nationalism as being political much too literally?

The second assumption—that we choose from existing models of nationhood—is so deep-seated within us in India that it has led to worrying consequences. In a chicken-and-egg situation, it has eroded our confidence in who we are as a community, and our imagination of the people we collectively and authentically want to be. We are not incapable of thinking about how we authentically and collectively feel about our country, so why have we given up? If a nation is an imagined community, why are we not imagining how our own nationalism could be?

The challenge faced by India these days is related to both these assumptions. We are losing our grip on the understanding of ourselves as a community that once came together to become India, and are running helter-skelter looking for meaning.

On the one hand, we are looking at our past in the hope that reviving ancient rituals, languages and decorum will lead us to our authentic selves. On the other hand, we are future-focused in attitude, and eager to align ourselves to the great seat of power that we believe India will surely have in the world. Yes, we realize that we need to find the nation first, in order to chart our own brand of nationalism. But until we are able to actually do so we seem to be lost, some more than others.

And so, as an easy way out, we have left it to the political folks to determine nationalism for us, following their ad hoc solutions influenced by the West that are useful for them to stay in power. Since the public assumes that nationalism is a political matter, we are following the ridiculous agenda of politicians and of them telling us 'how to be nationalistic'.

Let us see how.

We can recognize two dominant views on nationalism in contemporary India, of which neither is new. Both are led by the political class.

The first comes from mostly left-leaning thinkers and secularists who propose a secular and culturally neutral stance towards nationalism—a Nehruvian nationalism of sorts—in which every citizen belonging to a diverse group feels like a part of India. The people of Srinagar, on 19 July 1961, applauded Nehru as he remarked:

> Nationalism does not mean Hindu nationalism, Muslim nationalism or Sikh nationalism. As soon as you speak of Hindu, Sikh or Muslim, you do not speak for India. Each person has to ask himself the question: What do I want to make of India—one country, one nation or ten, twenty or twenty-five nations, a fragmented and divided nation without any strength or endurance, ready to break to pieces at the slightest shock?[6]

---

[6] Islam 2002; Nehru 2016.

The second view on nationalism emphasizes that the relationship between the people and the nation is based on shared ethnic and territorial roots. This is a puritan view where only those who belong to the original 'Akhand Bharat'—an entity with an imagined ethnic boundary, not the contemporary political one—must still be part of it, and no one else. This view considers Hindus to be the most 'authentic' inhabitants of the land, posits India as a great ancient civilization, and seeks to bring back the 'authentic' inhabitants and some of India's ancient practices and beliefs to contemporary times.

This second view has a very specific idea of the territory of India. It originates from the beliefs of independence activist Vinayak Damodar Savarkar. An atheist and a staunch rationalist, ironically, Savarkar had, in the early years of the twentieth century, coined the term 'Hindutva'. The term, he believed, referred to a collective Hindu identity as an imagined nation. For Savarkar, a Hindu is one who inhabits the land 'from the Indus to the seas'. India, for him, was the '*matribhoomi*' or motherland, '*pitribhoomi*' or fatherland, and also the '*punyabhoomi*' or Hindu holy land, whose sanctity is established by the rivers and mountains where pilgrims worship their gods. Therein lies Savarkar's distinction between Hindus on the one hand, and Muslims and Christians on the other: 'For though Hindustan to them is (pitribhoomi) fatherland as to any other Hindu, yet it is not to them a (punyabhoomi) holy land too. Their holy land is far away.'[7] Thus, the notion of nationalism came to be associated with the boundaries of an imagined ancient territory having a homogeneous Hindutva identity.

The form of nationalism propounded by Savarkar was developed further in free India. The Hindu right-wing organization, the Rashtriya Swayamsevak Sangh (RSS), took

---

[7] Jaffrelot 2016b.

forward Savarkar's vision of reinstating an imagined nation made up of those whose punyabhoomi it is. The RSS strengthened its presence and established an annual event—to be held on 14 August and called the Akhand Bharat Sankalp Diwas—for the formation of a reunited India. The event brought local people into the folds of their beliefs.[8] In 1966, the second RSS chief, M.S. Golwalkar, wrote in his book *Bunch of Thoughts*:

> Our epics and our Puranas also present us with the same expansive image of our motherland. Afghanistan was our ancient Upaganasthan. The modern Kabul and Kandahar were Gandhar. Even Iran was originally Aryan. Its previous king . . . was guided more by Aryan values than by Islam. The *Zend-Avesta*, the holy scripture of Parsis, is mostly the Atharva Veda. Coming to the east, Burma is our ancient Brahmadesha. The Mahabharata refers to Iraavat as being involved in that great war . . . In the south, Lanka has had the closest links and was never considered as different from the mainland.[9]

This view of nationalism refers to the greatness of India in another era and, indeed, another territorial boundary. Led by the right-wing political class, it unearths, strengthens and brings back many ancient Indian traditions and practices to contemporary times. While I find nothing wrong with a revivalist approach, its efficacy and legitimacy in a liberal environment depends on *how* these ancient traditions are presented and offered to ordinary citizens.

For instance, in 2014, the prime minister of India, at the United Nations General Assembly (UNGA) in New York,

---

[8] Jaffrelot 2016a.
[9] Golwalkar 1966.

proposed the establishment of an International Day of Yoga. Whatever an 'International Day of Yoga' meant, the proposal was dealt with in a democratic manner at the UNGA. It was discussed over several rounds of informal consultations convened by an assertive Indian delegation, and in the following year, 2015, the UNGA designated 21 June as the annual International Yoga Day.

Thereafter, in India, citizens woke up to messages sent by the 'Ministry of AYUSH', asking them to practise yoga. This new Ministry of AYUSH was created in 2014 by the government that had come to power at the centre that year. It was the same government that had established, via a democratic process, the International Yoga Day at the UNGA. The endeavour of this ministry was to promote Ayurveda, yoga and naturopathy, Unani, Siddha and homoeopathy, for which AYUSH is the acronym. Here is a sample of the messages from the government asking me to practise yoga, which I received on my cellular phone in New Delhi:

18 June 2015, 6.17 a.m.
Practice Yoga: It works on the body, mind, emotions and energy. Live life to its full potential. Ministry of AYUSH, Govt. of India.

19 June 2015, 3.04 a.m.
Practice Yoga: It can make you feel active, energetic and positive. Live life to its full potential. Ministry of AYUSH, Govt. of India.

20 June 2015, 3.04 a.m.
Rejuvenate with Yoga: It enriches the consciousness and makes one alert, aware and active. Live life to its full potential. Ministry of AYUSH, Govt. of India.

21 June 2015, 3.05 a.m.
Rejuvenate with Yoga: It helps to achieve control over the
mind and flexibility of the body. Live life to its full potential.
Ministry of AYUSH, Govt. of India.

Firstly, I considered it a breach of my privacy. I had not provided
my private cellular phone number to the government, so how
did the government procure it and find it appropriate to send me
messages in the wee hours of the morning? Second, signing off as
the 'Government of India' makes any message seem obligatory.
The message did not specify or provide a disclaimer that this was
a suggestion, and that I could use my discretion to do or not to
do yoga. Third, the entire drive—via phone messages, political
speeches, and the prime minister himself performing yoga at a
public event—to make yoga compulsory made me uncomfortable.
I practise meditation and do various forms of fitness activities every
day. However, I am uneasy if yoga or any other form of wellness is
foisted upon me, as if it were a badge of my nationalism.

Let us take another example. There has been a recent emphasis
by several Indian government officials on the 'saffronization' of
education.[10] This has often meant recalling and glorifying[11] ancient
Hindu cultural history in the education curriculum of our children,
raising a storm of malaise and anxiety among parents who would like
their children to get a more contemporary and balanced education.

This anxiety, aggravated by the overall low level of trust
in public institutions in India,[12] led citizens to suspect the
intentions of the government when Sanskrit was introduced

---

[10] Rashid 2016.
[11] For example, the 2016 draft of the National Policy of Education opens
with the statement that Vedic education is the earliest form of education,
which may be factually incorrect (Some Inputs for Draft National
Education Policy 2016).
[12] I have elaborated more on this topic in Chapter 7 titled 'Values'.

in the curriculum at IIT. It was added in April 2016 as an optional subject at the undergraduate level at India's most elite engineering school, which is also a public institution controlled by the government. Ordinary people wondered if this was part of the greater 'saffronization agenda'.

The worry of citizens was legitimate on another account: the ancient Indian language of Sanskrit holds the key to two doors placed at two opposite ends. Which of the two doors are opened depends on who holds the key.

One door leads to the vast literature, belonging to the millennia preceding and following Christ, on several technical topics including science, mathematics and political theory, which became the starting point for many advanced theories across various disciplines. It is estimated that even now, about thirty million texts of this rich knowledge are there in Sanskrit, the largest textual corpus of any existing human language.[13]

The second door leads to a specific section of the social world of Sanskrit that reeks of caste hierarchy, inequality and misogyny.[14] In an essay called 'The story of my Sanskrit', author Ananya Vajpeyi recounts how several Sanskritists and pandits in India have been left feeling misunderstood and alienated by the modern emphasis on science and technology, and so they resent liberal values.[15]

---

[13] Vajpeyi 2014.

[14] Ibid.

[15] Ibid. Vajpeyi, an Oxford and University of Chicago–educated Sanskrit reader who has taught at universities in New York and Boston, reminisces how as a young woman researcher she read Sanskrit in India with pandits and professors at *mathas*, Sanskrit colleges, oriental institutes and Sanskrit departments of universities, and the challenges she faced in doing so. She also describes the blatant attack on her by a well-known Sanskrit professor in Maharashtra who told her that only 'perverted women' became scholars.

If the liberal and secular community—who hold a Nehruvian view of nationalism—holds the key, they would open the first door that contains knowledge about India as her oldest and most authentic self. But if the key falls into the hands of those nursing a grudge, who are now supported by a right-wing political agenda, the effect would be starkly different.

In April 2017, a year after the inclusion of Sanskrit in the IIT curriculum, it was decreed that the ancient Indian science of architecture, vastu shastra, must also be included in the curriculum of IIT's campus in Kharagpur.[16] By teaching 'ancient Indian architectural traditions', it was said, the institute would train 'well-rounded architects'. Vastu shastra was developed between 6000 BC and 3000 BC, and has roots in the Rig Veda. It involves designing buildings keeping in mind the influence of the sun's light and heat, wind directions, the moon's position, and Earth's magnetic fields.

However, there is no agreement among practising architects that vastu shastra is a scientific system, or if it provides an accurate understanding of nature. Some architects have pointed out that, 'Vastu orders spaces and buildings based on geography in a caste-oriented and patriarchal way.

For example, the spaces it assigns for women and lower castes are towards the unfavourable elements of nature, while plentiful and favourable locations are provided for the "master".'[17] On what basis did the Indian government decide to alter the education curriculum?

In 2016, the Supreme Court of India ordered all cinema halls in the country to mandatorily play India's national anthem before

---

[16] Pandey 2017.

[17] Author's interview with architect Rajat Sodhi, 25 April 2017.

the screening of any film.[18] It also directed the audience to stand in respect so as to 'instil the feeling within one a sense (of) committed patriotism and nationalism'. The order was to be followed with the utmost seriousness, so much so that the government even issued guidelines for disabled people, saying they must not move and position themselves 'maintaining the maximum possible alertness physically' during the time that the national anthem was played.[19]

Indeed, our fundamental right as Indian citizens to free speech and expression also includes the right *not* to speak. We cannot be forced to sing the national anthem. Shouldn't patriotism come naturally to oneself? Can patriotism be invoked by force?

I don't think so. The order of the Supreme Court might have ensured that cinema audiences in India now stand while the national anthem plays. However, this is motivated by people's fear of being charged with 'anti-nationalism' and the heckling that follows if one does not stand rather than by any genuine feelings of nationalism.

The efforts of the ruling Indian political class have also contributed to dictating to citizens what must be considered 'anti-nationalistic'. In early 2016 at JNU, there had been a rally to protest the 2013 hanging of Mohammed Afzal Guru, a Kashmiri separatist convicted of the 2001 Indian Parliament attack. The president of the university's student union, Kanhaiya Kumar, was arrested and charged with sedition by the Delhi Police for allegedly raising anti-India slogans in a student rally. Kumar denied all the charges. He

---

[18] Shyam Narayan Chouksey vs Union of India, Writ Petition Civil no 855/2016, 20 November 2016. On 30 November 2016, the Supreme Court ordered all cinemas across the country, to play the national anthem, before movies (Rajagopal 2016). However on 23 October 2017 the Supreme Court said that people do not need to stand up in cinema halls to prove their patriotism, asking the Centre to consider amending the rules that regulate playing of the national anthem before a movie (NDTV 2017).

[19] Barry 2016.

was later released on interim bail on 2 March 2016 for lack of conclusive evidence, but the incident launched a nationwide debate about the value of free speech and the meaning of 'anti-nationalism'.

Would Dr B.R. Ambedkar, the man who led the writing of the Indian Constitution, be considered anti-national today? Ambedkar had an antagonistic relationship with Mahatma Gandhi and many other leaders of the freedom movement in the 1930s and 1940s. He had also rejected the Hindu religion. In 1939, Ambedkar said, 'Whenever there is any conflict of interest between the country and the untouchables, so far as I am concerned, the untouchables' interests will take precedence over the interests of the country,'[20] a statement that, among several others, clarified his allegiance to his cause over his country. All of these actions would be considered anti-national today!

Would the same tag also be placed on Rabindranath Tagore, the brilliant poet and Nobel laureate? After all, Tagore had rather radical views on nationalism. He believed that intense love for the nation, which manifests in the conviction of national superiority and the glorification of cultural heritage, is used to justify narrow-minded national interest. Writing in 1917, Tagore said, 'When this organization of politics and commerce, whose other name is the Nation, becomes all powerful at the cost of the harmony of higher social life, then it is an evil day for humanity.'[21]

And going by the reasoning rationale, would Gautama Buddha, the founder of Buddhism, also be considered anti-national? He went against the wishes of the ruler, his father, and abandoned his responsibility to govern Shakya. He must have been distinctly anti-establishment as well to have gone ahead and created a new religion!

---

[20] Jaffrelot 2016a.
[21] Dasgupta and Guha 2013.

But all these debates and arguments were quickly set aside.

The events of the last two years of right-wing political leadership in India have been such that in the name of nationalism we are now often told what we can and cannot eat,[22] what we can and cannot watch, what we can and cannot speak about, what we must sing and how. Couples who merely hold hands are harassed and attacked, because expressing love is not 'Indian'.[23] Are all notions of rights to be immobilized in the face of nationalism? Are we yet another nation state in the developing world that initially promised high ideals of emancipation and freedom to its citizens, and is later unable to do so? Or is 'nationalism', and even 'anti-nationalism', so abstract that its meaning can be manipulated to intimidate and beat down voices of dissent and criticism?

India is a diverse country, and its people have different views about the idea of India and their relationship with it. Instead of silencing those who hold a different view, why can we not respect these differences? And why can the reason for that not be the Constitution or our laws, but basic respect towards humanity and human diversity?

We have given enough importance to politics in regard to nationalism. Perhaps it is because we do not make enough of a distinction between 'nation' and 'nationalism'. As we know, nation states are a nineteenth-century European creation, and following in Europe's footsteps, India became one only seventy years ago. But nationalism is an emotion, it is a sense of relationship with the community that we agree to be governed with. Nationalism

---

[22] Here, I am referring to Article 48 of the Indian Constitution, which restricts or bans cow slaughter in twenty-four out of twenty-nine Indian states. See more on this in Chapter 15 titled 'Freedom'.

[23] Naidu 2017.

predates nation states. Our ancestors could have felt nationalistic towards their tribe or kingdom, just as we do towards our country. For various reasons, we agree to be part of a common governance structure, and so an entity that has political boundaries—tribe, kingdom, country—is created. Therein lies the link between politics and nationalism. But in a liberal set-up in any era, the way we feel towards a specific entity must not be defined by the political class. It is how we feel towards the entity that must define the agenda of the political class that governs us.

As I wrote early in this essay, I believe that part of the problem is that Indian citizens have lost their sense of themselves as a collective, and therefore, we are unable to establish an authentic and honest relationship with the group entity we call India.

What is India? How do we find her?

Much of our oldest wisdom is in Sanskrit, a language that we do not read any more. Most of our intellectuals for the past 300 years have been trained in Western thought. Indian science and mathematics weakened. Indian political traditions of a mixed Hindu and Islamic character, as theorized and practised in the precolonial kingdoms of the Mughals, Deccani Sultans, Nayaks, Marathas, Rajputs, Sikhs and many others, were delegitimized during the colonial period,[24] and have all effectively vanished now. A lot of the existing Sanskrit and Islamic philosophy is unavailable to India's intellectuals now, and whatever is available is in such an unfamiliar form and context that it is often perceived as irrelevant.

This has resulted in religion and custom emerging as the dominant survivors amidst the vast amounts of our rich wisdom in India. Religion and custom have hence been given a role—

---

[24] Vajpeyi 2012, xv.

encouraged by India's right-wing political class—to explain the meaning of India to anyone who wants to find her.

Moreover, who wants to search for India? Many of us are happy to let the political class take the lead and inform our opinions. Others seek education or work opportunities in the West, and are sceptical about anything Indian. Meanwhile, the majority is busy trying to somehow fill their empty stomachs instead of contemplating the idea of India.

The problem, therefore, is a very difficult one for us Indians. We cannot find India because we do not have the material, tools or the will to do so any more. Nor can we turn away from the West, as its institutions, such as nation states, democracy, and capitalism, are now available, acceptable and even desirable. This is the opportunity that the Indian right wing exploits. It steps in, bringing to us religion and customs as easy channels to know India once again, and forcing us to relate to our country through those lenses alone.

The truth is that we do not have to necessarily choose between polarities, such as India/West, modernity/tradition, traditional/organic, secular/religious, Hindu/Muslim and so on, to understand and relate to our country. These factors are not necessarily opposed to each other. We can straddle both or several of them in our own unique ways, gradually rendering the lead of the political class to guide us out of our confusion as pointless.

Our self-awareness and ability to make choices regarding our relationship with our country will only come when good quality education at school, in the family and in society is imparted to one and all in the country. This is the only way to ensure that it is not just the 10 per cent elite but even the general masses who are capable of taking informed decisions independent of the agenda of others. We will then be able to differentiate our understanding of nationalism from what we are told by people with an agenda. In a country where everyone is educated and has a rational head on their shoulders, it is hard to singularize 'one people'. Therefore, it will not be possible to thrust down our throats the idea of only one type of nationalism. Instead, in such a scenario, each of us will be able to leverage our intellectual and emotional breadth to sense how we really feel towards the India we know. *That* would be our nationalism.

References

Anderson, Benedict. 1991. *Imagined Communities: Reflections on the Origin and Spread of Nationalism* (Brooklyn: Verso Books).

Anderson, Benedict. 1998. *The Spectre of Comparisons: Nationalism, Southeast Asia and the World* (Brooklyn: Verso Books).

Barry, Ellen. 2016. Indian cinemas must play the national anthem, Supreme Court rules. *New York Times*, 30 November.

Chatterjee, Partha. 2014. The agenda for nationalism. *Centre for Studies in Social Sciences*, pp. 73–88.

Dasgupta, Sanjukta and Chinmoy Guha, eds. 2013. *Tagore: At Home in the World* (New Delhi: Sage Publications).

Golwalkar, Madhav Sadashiv. 1966. *Bunch of Thoughts* (Bangalore: Vikrama Prakashan; sole distributors: Rashtrotthana Sahitya).

Islam, Mozaffar. 2002. Nehru on national unity. *The Hindu,* 12 November.

Jaffrelot, Christophe. 2016b. This land, this nation. *Indian Express,* 12 January.

Jaffrelot, Christophe. 2016a. Ambedkar against nationalism. *Indian Express,* 14 April.

Naidu, Shiv. 2017. The war on V-day begins again; anti valentine. *Citizen*, 15 July.

NDTV. 2017. No need to stand at cinema to prove patriotism: Supreme Court on anthem. https://www.ndtv.com/india-news/no-need-for-anthem-at-cinema-for-patriotismcourt-asks-centre-to-decide-1766085.

Nehru, Jawaharlal. 2016. *Selected Speeches, September 1957–April 1963,* vol. 4 (New Delhi: Publications Division).

Pandey, Jhimli. 2017. IIT Kharagpur to introduce vastu shastra. *Times of India*, 17 April.

Rajagopal, Krishnadas. 2016. National anthem must be played before screening of films: Supreme Court. *The Hindu*, 30 November.

Rashid, Omar. 2016. Saffronisation of education good for India, says minister. *The Hindu,* 19 June.

Singh, Jyotsna G. 1996. *Colonial Narratives, Cultural Dialogues: 'Discoveries' of India in the Language of Colonialism* (Sussex: Psychology Press).

Some Inputs for Draft National Education Policy 2016: Issue brief, Ministry of Human Resource Development, Government of India. http://mhrd. gov.in/sites/upload_files/mhrd/files/nep/Inputs_Draft_NEP_2016. pdf.

Vajpeyi, Ananya. 2012. *Righteous Republic: The Political Foundations of Modern India* (Cambridge: Harvard University Press).

Vajpeyi, Ananya. 2014. The story of my Sanskrit. *The Hindu*, 16 August.

Part III

TRAPPED IN OUR OWN MAKING

9

Democracy

Discussing politics is a favoured pastime in India. The newspapers here are chock-full of all things political, with Indian television channels constantly blaring out 'breaking news' on politicians and the government, and it is common to hear the buzz of opinions, defence or criticism of politicians, parties and public government schemes.

There always seems to be so much going on in the governance of our own country that we have little bandwidth to learn about the domestic affairs of any other country. The public discourse overall tends to be dominated by an enormous focus on our politics and politicians' lives and problems.

As economist Amartya Sen has pointed out, we have a tradition in India of being discursive or 'argumentative'.[1] Over various works, Sen has delineated the historical recognition that public discussion has received in India. As one of the earliest examples of this, he mentions the organized discussion of the Buddhist Councils, started in the sixth century BC by Ashoka, which brought together different points of view represented by

---

[1] Sen 2005.

participants from across India and even abroad. In the sixteenth century, Emperor Akbar also organized public discussions on religious differences.[2] Referring to a less distant past, subalternist Ramachandra Guha extols the intellect of the leaders of India's freedom struggle to argue in subtle and sophisticated ways with each other.[3]

Indeed, intellectuals in India and abroad are delighted by public discussions about politics, which they often say is the basis for democracy. In saying so, they are not referring to the narrowly institutional view of democracy that characterizes it mainly in terms of elections, even though this view has its champions, including Samuel Huntington, who wrote: 'Elections, open, free and fair, are the essence of democracy, the inescapable sine qua non.'[4] But those who consider public discussion the basis of democracy believe that it is through the exchange of views concerning political questions that people broaden their understanding. They are enabled to make intelligent political choices, not just at the ballot, but also while participating in various other policy and governance decisions. John Rawls has called this 'the exercise of public reason', and in his book *A Theory of Justice* he laboriously argues how democracy is fundamentally linked to public deliberation.[5]

Making a case for Rawls's argument in the Indian context, Guha distinguishes between the 'hardware' and 'software' of democracy.[6] He writes that while the scholarly and popular understanding of democracy tends to focus on the 'hardware'—multiple political parties, free, fair and regular elections, freedom of the press, an

---

[2] Drèze and Sen 2013, 258.
[3] Guha 2016, 46.
[4] Huntington 1993, 9.
[5] Rawls 2001, 359.
[6] Guha 2016, 91.

independent judiciary, freedom of movement—little attention is paid to the 'software'. These are the cultural and emotional aspects of democracy, which include free public discourse on politics and governance.

Just this difference—Huntington's institutional definition of democracy versus Rawls's discursive view—highlights the various meanings of democracy in contemporary times, its debated areas of focus, and the plurality of ways to attain it. Intellectuals, as much as the public, have occupied themselves with thinking about this subject, leading to an enormous body of academic work on it the world over.

I would argue that democracy—in fact, governance as a whole—which was intended to be a means to an end, seems to have become the goal in our times. For centuries, governance systems—within tribes, kingdoms or nations—were established so that people could roam freely, speak and act in a way that allowed other members of that collective to do the same. Instead, in a Frankensteinian turn of events, today we excessively speak about and are bound to act in accordance with our governance systems that may or may not have our individual or collective interest in mind. This is the central point that I wish to expand upon in this essay.

In the early years of human evolution, it was our own idea to create some sort of a system that would support us in our instinctual activities of surviving, exploring, procreating—and we have discussed this in the first part of this book—in a free yet organized manner. Over thousands of years, we have experimented with creating and trying out various old and new forms of this 'system', and democracy is one of them.

Today, there is a near-unanimous acceptance globally—almost a moral imperative and missionary zeal—that every country must be a democracy, without having an equally unanimous agreement on what democracy means. In fact, the meaning of democracy varies so much that it is possible to trace its various 'versions' of democracy to different eras in time. For instance, the discursive democracy of the sixth century BC Buddhist Councils was not that of an elected government. Even in ancient Greece around the same period, only the minority of adult male citizens—excluding slaves—were involved in the consultative processes of governance, but the government itself was not voted into power. On the other hand, institutional democracy is said to have emerged much later, catalysed by the English Magna Carta charter in 1215, and the French and American revolutions of the eighteenth century. Ultimately, it took the form of adult franchise—initially male and eventually female citizens as well—in Europe and North America in the nineteenth and early twentieth centuries. It was only in the latter half of the twentieth century that democracy was established as a form of government.

In 1941, there were only eleven democracies in the world—Finland, Iceland, Ireland, Sweden, Switzerland, the UK, Australia, Canada, New Zealand, the US and Chile. This number went up in the second half of the century as democracies were established—in the most difficult circumstances possible—such as in Germany, India and South Africa. Further, decolonization created new democracies in Africa and Asia, and regimes became democratic in Greece (1974), Spain (1975), Argentina (1983), Brazil (1985) and Chile (1989). The Soviet Union collapsed, creating many more democratic countries in central Europe. Democracy took on varying institutional forms, based on the basic principle of a government made up 'of the people' as opposed to a composition of the elite, such that in the year 2000, American think tank Freedom House classified 120 countries, or 63 per cent of the world, as democracies.[7]

---

[7] *The Economist* 2014.

However, in this millennium, there have been many setbacks to the establishment of democracy. Hegemonic powers have initiated war on other countries in the name of establishing democracy, leading to millions of lives lost, and immense wealth and history destroyed.

It is true that dictators have been brought down in undemocratic regimes. The 'Arab Spring' began with the people's revolution in Tunisia in 2010 as they brought down a dictator and established a representative government. Other countries in the region, such as Egypt and Libya, also tried, but their fate was different.

It was 2011, and I was standing in the middle of Tahrir Square in Cairo, carrying a placard that read 'Indians for Egyptians'. Thousands of us were in the midst of the Egyptian uprising against President Hosni Mubarak, who had ruled the country for over thirty years. Standing amid a sea of humanity screaming for freedom and democracy, I was hit by the familiarity of these two words: 'freedom' and 'democracy'. I had missed hearing of them since I moved from Paris to Cairo a year and a half earlier.

At the time that I had relocated to Cairo, I was twenty-nine years old and had just quit the race to build a 'career'. I chose to exit my successful investment banking career, left my job managing a hedge fund in Paris, and moved towards doing everything that I truly loved. This meant that I chose to live in Cairo, where my partner at the time was also living, where I read books and wrote opinion pieces for various Indian newspapers on social issues, and developed my not-for-profit organization working for improving the status of women in the Middle East and India.

I thought I had adjusted to living in Mubarak's Egypt. In the old and dusty city of Cairo, even as an ordinary foreigner, my movements were always under the scanner. The local groceries

delivery boys, for instance, would report information about me to
the authorities, however irrelevant it may be to the working of the
Egyptian government. Inquiries would be made by government
officials each time the day after I had invited a large group of
non-Egyptian guests to my home. The government had a way
of knowing my change of home address or job, and they would
inform me with attempted subtlety that they were tracking
my movements. For example, just a day after my partner and I
relocated to a new apartment in Cairo, we found in our letterbox a
magazine whose cover loudly proclaimed 'India–Egypt friendship'.
It was published by the Foreign Ministry, and addressed to both
of us.

When I heard of the likelihood of the uprising one day
before it happened, I was tempted to brush it off as a rumour.
At that time it had seemed so implausible to believe that the
Egyptians would rebel against the regime. But it was a marvellous
phenomenon—on 25 January 2011, 90,000 people who had
never dared to raise a word against the establishment flocked
not just to Tahrir Square in Cairo, but also to the streets of
Aswan, Ismailiya, Mahallah and other Egyptian cities, screaming
'*kaifaya*' (enough).

On the second day of the uprising, I joined the Egyptians
at Tahrir Square—once a regular traffic roundabout, now a full-
fledged revolution ecosystem. The military with its guns, anti-
regime activists from every rank of society, the international media
with their cameras and, occasionally pro-regime supporters on
horse, donkey and camel back—they were all there. The picture
was complete and incredible.

I stood in Tahrir every day thereafter, adding my energy to the
masses. As journalists were being targeted by Mubarak's forces, I
sneaked out several editorials to the *Times of India* in New Delhi by
fax, reporting whatever I saw and felt. Emails were being scanned,

social media was completely blocked, mobile phone lines were cut, and low-flying choppers over our roofs watched us round the clock. At night, households in each neighbourhood would take turns to guard the roads, bridges, museums and other public property in their area. At daybreak, we would pick up brooms, sweep the streets and man the traffic intersections ourselves, because these public services had been suspended.

From this intimate perspective, in my view, the uprising was fuelled by the Egyptian people's great expectations of more jobs and prosperity, and they saw the fall of Mubarak and the establishment of democracy merely as a means to fulfil them. In comparison to the elite in their country, they felt so desperately deprived of resources, power, jobs and opportunities that they were now ready to lay down their lives to get them. They had been inspired by Tunisia, where a similar uprising had occurred just weeks earlier.

On the seventeenth day of Egypt's leaderless uprising, Mubarak stepped down with just a simple televised announcement late in the evening.

We marched out on to the streets, everyone headed for Tahrir. There, we climbed on to the military tanks and exchanged roses with the army. Everyone hugged each other and cried, proud of the achievement. No historian or academic could have explained to me even an iota of what it felt like to have been a part of history.

The jubilation was followed by the realization that now there was no one to take charge of the country, and no plan in place either to set up a government based on equal representation.

As the Egyptians set about their new way of life without Mubarak at the helm, they were woefully disillusioned. The wealth from his bank accounts was not distributed among the people, as they had naively expected. Even months after he was brought down, they were jobless. Many were dealing with the loss of family members—at least 846 people died and 6000 were injured during the seventeen days of the uprising.[8] After it ended, the spies on the streets were gone, along with the public security that came along with them. It was not uncommon to hear Egyptians confess that things under Mubarak were possibly better.

Governance in the country was a mess. The revolution resulted in the only existing organized political entity, the Muslim Brotherhood, briefly coming to power before the military took over in 2013. Since then, there has been hardly any respite from violence, and no progress has been made towards setting up a fair and effective governance system. The dictator has fallen, but whither democracy? Egypt's people today are neither happier nor freer.

Even in the West, it is time that we check our assumptions and reflection on the future of democracy. The American presidential election of 2016 was about making a forced choice between the country's two most 'disliked contestants',[9] and the European elite that same year put immense pressure on elected leaders in Greece who got in the way of fiscal orthodoxy.[10]

When India gained freedom, there were leaders who organized us into a democracy. Nehru was the chief architect, and he had a bevy of intellectuals to help him and even oppose and argue with him on various operational and fundamental issues. One such brilliant conversation stands out for me. I find it fascinating on two accounts. One, the existence of equally passionate yet opposing views on the relevance and indeed need of democracy in India, and two, the fact that it makes us think about the sort of intellectual deliberations that must have taken place at that time,

---

[8] BBC 2011.

[9] Wright 2016.

[10] Higgins and Kanter 2015.

deliberations that we cannot imagine among today's political leaders in India.

This delectable conversation is in the form of personal letters between Nehru and the social reformer Jayaprakash Narayan, found by historian Ramachandra Guha in the manuscripts of the Nehru Memorial Museum and Library in New Delhi.[11]

In his letters, Narayan asks Nehru to reconsider the sort of democracy he is establishing in India. He asks the prime minister to look beyond the party system. Narayan flags the need for a focused opposition to the ruling party, and suggests that democracy can be deepened by the energies of individuals and groups who are not themselves politicians.

Nehru, in response, warns of the disruptive dangers of an excess of identity politics, and presents a qualified defence of parliamentary democracy, saying it is not the perfect system of governance, but at least less harmful than the alternatives. He admits that democracy is 'full of faults', but had been adopted in India because 'in the balance, it was better than the other possible courses. Like any other system of governance, parliamentary democracy depended on the quality of the human beings who staffed it.'

'I do not think that the present system is a failure,' wrote Nehru to Narayan, 'though it may fail in the future for all I know. If it fails, it will not fail because the system in the theory is bad, but because we could not live up to it. Anyhow what is the alternative you suggest?'

Indeed, what *is* the alternative to democracy?

Certainly not autocracy.

As obvious as it might seem, it is important to reiterate this. Four decades after the Emergency was announced in India in

---

[11] Guha 2016, 46–49.

1975, by then-President Fakhruddin Ali Ahmed upon the advice of his prime minister, Indira Gandhi, there are still people in the country who suggest that a strong, even dictatorial, rule is the only way to achieve results in India and make economic progress. They feel that nothing will ever work unless there is someone at the helm to force things down our throats. We have not learnt our lesson, and are still mesmerized by authority. As I wrote in the previous essay, we quickly forget our discomfort with following government orders that make no sense for our individual or collective well-being.

Why is it that many Indians feel that being controlled and spoken down to by a strong political authority is a sign that all is well? The eminent psychoanalyst Sudhir Kakar ascribes this to 'an unconscious tendency to "submit" to an idealized omnipotent figure, both in the inner world of fantasy and in the outside world of making a living; the lifelong search for someone, a charismatic leader or a guru, who will provide mentorship and a guiding world-view, thereby restoring intimacy and authority to individual life.'[12]

As Kakar[13] puts it, this unconscious tendency to seek an authoritative leader appears even more sadistic when we realize that our human instinct is to roam free. Indeed, the basis of India's great struggle against the British was the longing for freedom. In fact, I find that in any modern 'free' nation, to defend freedom just because it is prescribed in our Constitution and laws—which are both of our own making—is an oxymoron. Instead, I believe that freedom must be guaranteed, first and foremost, because governance systems were created to ensure humans are free and living in harmony. Further, I think it is the modality of freedom that must be contained in our laws, not the justification of it!

---

[12] Varma 2005, 47.
[13] Kakar and Kakar 2007, 21.

We knew that collective freedom would be tricky to achieve and so we invented laws, codes, rules and constitutions. This is why modern governments were established—to ensure that humans as a collective are able to maintain our freedom—and not the other way around.

Alas, the latter is what we have come to. We have created a system in which feeding ourselves requires jobs and bank notes. We had probably thought this system would eliminate the need to go hunting each time we were hungry. It was created for our own convenience, but now it has trapped us. Jobs are hard to come by, as a consequence so are food and shelter. For those with an empty stomach, freedom is a lofty ideal. In the absence of bread, indeed freedom is easily forgotten. Our freedom is at the mercy of the government. If the government gets us our livelihood, even if it isn't accompanied by freedom, democracy and other ideals like equality and fraternity, we are ready to accept it. The consequences of this miserable desperation are dangerous.

Lest we forget what happened: on 12 June 1975, the Allahabad High Court ruled that Indira Gandhi was guilty of election malpractice and that she would have to resign.[14] Instead of resigning, Indira declared Emergency on the night of 25 June, just a few minutes before midnight. Before dawn the next day, police parties, acting on her orders, had her political opponents locked up in prison. Over the next thirty-six hours, India changed from a liberal democracy to a democracy that supported autocracy.[15]

Millions of Indians were outraged, but then they got used to it. There was press censorship, and so it was not very clear what was happening. Initially, public life began to improve visibly—

---

[14] *State of UP vs Raj Narain & Ors* on 24 January 1975. 1975 AIR 865; 1975 SCR (3) 333.
[15] Das 2002, 307.

government offices became more efficient, transportation began to run on time, factories became more productive. But soon, this short-lived efficiency declined. Disaster struck harder when the prime minister's beloved son, Sanjay Gandhi, stepped in. Sanjay ruled with his coterie of sycophantic ministers who unflinchingly obeyed his every order.[16]

Meanwhile, the number of Indira's political opponents in jail reached 1,00,000. Some of them were abused and tortured, while outside the jails every institution deteriorated.[17] All public and private media organizations were forced to relay only government propaganda.[18] Corruption became rampant. Ordinary people were arrested for no reason. Elections for Parliament and state governments were postponed, and in the meantime, Indira Gandhi was rewriting the nation's laws since the Congress party, with a two-thirds majority in Parliament, had the mandate required to do so. When she felt an existing law was not appropriate, she got the President to issue special ordinances, thereby bypassing Parliament and ruling by decree.

Sanjay then had the preposterous idea of controlling India's population by sterilizing the men of the country. Without consultation or planning, he immediately decreed that anyone with more than two children would be mandatorily sterilized, with no regard for age or marital status. The sterilizations were mostly done in makeshift and often extremely unhygienic conditions, and most cases were forced. Two thousand men died from the botched surgeries.[19] In just one year of the emergency 8.3 million Indian men were sterilized and lost the right to be

---

[16] Ibid, 173.
[17] Ibid.
[18] Ibid, 172–173.
[19] BBC News 2014.

fathers.[20] This order for compulsory sterilizations proved to be a death knell for Indira Gandhi's government as it incited a mass electoral revolt across north India and led to her loss in the 1977 polls.

Despite this, many Indians feel that Indira's authoritarian rule is what the country needs. They think it is the only medicine that would make things work here. They have forgotten the reign of terror during the Emergency, and believe that autocracy would have emerged a winner if it had not been for the excesses of the family planning programme. The perception is that Indira was the 'strong' leader India needed.

One of the most established Indologists of our times, under whose guidance I had the privilege of writing my master's, and later doctoral, thesis at Sciences Po in Paris, Christophe Jaffrelot, has for the past thirty years painstakingly followed the ascent of Prime Minister Narendra Modi. Jaffrelot's magnum opus, *The Hindu Nationalist Movement and Indian Politics*, published in French in 1993 and in English three years later, was the earliest serious study that accurately predicted the rise of right-wing politics in India.[21] In a riveting article, Jaffrelot points out that the styles of leadership represented by Modi and Indira Gandhi are very similar as they both epitomize two variants of populism.[22] This also goes to show that populism can be injected into right-leaning politics as much as the left-leaning variety.

Jaffrelot says that first, both Modi and Indira attempt to equate themselves with the Indian nation. While Indira's supporters claimed 'India is Indira and Indira is India', Modi's slogans evoke the notion 'I am the new India'. He quotes the work of political

---

[20] Researchgate 2012.
[21] Jaffrelot 1996.
[22] Jaffrelot 2017.

theoretician Ernesto Laclau[23] to show that this behaviour is typical of populist rhetoric, which relies on empty signifiers.

Another similarity, Jaffrelot notes, is in the high ideals evoked by both leaders. 'Both leaders relate to the people in the name of high ideals. While Indira Gandhi wanted to eradicate poverty, Narendra Modi resorted to demonetization to eradicate corruption. This decision could strike a moral chord among voters because of the extent to which they suffer from the curse of corruption. Its emotional impact was all the more significant as Prime Minister Modi congratulated Indian citizens for their national sacrifice, while they were suffering from his efforts to "clean" the country.'[24]

Jaffrelot points out, 'The nationalist rhetoric goes with a rejection of pluralism and alternative power centres—since the populist is the nation, any opposition is necessarily illegitimate. The judiciary is seen as an obstacle to the expression of the people's will. Students, academics, NGOs who protest in the street—like in Bihar and Gujarat in 1973 or JNU and DU today—can be disqualified as "anti-national". Similarly, some opposition parties are not only adversaries, but enemies who divide the nation. Hence, Indira's de-legitimization of the 1971 "reactionary" Grand Alliance, and the BJP's objective of a "Congress-mukt Bharat".'

Jaffrelot then notes a few important differences between Indira and Modi, notably the erosion of the over-representation of upper

---

[23] Ernesto Laclau (1935–2014) was an Argentine political theorist whose work focused on issues such as the importance of building popular movements and the possibility of revolution. Laclau's most significant book is *Hegemony and the Socialist Strategy*, co-authored with Chantal Mouffe in 1985.

[24] Jaffrelot 2017.

castes among members of Parliament and Legislative Assemblies; meanwhile, their percentage has risen in states the BJP won from 2014. In India's largest state, Uttar Pradesh, for example, he finds that the new assembly has 44 per cent upper caste MLAs—12 per cent more than in 2012, and the highest share since 1980.

The similarities, and even the differences, lead Jaffrelot to conclude that India's new populism relies on an ethno-religious definition of the nation. He notes that this is an 'ethnic democracy' model, a term formulated by Israeli social scientist Sammy Smooha to describe Israel's trajectory, where even though the regime remains in tune with the democratic constitution in practice, minorities are marginalized.

I agree with Jaffrelot's observations. But in my opinion, the fact that in free and democratic India, the styles of working of Indira and Modi (their forceful public policies and the unemotional way they deal with political opponents or those who fall from favour) have been accepted, or as Kakar says, 'submitted to', indicates a larger and more sinister issue—that democracy per se is not good enough. If, in our current governance system, there are not enough checks and balances to limit encroachments on freedom, it is time we reconsider the sort of governance system that works for us. The guarantee of collective freedom is not the only criterion for the viability of a governance system, but it is an important one. We cannot allow the bindings of the immense complexities we have ourselves created just to feed and shelter ourselves, to be the basis of another self-made trap in the form of a governance system that gives us bread but restricts our freedom.

Here, I would add that our tradition of public discourse—focused on domestic politics and politicians—is useful only if it serves in the immediate or even long term as an effective check on the government. Indeed a system of elections and voting is dependent on the people's understanding of the problems to be addressed and their perception of what others seek. This is a perspective put forward by John Stuart Mill, who emphasized on seeing democracy as 'government by discussion', a phrase that was coined later by Walter Bagehot.[25] In the context of India, then, is public discourse playing a major role in allowing us to freely express the changes we desire and expanding our collective understanding of the government our vote must elect? We certainly need to ask ourselves whether our habit of speaking about politics everywhere, from farms to buses, reading about it on eighteen out of twenty pages of the newspaper every day, and watching triple-deck bands of breaking news on television related to the politics of our land is helping us work with the government or other stakeholders to ensure our collective well-being.

This is an important question to ask because if the answer is 'no', there are two concerns: first, this is an enormous waste of public energy on a system that is of our own making, a case of 'much ado about nothing', and second, it raises the possibility of an information gap between the governors and the governed.

There is no point being 'argumentative Indians' if the information given out to the public is carefully censored. If the government seeks to influence the media, then what are we left to talk about except praising the government and giving subtle hints about our inconveniences. Even post-Independence nationalists in civil society could argue intelligently and mobilize different perspectives towards building institutions, because they had some sort of transparency on the goings-on and possibility of criticizing the powers that be if needed.

I worry that we are so caught up in the 'form' of democracy that we have forgotten that its essence is slipping.

---

[25] Drèze and Sen 2013, 258.

What I mean by 'form' is our assumption that declaring ourselves a democracy is enough, or that having plenty of public discourse on politics is beneficial. We stop short of assessing if the so-called hardware and software of democracy—to use Guha's terminology—are being respected.

The essence is the guarantee of our freedom. Ever since man decided to live in groups, we've asked ourselves—how do we live together in a way so that all of us can enjoy our freedom to immerse ourselves in our instinctual activities, and allow others to do the same as well? I reiterate this because we must remember that governance systems, old and new, were created to help us maintain that balance.

Now, if talking about governance has become our larger preoccupation without any productive use of that talk to effectively ensure our collective freedom or anything else we feel governance must provide we Indians have gone terribly off-track on our evolutionary ascent.

References

BBC News. 2014. India's dark history of sterilisation. 14 November. http://www.bbc.com/news/world-asia-india-30040790.

BBC News. 2011. Egypt: Cairo's Tahrir Square fills with protesters. 8 July.

Das, Gurcharan. 2002. *India Unbound*, first edition. (New York: Anchor Books).

Drèze, Jean, and Amartya Sen. 2013. *An Uncertain Glory: India and Its Contradictions* (Princeton: Princeton University Press).

Economist (US). 2014. What's gone wrong with democracy. 1 March.

Guha, Ramachandra. 2016. *Democrats and Dissenters* (Gurgaon: Penguin Random House India).

Higgins, Andrew, and James Kanter. 2015. Leaders from Eurozone work into morning on Greek crisis. *New York Times*, 12 July.

Huntington, Samuel P. 1993. *The Third Wave: Democratization in the Late Twentieth Century* (Norman: University of Oklahoma Press), p. 9.

Jaffrelot, Christophe. 1996. *The Hindu Nationalist Movement and Indian Politics, 1925 to the 1990s: Strategies of Identity-building, Implantation and mobilisation (with special reference to central India)* (London: C. Hurst and Company Publishers).

Jaffrelot, Christophe. 2017. Populism, remixed. *Indian Express*, 24 March.

Kakar, Sudhir, and Katarina Kakar. 2007. *The Indians: Portrait of a People* (New Delhi: Penguin Books India), p. 21.

Rawls, John. 2001. *The Law of Peoples: With, the Idea of Public Reason Revisited* (Cambridge: Harvard University Press).

Researchgate. 2012. Sterilization regret among married women in India. https://www.researchgate.net/publication/234133191_Sterilization_Regret_Among_Married_Women_in_India_Implications_for_the_Indian_National_Family_Planning_Program.

Sen, Amartya. 2005. *The Argumentative Indian: Writings on Indian History, Culture and Identity* (London: Macmillan).

Varma, Pavan K. 2005. *Being Indian: The Truth About Why the Twenty-first Century Will be India's* (New Delhi: Penguin Books India), p. 47.

Wright, David. 2016. Poll: Trump, Clinton score historic unfavorable ratings. *CNN,* 22 March.

10

Religion

In India, the cradle of four world religions, we somehow expect tolerance, peace and harmony to thrive. At school, we are taught that India is multicultural and that our strength lies in the diversity of languages, cultures and religious beliefs. Hinduism, India's most popular religion, is itself supposedly a collection of various regional practices and beliefs, and so it is assumed that it must be accepting of differences.

We hear mosques calling out prayers and temple bells chiming on the same street. The queues for langar at gurdwaras make a blessed and excited cacophony. We assume that the visitors to these institutions get along with each other, that there is fraternity despite diversity.

When I was six, our family lived a few years in Agra, the city that boasts of the Taj Mahal. A few kilometres away from this beauty, inside the air force camp, I would watch my father visit a cramped and modest local temple, more often when he needed a favour from the gods. I saw my mother pray harder and the box of sweets in my father's hand grow larger with each temple visit, as the desperation for the favour increased.

My parents were 'modern', a word that at the time meant being educated, English-speaking and Western in social habits. Yet, it was not out of character for them, no matter where we lived, to install a temple at home—a wooden holder placed in a corner of my parents' bedroom—and go to a local temple to offer sweets when the going got tougher. At the same time, they also offered me the lifelong freedom to visit neither the temple at home nor the one outside—as a child, I once told them that I could not understand why idols had to be worshipped because my faith resided within me.

Much later, living in a different part of the world, I would often hear inhabitants of foreign lands talk of India's 'spiritual' aspect. They would ask me about the sacred cow, karma, yoga, and mendicants in Benares. They would vociferously marvel at how even the poor were so content in India, assuming that the gratification, despite all that poverty, must be related to their belief in religion. Most of these people had not visited India.

Those living abroad and following the news are horrified by the news of the frequent rioting, violence and murder in the name of religion in India. They knew that through the seventy years of being independent, we have killed thousands of our fellow citizens for reasons related to defending our religion, by that coin opposing that of others.[1] Then, of course, there is the carnage of Partition in 1947, when one to two million people were killed, 75,000 women raped and mutilated, numerous villages set afire, and fifteen million people uprooted as Muslims were forced to trek to West and East Pakistan (the latter is now known as Bangladesh), while Hindus and Sikhs headed in the opposite direction.[2]

---

[1] Kumar 2011, 1.
[2] Dalrymple 2015.

My association with my Bengali Brahmin parents and the Muslim Farooqui family in Delhi has sensitized me to the angst and complex emotions on both sides of the divide.[3] In my twelve-year relationship with the Farooquis' son, we spent about eight years living together in various parts of the world. Every face-off between Hindus and Muslims would rock the chances of the societal acceptance of our relationship in India. This was despite the fact that the vicious hostility, based entirely on religious differences, of my family towards the Farooquis in the initial four years or so had gradually changed to fond friendship based on human values. My father discovered that he shared many typical middle-class Indian values with the Farooquis. 'They are the same as I,' he finally declared after six years of knowing them. Yet, this fortunate and uncommon reconciliation between the families could never drown out the condescending voices from the rest of society. A pandit once ousted my father from the temple after chiding him publicly for having 'given away' his daughter to a Mohammedan.

Caught between the two religions for so long, I have perhaps become more sceptical of the petty religious differences in our country. Indeed, my perspective on religion, as I write about it today, is a consequence of deeply private experiences, as much as it is of my intellectual curiosity. As I sought reasons I read and learnt about Hinduism and Islam in India. I painstakingly researched religion and eventually even wrote my master's thesis on the Indian Muslim community in Paris during my studies in the city.

Instances of religious violence in India are far too many and frequent to list, but here is just a glimpse. Millions of Hindus and Muslims died during the Partition of India, and in the riots that followed. A few decades after Independence, certain sections of

---

[3] Identity withheld.

Sikhs in Punjab were unhappy about domination by Hindus and started seeking political autonomy. In 1984, under orders from Indira Gandhi, the Indian army attacked the Golden Temple with tanks and armoured vehicles, killing many Sikhs. Thereafter, Indira Gandhi was assassinated on 31 October 1984 by two Sikh bodyguards. The assassination provoked unprecedented mass rioting in India against Sikhs—thousands were burnt alive or killed, and many displaced and injured.[4]

Communal violence in Kashmir continues too. While Kashmiris continue to live in constant fear for their lives, since the late 1980s, large numbers of Hindus who chose to remain in Kashmir have been driven out. Meanwhile, spurts of anti-Christian violence have frequently occurred in independent India as well. These days, even atheists are not spared. Recently in 2017 in Coimbatore, Farook, who had abandoned Islam and ran an atheist social media group with 400 members, was allegedly murdered by members of a Muslim radical group.[5]

It is a paradox that religious violence is rampant despite the subcontinent having historically been the womb of the Hindu, Buddhist, Jain and Sikh religions. But it is a greater paradox that the modern Indian nation state is constitutionally secular but even more inextricably trapped in the baffling, blinding and immense power of our own mortal creation—religion. This entrapment has, in a Frankensteinian turn of affairs has led to differences.

In other parts of the world too, at different points of time, religion has become larger than life, perhaps whenever we have forgotten that it is a man-made creation and not divinely ordained.

---

[4] Nelson 2014.
[5] Janardhanan 2017.

In Europe, during the Middle Ages, we killed each other in the Christian Crusades against Muslim invasions. A few centuries later, there were bloody wars between Roman Catholics and Protestants. More recently, we massacred innocents in terror attacks in the name of jihadist Islam. Nation states and corresponding governing structures, such as in Pakistan and Israel, have been created on the basis of religion, and committed atrocities on believers of minority religions. Each time we have felt justified in taking lives in the name of religion is when we have perceived religion as a cause much greater than ourselves.

So if the whole world is killing each other over religious differences, why should we be surprised when we Indians do the same?

But we *are* surprised, because somehow, we do not expect this in India. Just as those outside India presume there is spiritual peace here, we Indians believe in unity in our diversity.

There are two popular perspectives to Hinduism, which is followed by 79.8 per cent of Indians today[6]—a massive 966 million, approximately. One, pluralists envision a decentralized profusion of diverse ideas and practices that are happily incorporated under the big tent of Hinduism. I believe that this is the perspective that has made it to our school textbooks. The second perspective is the kind of Hinduism currently in practice, of the centralists who identify themselves as part of a single, pan-Indian, more or less hegemonic, orthodox tradition, centred on an ancient Vedic lineage of texts, transmitted primarily in Sanskrit by Brahmins. This orthodox manifestation of religious identity is prone to rejecting anyone who differs from it. It also points to a Hindu *rashtra*, deemed by divine ordinance, its purity measured

---

[6] Census of India 2011.

by the proximity of its inhabitants to the ancient Vedic culture, and polluted by anyone whose faith is different.

Ironically, the Hindu 'religious identity' is barely 200 years old. The practices that today constitute Hinduism can be traced back to about 1200 BC, but the emergence of Hinduism as a religious identity for Indian people is—and I will explain how—as recent as the nineteenth century.[7] Prior to this, neither did these groups have a name for themselves as a religious unity, nor did they consider themselves members of a single religious collective. Hindu religious identity is a recent phenomenon when compared to the establishment of other world religions such as Christianity, Islam, Buddhism or Jainism, which dates back to at least 1500 years. Yet, we can marvel at how in a comparatively short time, it has come to wield incredible power and taken the high ground of authority over various regional groups of vernacular languages and practices.

The history of the creation of the Hindu religious identity is fascinating. As recently as three centuries ago, 'Hinduism' was a largely geographical reference. It did not have a religious connotation. The term 'Hinduism' comes from the Indus river. Persians to the west of the Indus used the term, modifying it phonologically to 'Hind', to refer to the land of the Indus Valley. From Persian, it was borrowed by Greek and Latin, with India becoming the geographical designation for all unknown territories beyond the Indus. Meanwhile, Muslims used the term 'Hindu' to refer to the native people of South Asia, and more specifically, to those South Asians who did not convert to Islam, lending the term, for the first time, some religious significance.

It was only in the nineteenth century that the colonial British, in common parlance and later in their census, began to officially

---

[7] Lopez 1995.

use the word 'Hinduism' to refer to a supposed religious system, encompassing the beliefs and practices of Indian people who did not follow other 'named' religions such as Islam, Christianity, Buddhism or Jainism. By then, a series of distinct individual world religions had come to be defined, each with its own essence and historical timeline. A unifying umbrella of Hinduism as a religion, bringing together the various disparate practices of people living east of the Indus, was seen by locals in India too as a useful construct and counterpart to the seemingly monolithic Christianity of the colonizers.[8]

If we trace the origins of some religious practices in India that we now kill each other over, we can find explanations that point to a trivial incident or mortal whim in ancient times. Their origins forgotten, however, we now accord these incidents immense value with a blind fervour that has no place for reason, letting them legitimize atrocities, plunder and murder. Perhaps we cling to this blind fervour—or faith, as we call it—because it also provides us hope in hopeless times, makes us optimistic by offering ways to effect life-changing, logic-defying miracles, and lends itself as a pivot for our mortal life. Who then cares about its origins?

For those of us who do, let us take the example of the varna scheme, or the caste system, as we know it today, which is the basis of the Hindu stratification of society accorded by birth.

The first instance of the social institutionalization of Brahmin dominance—indeed, of the varna scheme or caste system—can be found in the *Purusha Sukta* hymn of the Rig Veda (10.90).[9]

When later Vedic texts such as the Yajur Veda further emphasized the role of sacrifices and prescribed sacrificial

---

[8] Ibid, 4.
[9] See Chapter 1 titled 'Survival'.

procedures ranging from modest domestic rites around home fires to elaborate public ceremonies sponsored by kings, the notion of sacrifice grew in importance.

As the role of sacrifice grew, so did the status of the new group of religious specialists who called themselves 'Brahmins'. The poets of the earlier Rig Veda had used the term 'Brahmin' to refer to the Vedic hymns—now popularly known as mantras. By extension, the Rig Veda poets also used the term to refer to those who fashioned and recited the hymns. The Brahmin reciters of the Rig Veda did not constitute a hereditary or endogamous social group. But gradually, towards the end of the Vedic era, the term 'Brahmin' came to be defined by the Brahmins themselves as a hereditary occupational social group, specializing in rituals and the teaching of the Vedas.

Not everyone agreed. Siddhartha Gautama, a Kshatriya born in the foothills of the Himalayas in about 566 BC, and the founder of the Buddhist religion, denounced the public sacrifices advocated by Brahmin specialists as overly costly, violent and unreliable. He ridiculed the Brahmins' claims to authority. He pointed out that anyone could see that Brahmins emerged not from the mouth of the Purusha, but from the same female bodily organ as everybody else. He also defied Brahminic claims to a special inborn authority, questioning other claims that the Vedas were 'revealed' texts. The Buddha, instead, emphasized that the Vedas were poems, not divine interventions, and human in origin.[10]

The Buddhists, Jains, later religious teachers such as Kabir and also the Bengali *bauls*—each originating and developing their specific philosophies in the Indian subcontinent—continued to question the authoritative claims of the Brahmins.

---

[10] Lopez 1995, 18.

Besides ideological difference, another plausible explanation of the rejection of the Brahminical order by Buddhists and Jains could be their stiff competition for the same pool of economic resources. Mendicants depend on alms, and the surplus production that could be offered to support various claimants—Hindus, Jains, Buddhists—was finite. So in this competitive situation, perhaps, the Buddhists and Jains developed a penetrating critique of Vedic practices.[11]

However, notwithstanding these criticisms, the Vedas became a gauge for Hindu orthodoxy in later times. As a consequence, many new Hindu groups, honouring new deities or new forms of worship, claimed allegiance to the Vedas. The epic Mahabharata posed as the 'fifth Veda', Vaishnava devotional poetry is said to be the 'Tamil Veda', and the nineteenth- and twentieth-century Brahmo Samaj and Arya Samaj movements sought to return Hinduism to what they claimed were its 'purer Vedic roots'. Gradually, it was established that those like the Brahmins, who adhered most closely to the Vedic tradition, had a status superior to 'others', such as the other Hindu castes or those following other religions, which were placed outside the Vedic fold.

Let us take another example: the origins of the Hindu concept of rebirth. Around the seventh century BC, at the conclusion of a royal sacrifice, a sage named Yajnavalkya declared to the king that he was the most knowledgeable in Vedic matters out of all those present. As a reward for his achievement, he demanded a thousand heads of cattle. A large number of people questioned him to test his claims, and Yajnavalkya proved himself each time. However, while doing so, he introduced several important concepts that were hitherto unknown in the earlier Vedic tradition. This included the notion that upon death

---

[11] Ibid.

a person is neither annihilated nor transported to some other world for perpetuity, but returns to worldly life to live again in a new mortal form. This concept of the succession of life, death and rebirth grew out of an earlier Vedic concern with the natural cycles of day, night and seasons, and was termed in the Upanishads as samsara or wandering.

But Yajnavalkya's notion of rebirth raised two new perplexing issues: What determines a person's subsequent form in rebirth? And is there an end to this cycle of rebirth?

To answer the first question, the all-knowing Yajnavalkya redefined the Vedic notion of *karman*, which simply meant 'action' in a very broad sense. In the Vedas, karman referred particularly to the sacrificial act. In Vedic sacrifice, all ritual actions have *phala* or fruits—consequences often not apparent at the time, but which will inevitably ripen. Yajnavalkya extended this notion of causality and gave it a moral dimension—that the moral character of one's actions in this life determines the status of one's rebirth in the next, a notion thereafter established as karma in Hinduism.

To answer the second question, Yajnavalkya suggested that a person may attain liberation by abstaining from desire, since desire is what engenders samsara in the first place, hence establishing for the first time the popular Hindu notion of moksha or salvation.[12]

After I returned to live in India three years ago, I decided to travel, explore and seek answers about the tremendous power of faith which fills us with hope for miracles, and makes us so blind to fact and reason.

I travelled widely and spoke to pilgrims and priests at various religious sites, delving into conversations—if they were

---

[12] Ibid, 11.

comfortable discussing these—about their personal faith and religious motivation. I felt that I needed to understand the subject from the perspective of those who perceived and experienced religion differently from me.

A year ago, I visited the Lord Venkateshwara temple, one of the holiest of all Hindu pilgrimage sites,[13] and by no coincidence considered among the wealthiest holy sites in the world as of 2016.[14] The temple is lavish, spread over 25 square kilometres atop the Tirumala hill, located in the south of India. It had a massive footfall of 27.3 million people who trekked up to visit the temple in 2016.[15]

My driver Irfan was a stubbled twenty-five-year-old dressed in denims and a loose chequered shirt, with a bunch of colourful lockets on golden chains around his neck. He was an employee of the temple guesthouse, where I was to stay. He was a chatty and helpful fellow who had picked me up from the airport of the nearby township of Tirupati. On our way up the 3000-foot winding road, he told me cheerfully that Lord Balaji—as Venkateshwara is fondly referred to by the locals—was in fact his brother-in-law.

'How so?' I asked, surprised.

'See, I was born in Tirupati town, right?' he began to explain.

'Right,' I said.

'So Lord Balaji's second wife, Bibi Nanchari, is Muslim like me. She also lives in Tirupati,' he clarified, pointing down the hill to the town we had left behind an hour ago.

'She lives there? The Hindu god's wife is Muslim?!' I found it hard to hide my astonishment.

---

[13] *Time* 2008.

[14] Indiatoday.in 2016; NDTV 2009.

[15] News Minute 2017.

'Yes. She is the daughter of a sultan. She saw the Lord Balaji's idol and fell in love with him. She was dedicated to Balaji, even though she had never seen him in person. The sultan was angry, but then Balaji appeared in the sultan's dream and told him he would marry his daughter. The sultan agreed.'[16]

Bibi Nanchari's story reminded me of any contemporary fangirl tale. 'Okay. So why does she live down there, then?'

'At his feet,' he replied. 'The lord's first wife, Padmavati, lives in his heart in Tirumala temple, and his second wife, Bibi Nanchari, lives at his feet down the hill in Tirupati.'

'Indeed,' I said.

At Tirumala, I was greeted by the exuberant guesthouse manager, former army subedar Surender Reddy. He wore a beaming smile, besides a loose white shirt and dull grey trousers on his short, portly body.

'The gods have brought you to us, maa,' he said, welcoming me.

Surender Reddy, aided by Irfan, would be my guide at the temple. That evening, we walked around the temple city of Tirumala—barefoot, as per the rules—so that I could understand the various structures and facilities.

One of the most striking aspects of Tirumala is its self-sufficiency. Transportation is free of cost to pilgrims as the publicly run electric buses have been gifted by donors. Electricity is provided by wind turbines set up on their own premises. Food is cooked using solar power generated by panels on the campus, and the meal ingredients are either homegrown or sent by donors as well.

---

[16] There are several versions of this story about Bibi Nanchari and Lord Venkateshwara.

The temple city premises and its facilities, including hospitals and schools, as well as more complex processes such as budgets, donor relations, pilgrim accommodation are overseen by the Tirumala Tirupati Devasthanams, popularly known by the abbreviation TTD. They have taken religion online with all seriousness, offering 'e-seva', 'e-hundi', online auction of hair, and even a virtual queue system.

'TTD employees do not suffer from blood pressure, ulcers or other workplace stress ailments because employees are volunteers on rotation. We are here because we love working here. Moreover, everything is getting digitized,' said Madhu, an employee at TTD's donation cell, almost reading the questions on my mind.

Religion—in ancient and modern India—receives the largest chunk of philanthropic funds,[17] and Tirumala's wealth is at stratospheric levels. One of the wealthiest holy places in the world, Tirumala's budget for the financial year 2015–16, approved by TTD, was a massive Rs 2530.10 crore, or approximately $392 million.[18] In comparison, even the Vatican's total annual budget was far less, at about $274 million for the same period![19]

Madhu handed me the donor brochure, a handbook providing guidelines for pilgrims about donation amounts and the corresponding privileges. It read as follows:

> Privileges for donations of Rupees 1 crore and above
>
> Donor and family (not exceeding five members) will be provided free accommodation for three days in a year in VIP suit of value of Rupees 2500. Donor and family will be admitted for Break Darshan and Suprabhat Darshan for

---

[17] Cantegreil, Chanana and Kattumuri 2013.
[18] TTD News, 2016. Conversion rate as of 17 August 2017.
[19] Parrish 2016.

3 days each in a year free of cost. On any one day in a year chosen by donor, Veda Ashirvachanam will be given by Veda Pandits at the temple. Ten big laddus will be issued to the donor. One dupatta and blouse piece will be presented to the donor. One gold dollar of 5 grams in addition to one gold plated silver medallion will be given at the time of the donor's first visit only. Ten mahaprasadam packets will be issued to the donor once a year during donor's visit. Sarvakamaprada Lakshmi Srinivasa Maha Yagnam will be performed at Srinivasa Dangapuram as desired by donor on any one occasion. These privileges are for lifetime of the donor in case of individuals, and for 20 years in case of companies.

Surender Reddy announced to me proudly that just a few days ago, the chief minister of India's newest state, Telangana, had donated gold ornaments worth Rs 5.6 crore to Lord Balaji at the Tirumala temple. The chief minister was fulfilling a vow he had made earlier that he would present gold ornaments to various deities if a separate state of Telangana was indeed formed.[20]

The Lord Venkateshwara temple's annual budget showed that in 2015 alone, donations amounted to Rs 905 crore, and in 2016 they increased further to Rs 1010 crore![21] These numbers did not include contributions from pilgrims through tonsure and the sale of thousands of kilos of their hair each year, entry tickets, the enormous amounts of cash collected in the *hundi* from visitors donating inside the temple, or the sale of the laddu *prasadam*—famed and so coveted that the temple

---

[20] *Indian Express* 2017.
[21] TTD News 2016.

has patented its laddu under the Registration and Protection Act.[22]

In a country that today accounts for the largest number of malnourished children and people living below the poverty line in the world (in 2013)[23]—adding up to almost 800 million poverty-stricken people—crores of rupees are donated every day at this temple. Was this not a failure of India's wealth distribution?

'We do not send financial statements to donors about their money,' Madhu told me. 'The donor tells us which aspect of the temple facilities they want their money to go to, and we do that. We do not reveal money details to anyone.'

'Why not?' I asked. TTD's donor cell is open for pilgrims to visit 24/7—clearly the staff could use some of their time for transparency and reporting.

'God is watching us. We don't need security cameras or managers or donors overseeing us,' Madhu explained.

Glancing over my shoulder at the queue of pilgrim donors waiting to be attended to, Madhu smiled at me impatiently.

I stepped outside the TTD donor cell office, slightly cold in the winter breeze blowing in from the surrounding hills. Night had fallen, and the sounds of devotional songs resounded from Lord Balaji's temple a few hundred metres away. The mood was calm. It seemed that the flurry of devotional activities of the day had eased.

However, as Irfan, Surender Reddy and I drove to the residential premises of the temple city, the action picked up.

Along the roads, there were a few large, hygienic night shelters—similar to Indian bus depots—providing nothing but a

---

[22] *Times of India* 2009.
[23] *Business Today* 2016.

roof to pilgrims. Men and women slept on the floor here, with a bundle of clothes under their head as pillows.

Sprinkled across the temple hill town of Tirumala were modest yet clean rooms, crammed into a few dozen three-storey buildings, with shared toilets and freshly washed clothes hanging on strings outside common corridors. Residents, often neighbours just for a day, spoke a medley of languages, and planned their temple visits together. Irfan and I ate with the pilgrims that night, in a massive public dining facility that efficiently fed 5000 people every ten minutes.

A little farther away were the bungalows of a bevy of Indian billionaires. The Ambanis, Birlas, Mahindras, Jindals, Shiv Nadar, the Sannareddys of Sri Cement, Ramesh Chandra of Unitech, the Singhanias of Raymonds—they were all there. You could name any billionaire industrialist in India, and chances were they had a glistening home here at the feet of the lord. Each bungalow was distinct in design or in the display of expensive art inside, and unlike the crammed shelters and buildings for the masses, they seemed rather vacant. En route to our guesthouse, we stopped to visit Vijay Mallya's bungalow. Irfan was excited—he said that Mallya's bungalow was auspicious as it had the best view of the temple.

As I went to bed later and recounted the events of the day, I found it hard not to be dismayed and saddened at this glaring contrast in resources and status, even in the house of God.

While the dew was still fresh the next morning, Surender Reddy and I set off with Irfan at the wheel for a sighting of the lord.

Irfan drove us to the entry point. Ditching the quick VIP entry, we decided to take the scenic route through the long queues and pilgrim waiting rooms, a winding row of fully covered 'compartments', each entirely digitized for security and replete with provisions of food, fresh milk and water.

However, there was no way to ascertain the number of hours the journey would take. The TTD continuously adjusts the sequence of compartments according to the number of pilgrims in queue, adding more compartments to the route and opening up more waiting rooms as the numbers increase—so we were now, quite literally, at the lord's mercy.

Before we embarked on the journey, Surender Reddy and I sat on the carpeted floor at the first entrance gate. We sipped glasses of hot milk offered free of cost by volunteers, and watched the pilgrims arriving in hordes every few minutes.

'There, you can ask all of them your questions,' Surender Reddy teased me, wearing his usual broad grin while pointing towards the newly arrived crowd.

'Yes, depends on how long TTD keeps us waiting!' I agreed.

Surender Reddy was almost right. I spoke to at least 120 pilgrims that day during a journey to the lord's statue, which took us about six hours.

'Is this your first time here?' I asked a woman standing next to me in the compartment. She was accompanied by her husband and pre-teen daughter.

'No, it's my fourth,' she said. 'My husband is a devotee of Lord Balaji and he has been here more than twenty times. Since we got married, we come as a family as often as we can.'

'Do you have a *mannat* to ask of the lord?' I asked another girl in the crowd. She seemed to be in her early twenties and was accompanied by her mother.

'Yes, to pass my chartered accountancy exam.'

'And you? Do you have a specific wish as well?' I asked the man behind me, who was evidently finding it a challenge to keep silent while waiting in the queue. He spoke and joked with everyone around him, his voice booming over everyone else's.

'I do!' he declared. 'I want a job at the World Bank!'

'That is rather specific, no?'

'Not at all. There is a technique to ask Lord Balaji for your wish. One has to be clear-headed and specific in the ask. And then it takes about thirty-five days for fruition. Lord Balaji needs that much time.'

'How do you know?'

'This is my fifth time here! Each time, all my wishes have come true. Last time, I wished for a job switch, and it happened! And before that, I had wished for a US visa . . .'

His testimonial of the lord's miracles immediately became a popular subject among the crowd where we stood. Some exchanged notes about their own experiences with miracles, and took tips on how to make wishes come true.

However, the majority of those I spoke with came to Tirumala with no specific wish. Some told me it was a 'divine call'. Many said simply seeing the lord gave them peace. Most pilgrims said they came because of devotion and not wishes.

One man explained, 'But Lord Balaji knows everything. He probably even knows the wishes in my heart that my brain does not. So no need for me to ask Lord Balaji anything; he already knows.'

Faith to them meant devotion, an unquestioning and unconditional belief in something.

'When we are up in the sky, travelling in something as dangerous as an airplane, we have faith in the pilot, don't we?' explained another pilgrim who was a professor of engineering from Karnataka. 'It is that faith that keeps us calm all through the journey.'

It seemed that living with faith in God, a spouse, or even an airline pilot, made their lives simpler and perhaps happier. They abandoned questioning and relinquished doubts about the object of their faith. Their devotion to one central cause seemed to bring them unending stability—and that cause could be anything, as devotion to 'God', it seemed, was but a metaphor. In a way, it was beautiful, I thought—the clarity of mind that faith can bring. On the other hand, I realized that the proof of success of religion over centuries was in providing people with convenient truths, leaving no room for doubt.

At last, at the entrance to the chamber of Lord Balaji, the mass slowed down in its pace, as if readying for the grand finale. I turned to my neighbour and asked him why he was here.

'I have been coming here every year for the last fifty-eight years. This is my annual health check-up,' he said.

'How is that?'

'Every year, I walk here from Chennai,' he said. 'I walk a distance of 140 kilometres from Chennai up to the temple here in Tirumala. While doing so, I discover amazing things about my own body. Are my knees aching? Am I short of breath? The answers point to the state of my health.'

Just then, Surender Reddy grabbed me by the arm and pulled me inside. As I inched towards the statue, he stood behind me, whispering continuously in my ear.

'Watch him closely, observe, remember what you see forever. Look at his eyes, this is energy, it will protect you.'

And then we were out in the sun. The darshan was over.

Sitting cross-legged atop a platform out in the courtyard of the temple, Professor Prashanth Sharma was chanting Vedic verses on a microphone. Surender Reddy had already explained to me that Professor Sharma was the deputy head priest, and in charge of temple affairs these days as the head priest was away travelling.

I climbed the platform and sat beside the professor, who decided to take a quick break.

'We do not understand the language of the Vedas. Then why do you recite them?' I asked.

'Vedic hymns and rituals are like pure mathematics. We pandits know and understand it. But other people do not need to understand what these rituals mean. It is just like how people need to know only applied mathematics, and have no need to understand pure mathematics.'

He added, 'See, religion needs to be led responsibly. It is like gold, which is great but also dangerous.'

'What does religion mean to you?' I probed.

'The meaning of religion differs according to one's experience. At the crux of it, it is to live happily and make others happy. We call this ananda. The Vedic meaning of ananda is different from the popular one, which refers to a person who has sufficient money, worldly resources, and is enjoying the world. Instead, ananda in the Vedas means the shape and size of the universe itself.'

I gathered that the professor was articulating an important and recurrent theme in Indian religious philosophy, that true happiness is often not accessible through ordinary human experience, but must be achieved through some other transcendental means, which can be yoga, meditation, devotion or rituals. For example, from as early as the seventh century, tantriks have viewed the human body as a microcosm of the universe, focusing on it as the only vehicle for attaining power and liberation. Later, the Bhakti Movement, developed between the twelfth and sixteenth centuries in India, brought in a deeply devotionalist trend, which also included techniques to not only worship but interact with God, the higher levels of which would include a variety of psychological states and emotional responses. The conquests of the Turkish, Afghan and Central Asian Muslim warriors between the twelfth and seventeenth centuries have had a significant effect on India's political history, establishing Islam as a major religion in India. Yet, there are also the more conciliatory and assimilative activities of the Sufis, which have incorporated yogic techniques and devotionalism, similar to Hindu transcendental practices, to implant Islam as a more customized Indian religion. The monist cosmological formulations of Ibn-al Arabi, the personalization of Allah in Sufi poetry, as well as the renunciatory practices of Sufi masters—all of these have created a mystical form of Islam in India. Even though Sufism originated during the earliest phases of Arab Islam, and flourished throughout the medieval Islamic world, it seemed in many ways uniquely suited to the Indian religious setting.

The professor was also right in pointing out that ultimately, the meaning of religion for each of us hinges on personal experiences with religion. On my way back from Tirumala to Delhi, I realized that over the past three years living in India, I had learnt to distinguish between my individual experience with religion—which had been full of conflict—from that of the meanings religion has for others in the country. Religion without faith is shallow and meaningless ritualism, whereas faith in itself is powerful. In India, I met people who were spiritual and inspiring, and the source of their faith was their religion. There were those who, using the power of their faith for a positive outcome, had fought enormous challenges and terminal diseases with extreme stoicism, spirit and peace of mind. There were people across economic classes who had drawn strength from their faith to overcome great personal loss from floods and rebuilt their lives. There were also those who had risen from refugee camps and slums to become millionaires, drawing power from unflinching faith in their own capabilities.

In each case, there was nothing rational about the source of their faith. It was inexplicable what made them so certain of their beliefs. Their faith, I found, was the very negation of reason. It was not supported by facts. Yet, such a faith was beneficial to them, when they used it to improve their life in a country where, usually, nothing is easy.

On the other hand, must we forget the killings in the name of religion in India? Can faith be constructive only when we bury our memories of communal violence? I don't think so. Instead, we need to make a greater effort to remind ourselves all the time that it is the same absolute sense of certainty that can empowers us with so much positivity which also shuts down scientific reasoning such that it has given legitimacy to humans to take the life of another human. So much so that a victim of religious violence is often seen as the criminal, while the ideologies that justify such violence enjoy the patronage of our society, if not of the state.

Ultimately, the problem is that we find less and less room in India for a middle ground between religion's two extreme faces—one supremely constructive and the other morbidly destructive. Those squeezed in the middle are looked at suspiciously. Who can be labelled secular has become a great puzzle in India.

For one who holds secularism as a personal virtue, it means having no prejudice against any other community. But this is possible only if this person also has solid national institutions supporting this secularism. In India, however, secularism does not include an institutional commitment to upholding individual rights, freedom of expression, dignity, equal treatment by the state, and rule of law.

For one who nurtures secularism as a societal value, secularism means living in religious harmony. But even though India's founding fathers had initially envisaged such an ethic for the nation, we have not been able to get past the bloody memories of Partition.

For those who see secularism as a political orientation, these days it popularly means subscribing to the Congress's narrative of Indian history. But this is a fallacy as well. Indira and Rajiv Gandhi's regimes took decisions which affected every minority community in India. I have written in this essay how there has been religious strife and conflict in different eras of India's past, irrespective of which political party was in power. Only during elections are certain minorities appeased. And so in truth, in India, we do not have any national political party that we can really call secular.

For those who perceive secularism as a nationalist agenda, it demands putting India first. But this raises the important question: What is India? Do we define India by the ethno-territorial interpretation conceived by Veer Savarkar in the early years of the twentieth century?[24] When Savarkar coined the term 'Hindutva', he believed it referred to a collective Hindu identity as an imagined nation. Clearly, we have given powers to religion—both constructive and destructive—that are larger than life. We choose to ignore the fact that every religion is merely a human creation. We forget that religion was founded as an early form of philosophy, as man's attempts to explain the world and give some sort of a coherent frame of reference to life and how to lead it.

Instead, we have utterly complicated the matter, and allowed ourselves to be overpowered—for good or for bad—by a phenomenon of our own making. We have minimized the chances for anyone slipping out of the game. We have given legitimacy to religion's monopoly on our ethics, and increasingly on our politics—and it is this deadly combination that we should collectively fight against.

---

[24] See more on this topic in Chapter 8 titled 'Nationalism'.

References

Business Today. 2016. India has highest number of people living below poverty line: World Bank. 3 October.

Cantegreil, Mathieu, Dweep Chanana and Ruth Kattumuri, eds. 2013. *Revealing Indian Philanthropy* (London: Alliance Publishing Trust).

Census of India 2011. http://www.censusindia.gov.in/2011-Common/CensusData2011.html.

Dalrymple, William. 2015. The great divide. *New Yorker*, 29 June.

Indiatoday.in. 2016. Devotees to Tirupati get free food, water after 500, 1000 rupee notes banned. 10 November. http://indiatoday.intoday.in/story/tirupati-tirumala-devasthanam-tirupati-demonetisation-of-500-and-1000-rupee-notes-temple-donations/1/807004.html.

Indian Express. 2017. Telangana CM KCR makes another massive donation—gold ornaments worth Rs 5.6 cr—at Tirupati temple. 22 February.

Janardhanan, Arun. 2017. Tamil Nadu youth killed for being an atheist, father says he too will become one. *Indian Express,* 27 March.

Kumar, Rohit. 2011. Vital stats: Communal violence in India. *PRS Legislative Research*: 1.

Lopez, Donald S. 1995. *Religions of India in Practice* (Princeton: Princeton University Press).

NDTV. 2009. World's richest temple adds gold, crores, and hopefully, Rahman. 2 December. https://www.ndtv.com/india-news/worlds-richest-temple-adds-gold-crores-and-hopefully-rahman-405921.

Nelson, Dean. 2014. Delhi to reopen inquiry into massacre of Sikhs in 1984 riots. *Telegraph,* 30 January.

News Minute. 2017. With 2.73 crore visitors in 2016, Tirumala temple sees pilgrim footfall rise. http://www.thenewsminute.com/article/273-crore-visitors-2016-tirumala-temple-sees-pilgrim-footfall-rise-55365.

Parrish, Andrew. 2016. Saudi Arabia spends 32 times the Vatican budget to spread Islam. Stream, 6 October.

TTD News. 2016. TTD approves Rs. 2678 crores annual budget for 2016–17. 30 January.

The Hindu. 2016. TTD approves Rs. 2,530-cr annual budget. 28 March.

Time. 2008. India's temples go green. 7 July. http://content.time.com/time/
world/article/0,8599,1820844,00.html.

Times of India. 2009. Tirupati laddu gets global patent. 16 September.

11

Corporations

India's unique 24/7 corporate culture is in stark contrast to other laid-back aspects of the country. Indian corporates consider it a badge of honour to be busy, high-strung and available at all times to the call of duty. This is despite the facts that our government is sluggish when it comes to putting systems in place, courts procrastinate for years in many cases and the country ranks as one of the most difficult and slowest countries to start a new business in.[1]

It is considered a sign of success for exuberant Indian executives to be in an endless frenetic hustle. A 'job'—once a smart solution invented by humans to earn a currency by which goods could be bartered now has the supreme power to shape lives. In a country that enjoys the largest number of public holidays in the world,[2] executives consider 'off day' a dirty word, and hardly ever dream of taking a vacation. While it is an arduous task to find Indian government clerks at their desks during office hours, it is not

---

[1] Doing Business 2018.
[2] Plush 2017.

uncommon to see corporate employees working round the clock all days of the week. We have even made a business out of this enthusiasm, grabbing $28 billion worth of global commerce a year by being the world's largest base for 'back offices' working all through the day and night.[3]

In 2014, when I joined the Jindal Group, I had never worked in India, or for that matter, in an Indian company. For fourteen years previously, I had worked across eight countries— first in French politics, then at investment banks in New York, London and Paris, followed by Geneva at the World Economic Forum, which is known to be a highly political and complex organization. Yet, when I moved to India, I expected to be surprised and utterly outwitted by my 'cultural experience' at the workplace.

I knew that in fast-developing economies,[4] corporate culture has a strong and unique identity. In countries where the economy is creating opportunities for societal change, there is often a lag between corporate culture and the accepted behaviour in the rest of society. Corporate culture is not always a reflection of what people believe in and expect of others outside the workplace. We have seen this happen most recently in the post-Soviet states, where the communist societal structure was gradually transformed by the advent of capitalism in the markets. There, capitalism came first to the markets, ushering in a competitive attitude for profit-making

---

[3] *Economic Times* 2016.
[4] While India's GDP growth rate in the period 1960–2000 averaged 4.5 per cent, the average GDP growth rate thereafter, until 2015, was 7.198 per cent, making India the seventh largest economy by GDP in the world. As of 2016, India has one of the fastest-growing service sectors in the world and the manufacturing industry is expanding, contributing to almost a quarter of India's GDP (Khan 2016).

in the corporate culture, and then social mindsets gradually began to change.

In liberalized India, where corporate governance is weak and regulations poorly implemented, the private sector has developed in a fairly independent manner, which is not entirely similar in trajectory to the change in society. For example, one of the first things I realized here was that in a country of 420 million people between the ages of fifteen and thirty-four,[5] being sixty is still an essential criterion for being considered for a leadership position in business. On the other hand, while some fathers in India kill their infant girls, considering them a financial burden, corporate India is more accepting of women, even in leadership roles. Indeed, in Indian businesses, power is still associated with virility and manliness, but not with gender per se. A woman willing to be forceful and insistent on simply getting the job done with machismo is accepted in business, but not at home. My point here is that we cannot presuppose that corporate culture in India has the same values as Indian society.

Clearly, I had made a rather dramatic re-entry into India. From the Swiss Alps at Davos, I moved overnight to the sweat and grime of the factory floor. I was working at Jindal's headquarters in Delhi on strategic issues for the company as well as those that were pan-industry, often meeting and collaborating with trade associations and other companies in relevant sectors. On most days each month, I would set out wearing my yellow hard hat and fluorescent orange safety vest to oversee several thousand employees at iron ore mines, steel factories, power plants, training centres, and schools and hospitals in the most far-flung parts of Odisha, Chhattisgarh and Jharkhand.

---

[5] Sengupta 2016.

Atop the Sundargarh hills, our iron ore mines were deep craters dug into the earth—carefully engineered so as to reforest the entire area back to its natural flora once the minerals had been extracted. Our factories would cull out the extracts and process hot, molten, raw iron to manufacture large steel plates, beams and columns, among other products. These we would sell to buyers such as ship and aeroplane builders, infrastructure projects for constructing bridges, wind power projects and large turbines. I would be involved in every part of the manufacturing process as well as in sales, putting in place checks and balances to ensure the company's holistic growth. Usually, I would be the lone woman in a group of a few thousand male employees. It was baptism by fire, quite literally, as I learnt how business is done in India. There was never a day I did not make a comparison with everything I had experienced in other countries.

Some of the new friends I became closest to were owners of other large Indian companies. I had first met many of them while working for the World Economic Forum, but it was in India that we became friends. When they shared with me their triumphs as well as woes about life and business, my mind would automatically extract significant lessons for my own self. As a friend, I would offer my affection, and as an apprentice, I would learn about why and how they made decisions, the manner in which they reacted to a crisis or challenge, and their motivation to work.

When I travelled out of Delhi to visit schools and universities that I managed on behalf of the Jindals, and at the ones in Delhi where I occasionally lectured, I would meet and speak to as many young Indians as possible. I was curious to know their interests and aspirations, and I wondered if I could help them in any way. I wanted to know how they felt about the future of their locality, city and country. Their challenges were, I discovered, a reflection of my own in the past, but their future was to shape our country's fortunes.

The economist Amartya Sen has pointed out that in India, there is indeed an emphasis on primary education for children, even in the poorest of families. He has written that the common assumption that Indian parents are often uninterested in the schooling of their girl child is not true. He substantiates this by mentioning one of the main findings of the Public Report on Basic Education, published in 1999, and also those of more recent investigations by the Pratichi Trust—that there was no serious reluctance of parents to send their children, daughters or sons, to school, provided that affordable, effective and safe schooling opportunities were available in their neighbourhood.[6]

I differ from Sen's observation on two counts.

First, the measurement of the gender gap in education—or, for that matter, at the workplace—needs to be redefined as this cannot be conclusively assessed only by data related to the headcount of those going to school. There are many other variables that need to be considered. For example, in India today, everyone is indeed likely to be enrolled for primary education, but boys are more likely than girls to be enrolled in private schools, and more likely to have more money spent on their education.[7] Further, surveys do not measure what boys and girls *do* with their education. Are they equally empowered to understand the same life choices, effectively evaluate those choices, and implement the choice that works best for them? I do not think so!

Second, the good news lies only in primary education data. According to UNICEF data from 2013, while the enrolment

---

[6] Drèze and Sen 2013, 110.

[7] Boyden and Dercon 2012, 3.

ratio of girls as a percentage of boys[8] for primary education is a fantastic 99.9 per cent; this drops to 91.8 per cent for secondary education. Thereafter, there is no guarantee that the girls who have been enrolled will complete their education. The survival rate at secondary school for girls is 48.7 per cent, as compared to 58.5 per cent for boys.[9] Consequently, fewer women have jobs in cities, compared to women who work in farms in rural India. According to a Catalyst report, a meagre 16.2 per cent of urban workers are women (2015–16)![10] In contrast, a whopping 30 per cent of India's adolescent girls are already married, as compared to 4.6 per cent married adolescent boys.[11] Clearly, the primary role of girls in urban and rural India is perceived to be at home.

During board meetings in the early days of my tenure at the Jindals', the office pantry boys would skip serving me a cup of tea. This was because they were not habituated to seeing a young girl taking a seat in the boardroom. They thought I was an assistant to one of the board members, and therefore undeserving of tea.

A number of general practices were not even recognized by employees as gender-insensitive, but were inconvenient for women employees. Some of these practices would be considered terribly odd in most other parts of the world. General electronic communication to the company's men and women employees usually went out with the greeting 'Dear Sir'. My boarding pass on our company

---

[8] The enrolment ratio of girls as a percentage of boys is calculated by the girls' enrolment ratio divided by that of boys as a percentage. The enrolment ratio is the number of children enrolled in a schooling level divided by the population of the age group that officially corresponds to that level (UNICEF 2013).

[9] UNICEF 2013.

[10] Catalyst 2017.

[11] UNICEF 2013.

aeroplane had me titled as 'Mister'—they were not used to women passengers in a private jet. Some of our offices had the customary two toilets standing side by side—both for men.

There is also a peculiar practice in many Indian companies to celebrate employee birthdays inside an office meeting room with a cake, Coke, potato chips and a bouquet of flowers. Colleagues awkwardly line up at the designated time, the more enthusiastic ones start to sing the birthday song, and the cake is cut and subsequently smeared on the face of the employee whose birthday it is. Then comes the moment when it must be decided who will slice and serve the cake to everyone. All eyes turn to the women in the room. Even if there is one woman in a room full of men, and even if all the men are in greater proximity to the cake than the woman, the role of slicing and serving must be hers.

'But this is not about gender, it is about the skill set!' the company's baffled head of human resources explained to me after I sent out company-wide instructions that whoever—man or woman—happened to be closest to the cake must slice it.

So do we capture these biases in our data on the workplace gender gap? We do not. And so my view is that, really, it is not just all about the headcount.

We know that 24 per cent of entry-level employees in India today are women, and 14 per cent women make it to considerable levels of seniority.[12] To me, these numbers are inconclusive. They tell me nothing about the experience of these women at work. Is their role in line with their aspirations? Do they get equal access as the men to leadership opportunities? Can they be their authentic selves at work—no matter how feminine or geeky that might be? Or do they need to coerce themselves into becoming a clone of the

---

[12] Shyamsunder, Pollack and Travis 2015, 5.

majority personality type at work (as in most parts of the world) so as to 'fit in' and get the job done?

I have found that what men and women actually do and get at the workplace can be traced back to our education system.

Boxing young children of varying aptitudes and interests into a classroom of forty to teach them all the same content in the same manner is a sure-shot recipe for producing adults who are devoid of authenticity and programmed to wear blinders at the workplace.

When a four-year-old is told to fill the colour of his crayons within the boundary lines of the drawing in his colouring book, or that he needs to wear a uniform, walk in a queue, and greet his teacher 'good morning' without quite knowing the meaning of it, he is learning important lessons for life. A few years later, he is asked to learn by rote answers to questions, whereas he should have been taught to ask questions for the answers he seeks. Everywhere in the world—except in the Scandinavian countries, where some of the traditional subjects and teaching methods are being abandoned—education is designed to create an army of clones. It probably worked in the industrial era when we needed like-minded, hard-working employees who would obey orders without question. But in the knowledge era, especially in a country like India which wants to establish itself as a knowledge economy, furnishing the economy with zombies who work all day and night will not work.

One of the first things we are taught as young adults is the concept of 'work culture'. We are made to understand that we need to spend a large chunk of our day on earning our living. We are told that the socially accepted way to do so is by getting a 'job' (rather than being a sportsperson or an artist, for instance), and dedicating our life towards adding one line at a time to our curriculum vitae. We give the entire process a name—'career'.

When star employees switch jobs, they are applauded at their stellar ability to unlearn all behaviour patterns imbibed in their previous organization, and observe and correctly mimic the dominant mannerisms of colleagues in their new environment.

And hence, a herd mentality develops. Employees start to display similar behaviour patterns, and make similar choices at the workplace.

Since the early part of the millennium, well-educated Indians with degrees from India and abroad have been less enthusiastic about working for the government or in academia, and have chosen to ride the wave of business and commerce instead. Social mobilization has also raised aspirations,[13] and economic development has increased the capacity of society to satisfy those aspirations. At the corporations that these educated Indians create or join, they bring with them their habits of hard work and rigour, as well as stamina and ambition to build their career.

Resources are few, however, and the claimants are many. Indeed, in a country where one million people will turn eighteen every month for the next several years, job openings in corporations don't yet match up to the demand, and the leadership pipeline is clogged.[14] In the long run, economic development produces a more equitable distribution of income. In the short run, however, the immediate impact of economic growth often exacerbates the difference between the 'haves' and 'have-nots'.

Those lucky enough to get these coveted corporate jobs work harder to keep their livelihood and to ensure professional growth. They multitask at work and adapt to gruelling work hours. As a result, while we are yet to excel at the Olympics, some

---

[13] See Chapter 2 titled 'Evolution'.
[14] Sengupta 2016.

domestic Indian companies which had modest beginnings about fifty years ago, such as the Tata Group, Bharti Airtel, the Jindal Group, Reliance, have thrived, provided value and employment to millions, and expanded globally.

Many of these large business houses in India are family-owned, which means that the founding family owns the largest stock among shareholders in the market. Majority shareholding, coupled with weaknesses in the implementation of labour laws, governance structures, reporting practices and government regulations in India gives these corporations vast powers to hire, fire and almost always do whatever they please.

As far as the employees at some of these organizations are concerned, the fragile nature of their fate at the hands of the company owner breeds a culture of fear, creating a 'motivation vacuum', often turning them into sycophants who seemingly work hard and long, but only when the boss is around. On the other hand, few Indian large business owners would be able to hold a candle to the vision, grit and patience of the founder, who is often the current owner's father or ancestor.

Pooja Jain is the forty-year-old heiress of the $80 million Luxor writing instruments company, whose crayons have coloured the lives of children across India, and whose pens can be found in almost every literate household. The company was founded in 1963 by her deceased father, Davinder Kumar Jain, with five employees and an initial investment of Rs 5000.

Pooja's father was known to be humble, polite and patient. He was methodical in his ways and caring towards his employees.

'He only looked at the balance sheet and took the larger decisions,' says Iyer, D.K. Jain's former assistant.[15]

---

[15] Hussain 2014.

In contrast, this was how international business magazine *Forbes* described Pooja in 2014:

> Pooja likes to micromanage and is demanding of her employees. She is known to work almost twenty-four hours a day, even on Sundays . . . Her colleagues say they can expect calls from her at any time of the day or night, even on weekends . . . It's not unusual for Pooja to call them at 1 a.m. to talk about the business or brainstorm for new ideas.[16]

I had known Pooja well for half a decade, but we became closer after I moved to India to join the Jindals in 2014, the same year that her father passed away. At that time, D.K. Jain's last will had instructed that the company be passed on to his wife, Pooja's mother. Pooja used to run a part of the business with her father, and after he was gone, her role expanded to overseeing the entire group.

Pooja and I met often. I noticed that for the a few months after her father's death, she would go about her day in a perpetual daze, without registering much of what was being said to her. Clearly distraught, she sought to rely on the company's old guards at work for a while. Gradually, she regained her strength and her character. Emotional and affectionate in private, she was hardworking, boisterous and impatient when it came to getting things done at work.

'Why are second-generation family business owners so erratic in their decisions at the company?' I asked her while we were driving in Delhi's Mehrauli area.

'We are disruptors,' she replied. 'We shake up the company and make it open to constant change.'

---

[16] Ibid. This is not the opinion of the author of this book.

'How so?'

'The company has to get used to quick decisions and action. Employees can expect a call at any time from me—it keeps them on their toes.'

'But is that fair? To call employees at all hours?'

'Of course—they get paid for it,' she said, surprised.

Let us take another example. On 11 June 2008, Daiichi Sankyo, the third largest pharmaceutical company in Japan, made an offer to buy a controlling stake in Ranbaxy, the largest drug maker by revenue at that time in India.[17] Daiichi's purchase price of Rs 737 per share represented an enormous premium of 53.5 per cent over Ranbaxy's average daily closing price on the National Stock Exchange for the three months ending 10 June 2008. The Japanese company was clearly excited about the deal.[18]

By November 2008, Daiichi ended up acquiring 63.92 per cent shares of Ranbaxy.[19] Daiichi hoped that this acquisition would help the company establish itself in the fast-moving emerging markets as well as in the generic drugs sector of the pharmaceutical value chain. The acquisition also gave Daiichi access to Ranbaxy's basket of thirty drugs, for which the company had approvals in the US.

Trouble began to brew in this deal—which had initially seemed to be an incredible win-win for both companies— when, in September 2008, the United States Food and Drug Administration (FDA) sent Ranbaxy warning letters regarding manufacturing practice violations at two of its plants, Paonta Sahib and Dewas. The FDA put restrictions on the import of

---

[17] *Business Standard* 2017.

[18] *New York Times* 2008; Jacob and Balakrishnan 2016.

[19] Including transaction costs, the deal cost Daiichi $4.98 billion with a recorded goodwill of $4.17 billion (*UK Essays* 2015).

drugs manufactured at these plants. In February 2009, the FDA also invoked its Application Integrity Policy against the Paonta Sahib facility. According to the FDA report, Ranbaxy's quality control scientists took short-cuts on stability tests for at least two major drugs.[20] They found that Ranbaxy conducted these tests on the same day or within a few days of each other, not over nine months, as claimed by the company. The FDA also alleged that Ranbaxy had submitted manipulated data as part of its application to market new generic drugs in the US, as well as kept hundreds of improperly stored samples in its factories in Paonta Sahib and Dewas.[21] At the time the deal between Ranbaxy and Daiichi was signed, the inquiry did not come as a surprise to either of the two companies, since the FDA had started it in 2006.

At this point, the question being asked by everyone, from trade analysts to the media and the general public, was 'Did Daiichi Sankyo get sold a lemon?' No such ruckus was made over the question: 'How did Ranbaxy get away with selling allegedly inferior quality medicines in India?'

Why did we need the US FDA to reveal the possibility of errors made in our own backyard? I wonder how Indian regulators never got wind of these alleged malpractices.

Ranbaxy, founded by Ranbir Singh and Gurbax Singh in 1937, had grown rapidly amid a weak corporate and government regulatory environment in India. Three generations later, in January 2006, Delhi-based Malvinder Singh—whom I have known as a good friend for some years now—took over as Ranbaxy's managing director and CEO. While his grandfather was a visionary and patient with employees, Malvinder had earned a reputation in the company for being different.

---

[20] Eban 2013.
[21] Ibid.

In 2013, *Fortune* magazine profiled Malvinder in this manner:

> Singh was brash and competitive. The Indian business press
> dubbed him the Pharaoh of Pharma. Others viewed Singh as
> petulant and immature.[22]

Malvinder's profile in *Fortune* was part of the magazine's
nearly 10,000-word sensational investigative essay on Ranbaxy
by Katherine Eban titled 'Dirty Medicine', which revealed
the company's failure to conduct safety and quality tests on
several drugs.[23]

Eban quoted whistle-blower and former Ranbaxy employee
Dinesh Thakur in her essay, writing:

> Thakur says that the company culture was for management
> to dictate the results it wanted and for those beneath to
> bend the process to achieve it. He described how Ranbaxy
> took its greatest liberties in markets where regulation
> was weakest and the risk of discovery was lowest. He
> acknowledged there was no data supporting some of
> Ranbaxy's drug applications in those regions and that
> management knew that.

Malvinder is one of the warmest, most generous, ethical and
perennially optimistic people I have known. Yet, he is an
astute businessman at work. There is nothing that gladdens his
heart more than being terribly busy with work. He discusses
business with his closest ally, his younger brother Shivender,
and trusts no one else more. In 2008, when the brothers sold

---

[22] Ibid. This is not the opinion of the author of this book.
[23] Ibid.

their 34.82 per cent stake in the family company to Daiichi
Sankyo, they together announced the sale even to their own
family only a night before the actual transaction. They had
kept the results of this crucial deal close to their chests until it
was fully realized.

After the FDA accusations, Malvinder refuted any claims of
fraud. 'The kind of malignment, or whatever is the right word,
the kind of perception getting created that the data was falsified,
is not correct. Secondly, if Daiichi Sankyo is saying they were not
aware of whatever was linked to the FDA, that is not correct,'
he said.[24]

'They (Daiichi Sankyo) have mismanaged it. They have not
been able to deal with it. And now they are trying to put a blame
for things of the past. For what? They did their due diligence.
They bought a company but have not been able to run it,'[25] he
added.

The ping-pong between Daiichi and Ranbaxy's founding
family continues even in 2017, with each party throwing the
blame on the other. In the meantime, many legal battles have been
fought. Media agencies have written sensational stories and made
an extra buck but ultimately it is the consumers who have lost.

While American consumers are protected by strict and
alert regulatory agencies, in India this is clearly not the case.
I think the biggest lesson in the entire Ranbaxy saga is that
Ranbaxy could easily clear Indian drug regulations, but not
US FDA regulations. It could skip procedures and exercise
allegedly poor quality control to manufacture drugs at a low
cost and sell these drugs in India. Many factors made Ranbaxy
successful in India. One of them was that the earnings of

---

[24] Kalbag 2013.
[25] Ibid.

citizens were not high enough to buy costly patented drugs, and so competitively priced drugs, such as those from Ranbaxy, made up a majority of the drug market in India. If costs (and therefore prices) are controlled by increasing process efficiency, that should be lauded, but if costs are low because of a lack of rigour in the manufacturing process, it should be unacceptable. But the Indian market is lucrative perhaps precisely because corporate governance, integrity and government oversight are so weak.

Malvinder Singh resigned in 2009. Atul Sobti, Ranbaxy's new CEO, was brought to the Daiichi-acquired company. At that time, Sobti told *Forbes*, 'The Japanese are very process-oriented . . . On compliances and quality, there can be no compromises . . . Culturally, those are not our country's biggest strengths.'[26] But he had no way of knowing then that the alleged slack in compliances at Ranbaxy would cost Daiichi much more than the Japanese company could ever have imagined.

In a catch-22 situation, many companies in India perhaps grew too fast too soon, despite and because of the fact that internal or external governance structures could not catch up and support that growth.

Here is another example of this. In July 1992, when India was in the early stages of privatizing its erstwhile closed economy, the coal ministry ordered the setting up of a screening committee to consider proposals from private power companies for captive mining on a first-come-first-serve basis. The committee guidelines gave preference to the large projects of power and steel companies. During the course of that month, coal blocks that were not in the production plan of the government-owned Coal India Limited (CIL) and Singareni Collieries Company Limited were identified.

---

[26] Goyal 2009.

Between 1993 and 2011, these coal blocks were allocated to various companies.[27]

In March 2012, a draft report by the Comptroller and Auditor General (CAG), an institution established by the Constitution of India, accused the government of inefficient allocation of coal blocks from 2004 to 2009.[28] It estimated that because of this, gains of Rs 10.67 lakh crore had been made by the allottees.[29]

This was when a matter of inefficient government procedures became a political issue. On a complaint by two members of Parliament from the opposition, the Bharatiya Janata Party, the Central Vigilance Commission directed an enquiry into the matter, to be conducted by the Central Bureau of Investigation (CBI). Meanwhile, the prime minister at the time, Manmohan Singh of the Congress, offered to give up public life if found guilty of any misconduct related to the coal blocks allocation.

In August 2012, the CAG's final report was tabled in Parliament. The report toned down the 'potential' losses to the exchequer in the draft report, earlier calculated to be Rs 10.67 lakh crores, to Rs 1.86 lakh crore.[30] This amount was arrived at in the following way: 6.2 billion tonnes of coal reserves x Rs 295 per tonne = Rs 1.86 lakh crore.

---

[27] The Coal Mines (Nationalization) Amendment Act, 1993, passed in June 1993, allowed Indian companies engaged in the generation of power, as well as iron and steel producers, to engage in coal mining for their captive use (Rai 2014); *Hindustan Times* 2012.

[28] Draft CAG report 2011–12.

[29] Ibid, 34.

[30] Performance Audit of Allocation of Coal Blocks and Augmentation of Coal Production 2012–13, 30.

But there is a problem with the 6.2 billion tonnes figure, because it assumes that 100 per cent of the estimated reserves of all 218 captive coal blocks had been mined over thirty years. This, despite the fact—which even the CAG writes it in its report—that only forty of the total 218 blocks were operational, whereas the remaining had been lying undeveloped. Therefore, a much lesser amount of coal would have been 'potentially' mined from the operational captive coal blocks over twenty years, and not 6.2 billion tonnes as assumed by the CAG. The government also pointed out that the CAG's presumptive loss theory was flawed, as mining in many of the coal blocks mentioned had not even begun yet.[31]

I even see a problem with the Rs 295 per tonne figure. The calculation methodology used to arrive at this figure is based on the difference between the average price realization of CIL and the average cost of CIL only in 2010–11. However, firstly, CIL's annual reports between 1993 and 2010 show that its margins have been significantly lower than Rs 295 per tonne. Secondly, many of the private companies were mining coal of a much lower grade than what CIL was mining, and the prices of this low-grade coal were much lower than that of CIL in 2010–11.

Is it illegal in this country for private companies to make legally accrued financial gains? In case corrupt or unfair practices have been used in the allotment procedure, by all means those cases must be investigated. But what about those who followed due legal procedures to develop their mines? If we consider the allegation that the government had allocated coal blocks to companies in a highly unsystematic way, why are private companies to pay the penalty for the inefficiency of

---

[31] India News Tickr 2012.

the government? We often tend to skim the surface of an issue and take away a simplistic reading of it. For example, the CAG report of 2012 implied that if competitive bidding had been held by the government since 1993, a part of the Rs 1.86 lakh crore would have gone to the government. It did not say that the government incurred a 'loss' of Rs 1.86 lakh crore, which was the popular assumption.

More dramatic events were to follow. In April 2013, a report from the Standing Committee on Coal and Steel said that from 1993 to 2010, natural resources had been distributed without following a transparent system and without generating revenue for the central government.[32]

In May 2014, the BJP-led coalition government had come into power. On 25 August 2014, the Supreme Court ruled that all coal blocks allocated by the government between 1993 and 2010 were 'illegal'.[33] Within weeks, on 24 September, the Supreme Court de-allocated all coal blocks allocated between 1993 and 2010 with the exception of those allotted to government companies with no joint ventures, and the ones used for large power projects classified as Ultra Mega Power Projects.[34] Forty of these blocks were coal-producing blocks. Further, the popular perception of the Rs 1.86 lakh crore 'loss' to the government led to a Supreme Court order, in September 2014, that all private coal producers whose operational mines had been de-allocated must pay the government Rs 295 per metric tonne of coal they had ever extracted in the past from the coal block.

---

[32] Standing Committee on Coal and Steel report 2012–13.
[33] *The Hindu* 2014a.
[34] *The Hindu* 2014b.

Such a retrospective amendment of the law caused mayhem. Banks that had lent money to these businesses panicked.[35] Investor confidence in India dropped—foreign investors were aghast that Indian courts could just scrap 204 of 218 coal blocks, allotted by the government to different companies over more than twenty years, without any investigation of individual cases. They asked if there was any guarantee that some court would not scrap a deal sanctioned by the government on the basis of a report in the future.[36] Why did the government not salvage at least the coal-producing mines that producers had worked hard to develop with technology and investments? Why were coal producers being retrospectively charged for extracting coal, as if it was their fault to have developed the mines? The alleged 'illegality' of mines that were duly allocated by the government just did not make sense to investors.

As part of the top management at the Jindal Group, I was right in the eye of this storm. From this vantage point, I was amazed to watch how a matter of alleged government inefficiency (in the allocation of coal blocks since 1993) was conveniently turned into one of corruption by individuals. The entire narrative, I felt, had been transformed to feed a simplistic story to the masses. The 'presumptive' loss to the government estimated by the CAG was an amount that 'would have been gained' in case the allocation had been done efficiently—but this came to be understood by the public as actual losses incurred. It worried me how, in a democracy, politicians were prepared even to hinder economic development if it benefits them in running down their opponents.

---

[35] *Economic Times* 2014.
[36] Ibid.

Corporations are also to be blamed for poor compliance and regulatory frameworks. Large family-owned companies in India struggle to trust professionalism and organizational procedures. Their companies had probably expanded in a very different era—one fraught with crony capitalism and often driven by the fathers of the current owners. The nature and pace of growth of these businesses at that time were, therefore, often different from what was expected of them now.

To stay in step with changing times, Indian family-owned companies have, over the past few decades, made the switch to hiring CEOs with professional credentials. However, in many of these cases, the relationship between the company owner and the CEO has not been easy. Usually, the management styles of the owner and CEO differ depending on the pace of organizational growth they desire. Often, the employees of the 'old establishment' are also difficult to bring on board to a more professional working environment. These employees then become troublemakers, obstructing the transition to ethical, transparent, systems-based corporate practices. Any bad business deal, poor performance in profits, or undesired change in working style is blamed on the 'new way of doing things', which is quick to be deemed a failure by its opponents in the company. Either the owner or the CEO is unable to endure these pressures of changing work culture, and caves in.

For example, India's largest business conglomerate by revenue, the Tata Group, surprised everyone when, on 24 October 2016, the Tata Sons board approved a resolution to remove Cyrus Mistry as chairman of Tata Sons, only four years after he was brought in to replace Ratan Tata. Mistry, educated at Imperial College and London Business School, was the sixth chairman of the group, and only the second to not bear the family surname. The Tatas said that Mistry was ousted because the board lost confidence in him, while Mistry has maintained that the Tatas were afraid of his clean-up drive, which resulted in his dismissal. Mistry has also raised various corporate governance issues in the Tata Group since his expulsion.[37] Immediately, Ratan Tata, of the founding Tata family, resumed chairmanship of the company for the subsequent four months.

On the one hand, India offers one of the most tiresome conditions in the world for business—if done ethically. On the other, the loose set of ever-changing rules and massive market opportunities make it easy to exploit the loopholes and make a profit. This is the brittle structure many Indian corporates are built on today. They have looked for loopholes in the law, at times taken advantage of the weak regulatory oversight, and capitalized on the enormous Indian demographic dividend. It is a risky game, but the rules are so weak that the game becomes easy. However, in a crisis, the lack of organizational coherence, both internally and in the external regulatory environment, leads to institutional accidents. As a result, there is a heightened risk of the collapse of the parts holding the corporation together.

By no means am I maligning corporations, or saying that being astute in making profits is a bad thing. Instead, my point is that for profits to be conducive for economic development, the manner in which they are earned and distributed needs to be fair.

Fair distribution of profits can only happen when economic development is not driven by the whims of individuals, and is combined with institutional checks and balances. Why? If the appropriate checks and balances are not in place, three things will happen. First, the gains will be concentrated among a few while the losses will be diffused among many. As a result, the

---

[37] Firstpost 2016.

number of people getting poorer will only increase. Second, the nouveaux riches who are often imperfectly adjusted to the existing order will keep wanting more power and social status commensurate with their new economic position, which will then widen the socio-economic gap between rich and poor. Third, eventually, increased literacy, education and exposure to mass media will allow people to recognize the widening wealth gap, causing frustration and hopelessness amongst the have-nots.

At the crux of it, just like democracy is as ineffective as a dictatorship if it does not represent consensus, legitimacy and justice, private enterprise is a disastrous form of crony capitalism if the people implementing checks and balances—in the corporations and the government—are not ethical and mindful. Indeed, in corporations, as in politics, it is not just the form but also the degree of governance that is important.

Ultimately, governments and corporations are made up of people who can neglect or pay lip service to ethics, compliances and regulations mechanically without applying their minds. The dwindling capacity of each of us to think, evaluate and choose affects our values, ethics, emotions and volition. If our education—at home, at school and in society—forbids us to think for ourselves, then we end up being replicas of one another, trying to mimic others but failing, because it is impossible to be entirely like another person. So we become second-handers, allowing ourselves to be run by the others, in our eternal quest to be like the other. But we will constantly be told that we are still not good enough, making us work harder to resemble the prototype. This is the dysfunctional utopia that corporations thrive on.

By the time we join an organization as executives, our faculty of reasoning is so rusted that we cannot assess how we truly feel about what we do. That which was supposed to be a rather basic activity of earning a currency, to barter for the goods we ourselves cannot ourselves produce, now governs our life. We ferociously chase career choices that the majority around us desires, each person in the crowd not knowing why they want it so badly. We are ready to make great sacrifices—choosing where to live, what to do with the major chunk of each day of our lives—according to the dictates of corporations.

Just like religion, a 'corporate job' has usurped a high moral status. It is supposedly our moral duty to offer obeisance to God and the boss. We blindly follow what others do, and cannot apply our minds to appreciate diversity in terms of gender, culture and other aspects. We are unable to decipher the direction of our personal moral compass when confronted with ethical dilemmas at work. We simply reproduce the mannerisms of others, or merely and thoughtlessly do whatever gets us to our goal quicker, so that we can all fit into one homogeneous blotch of nothingness.

It is this highest level of our emotions that has to be redeemed from the challenges of corporate life.

References

Boyden, Jo, and Stefan Dercon. 2012. *Child development and economic development: Lessons and future challenges* (Oxford: Young Lives).

Business Standard. 2017. Ranbaxy's Singh brothers known for lucky timing find time in short supply. 29 March. http://www.business-standard.com/article/companies/ranbaxy-s-singh-brothers-known-for-lucky-timing-find-time-in-short-supply-117032900027_1.html.

Catalyst.org. 2017. Women in the labour force: India. 27 June.

Doing Business 2018: Economy profile, India. World Bank Group, http://www.doingbusiness.org/data/exploreeconomies/india.

Draft CAG report. 2011–12.https://timesofindia.indiatimes.com/realtime/Draft_CAG_report.pdf.

Drèze, Jean, and Amartya Sen. 2013. *An Uncertain Glory: India and its Contradictions* (Princeton: Princeton University Press).

Eban, Katherine. 2013. Dirty medicine. *Fortune.* 15 May.

Economic Times. 2014. Investor confidence goes with coal blocks. 25 September.

Economic Times. 2016. India's back office sector remains largest worldwide. 22 September.

Firstpost. 2016. Ratan Tata–Cyrus Mistry spat: Here's the timeline of biggest corporate battle of 2016 in a graphic. 28 December.

Goyal, Malini. 2009. Ranbaxy's new CEO: I can't ask for a better signoff. *Forbes India.* 5 June.

Hindustan Times. 2012. Coal scam: Chronology of events. 24 August.

Hussain, Shabana. 2014. Pooja Jain is rewriting Luxor's future. *Forbes India*, 2 September.

India News Tickr. 2012. CAG Views On Coal Blocks Flawed: Govt. https://indianewstickr.com/cag-views-coal-blocks-flawed-govt.

Jacob, Shine, and Reghu Balakrishnan. 2016. Singh brothers have to pay Rs 3,500 cr for hiding facts in Ranbaxy sale: Daiichi. Livemint, 7 May.

Kalbag, Chaitanya. 2013. Ranbaxy is not a lemon: Malvinder Singh. *Business Today,* 23 June.

Khan, Mehreen. 2016. Growth star India overtakes China as world's fastest growing major economy. *Telegraph*, 8 February.

New York Times. 2008. Daiichi Sankyo to buy control of Ranbaxy of India for up to $4.6 billion. http://www.nytimes.com/2008/06/11/business/worldbusiness/11iht-drug.4.13640244.html.

Performance Audit of Allocation of Coal Blocks and Augmentation of Coal Production, Ministry of Coal. 2013. http://bit.ly/2yrhR89.

Plush, Hazel. 2017. Mapped: The countries with the most public holidays. *Telegraph*, 30 April.

Rai, Vinod. 2014. *Not Just an Accountant* (New Delhi: Rupa Publications).

Sengupta, Somini. 2016. Every month for the next several years, 1 million Indians will turn 18. *Guardian*, 24 April.

Shyamsunder, Aarti, Alixandra Pollack and Dnika Travis. 2015. India Inc.: From intention to impact. Catalyst.org.

Standing Committee on Coal and Steel report. 2013. http://www.indiaenvironmentportal.org.in/files/file/Report%20on%20allocation%20of%20coal%20blocks.pdf.

The Hindu. 2014a. Coal block allocations since 1993 illegal: Supreme Court. 25 August. http://www.thehindu.com/news/national/supreme-court-cancels-all-coal-block-allocations/article6349454.ece.

The Hindu. 2014b. Supreme Court quashes allocation of 214 coal blocks. 24 September.   http://www.thehindu.com/news/national/supreme-court-quashes-allocation-of-all-but-four-of-218-coal-blocks/article6441855.ece

UNICEF Statistics. 2013. https://www.unicef.org/infobycountry/india_statistics.html.

UK Essays. 2015. Daiichi Sankyo's Ranbaxy acquisition analysis. 23 March.

Part IV

CHAOS

12

Money

I first met Chirag at the crowded rooftop bar of a friend's restaurant in Delhi. Towering over everyone else with his tall, slim, muscular frame, he had approached me almost immediately after stepping on to the terrace. He was dressed in a pair of cream-coloured faded jeans paired with a plain mauve cotton shirt, and his brown hair was lightly brushed back over his broad forehead. He seemed to be in his late twenties, I estimated quickly, as he came closer. Wearing a boyish smile—which I later learnt was a permanent feature of his face—he effortlessly struck up a friendly conversation with me. He had a polite, cool-headed, frank demeanour when he spoke, completely unlike the Delhi boys I had met thus far. So it was no surprise when he told me he was only visiting Delhi for a few days—here for the second time in his life, in fact—to check out a prospective investment in the very restaurant where we stood.

I told him I was pleased to make his acquaintance, and then wandered off into the crowd with my girlfriends.

Two days later, it was by providence that we met again— Chirag came by unannounced to a party I had been invited to. We had not planned to meet there. The loud music made it the worst place for a conversation, keeping us on our feet and dancing instead.

And so it was only the day after when he took me out to dinner that we really talked.

From across an oversized platter of sushi and dumplings, Chirag patiently explained to me that forty years ago his father, barely seventeen years of age then, had jumped on a ship that had taken him from India to the shores of opportunity in Dubai. Illiterate and without a coin in his pocket, his father had earned his living initially on a shop floor selling Indian saris in Dubai. Later he joined an electrical and waterworks company and fixed electrical appliances and pipes in people's houses. Chirag's mother, a graduate from Bombay University, belonged to the Sindhi community like his father, but until they married in Dubai, they did not know each other. She was sent to him from India, a marriage arranged by Chirag's grandparents. She bore him a son and a daughter in Dubai.

When Chirag turned fourteen, his father packed him off to faraway New Zealand, accompanied by his mother and infant sister. That country seemed to offer better education and living conditions than impoverished India and the cultural 'bling' of the UAE at the time. Meanwhile, his father stayed on in Dubai. The oil economy was taking off, and the desert was being transformed into a peninsula of multi-storey modern homes, offices, shopping malls and entertainment centres, flanked by the sea on both sides.

His father felt that the opportunities for profit in Dubai were unparalleled anywhere else in the world. He established a small company, employing about a hundred labourers and two dozen engineers—all migrants from India, like himself—who installed electrical and water equipment in large infrastructure projects across Dubai.

I understood that Chirag was distinctly entrepreneurial in his own right, despite living in the shadow of a rather strong-willed father. Hardly had he turned twenty than Chirag set up his own business in real estate and construction in Auckland. He also began to shuttle between Auckland and Dubai, where he helped his father in the business.

After dinner that night, I drove Chirag around central Delhi for his first glimpse of the magnificent treasures of the old and dusty city I lived in. I wished he would see—as I did—that no other city in the world could hold a candle to the elegance of Delhi by night.

Red palash flowers swung from the trees, bowing towards the road. Monumental relics in carved stone from the times of the Mughal emperors sat firmly on the crossroads like old guards of the city. Sprawling bungalows watched us from behind iron gates as we drove past. A gurdwara and a few temples decorated with strings of coloured bulbs shone in the dark. The public gardens were coquettish, promising to reveal lawns sprinkled with more Mughal relics only at dawn. So for now, the black night came alive solely by the blazing force of the neon-lit circular pandemonium around India Gate.

Parking our car by the kerb, we paused to take a good look at the war memorial. I came here often to watch the crowds, I confessed to Chirag. Here, people old and young, driving Rolls Royces, BMWs and rickshaws, speaking in different languages about different things, were united in their love for ice cream, *kabuli chana* and the hullabaloo. The memorial's history largely forgotten, it was the congregation of a heterogeneous and unrelated mass of people that had breathed new meaning into the space. This spot, for me, was India's epicentre. It throbbed with extraordinary diversity, and the deeply distressing contrasts between the exorbitantly rich and the despicably poor that co-exist in India, I told Chirag.

I was neck-deep in work the following day when I received a message on my phone from Chirag—at an hour past the time of his flight back to Dubai. He asked if he could take me out for dinner once more.

It was not the only time that Chirag would forsake his flight out of Delhi for me, and certainly not the last of our dinners. Over the next three months, our weekends were spent together, either in Dubai or Delhi. Chirag's trips to Delhi would usually be extended by a few days, each visit longer than the last, until the evening he unilaterally took a decision and announced it to me in the parking lot of Khan Market when I reached there after work to pick him up and go home.

'I have decided I am not leaving!' declared Chirag, hastening towards me in the characteristic duck walk he does when he is excited.

'How come?' I replied, surprised, looking at him through the window of the driver's seat.

'I just spoke to dad and told him that the market is great here in India, and I'm setting up my own business,' he said, his face beaming as he got in the car and gave me a peck on the cheek.

'That is a wonderful surprise,' I said, after taking a few moments to realize that both our lives would now change forever.

It was also hard for me to miss the irony: the land his father had once desperately quit to sail off to more lucrative pastures in Dubai now seemed to Chirag a bed of business opportunities—far more than Dubai.

Chirag's business idea was to manufacture and set up India's first isolation tank at a central location in Delhi. He described it as 'a well-established medical procedure for mental wellness that replicates the Dead Sea in a controlled environment.' Isolation tanks were popular in the US and a few other parts of the world, including New Zealand, where Chirag had experienced it, but he had discovered that they were not yet available in India. Chirag felt there was a ready market in Delhi for this luxury experience, not only for those Indians who had tried it while travelling or living abroad, but also the increasing number of Delhi residents who had the money to spare.

Our discovery of Delhi from that moment on was of a different face of the city. The volume of money flowing into Delhi was massive. Investors had come in with fat chequebooks, vying for projects that promised them a windfall of profits. Government officials had padded up their bank balances, middlemen had flourished, and some businessmen seemed to have struck pure gold. While the centre was calm, it seemed that Delhi was stretching at the seams. New roads, bridges and overground and underground Metro lines were being constructed to connect the expanding corners of the city. As Chirag went across town looking for locations to set up shop, we learnt of all the action on the city's periphery. On the fringes of the city, several hundred apartment buildings were being built and many more were needed, to cater to a wide range in terms of affordability. Large global firms had set up offices here, attracting talent from around the world to live in the neighbourhood. These people wanted the services and goods they might have seen when they travelled or lived abroad, creating new opportunities for businesses. There was more of a demand than supply of hospitals and doctors, as also of new schools in every budget bracket. Everywhere, there was a thirst for newer malls, shopping choices, cinema halls and fresh entertainment. Yet the money and opportunities coming into the city did nothing to reduce the numbers of children sleeping on the streets. Entire families would be living under bridges, exposed to the harsh Delhi sun and the fuming vehicle engines on all sides. Twenty-something men would be sitting on pavements outside marketplaces with nothing to do.

Flush with new money, filled with destitute poverty, the ugly contrast in Delhi seemed to have created ample room for not just entrepreneurship, but also exploitation, bribery, extortion and nepotism.

Thousands of Indians—about 2,85,000 a year[1]—were moving to the Indian capital, whose population swelled to three times that of Switzerland and double that of Sweden! People's motivations were varied—labour, skilled jobs, education, marriage . . . They felt there were opportunities for everyone, and so they would come here from various towns and villages. While some came to roll out big businesses, others were searching for just a livelihood, having relinquished their small towns to move here. All arrived with hope in their eyes and a few things or skills to sell. In a big city, chance is blind, the stakes are high, and fortune can favour anyone who dares to try. As Chirag ventured out to procure land, government permits, manufacturers and labour for construction, we noticed a dire eagerness among the people we met—wealthy or impoverished—to bend every rule for profit. There was no rule written in stone—this 'flexibility' created both confusion and opportunity, depending on how one leveraged it.

The combined force of the deluge of manpower and financial capital was clearly transforming the architectural landscape as well as the ethical boundaries of the city. And what we experienced intimately in Delhi while setting up a small business was a clear reflection of the broadening income inequality I saw as I travelled to many places in India, working for the Jindal Group and interacting with other large companies.

---

[1] Data as of 2001 (World Population Review 2017).

In India, the richest 1 per cent own 53 per cent of the country's wealth, the richest 5 per cent own 68.6 per cent, while the top 10 per cent have 76.3 per cent. At the other end of the pyramid, the poor half jostles for a mere 4.1 per cent of the national wealth.[2] India dominates the world's poorest 10 per cent with 22 per cent of the population living below the international poverty line. We even had the unfortunate honour of being home to the largest number of malnourished children in the world in 2016.[3] India is already the second most unequal country globally,[4] and the rich are only getting richer.[5] I believe that if the incomes of all Indians congregating on a Friday evening at India Gate are to be compared, then the spectrum would well reflect the overall inequality of the entire country, and also show that it has only widened over the past seven decades.

It seems that as long as inequality thrives, businesses in India profit. Take a look around and you will see that successful businesses are those that have tapped into the country's obscene income gap—producing where incomes are low and selling where they are high. For example, the labour cost for the production of, say, wooden furniture is a pittance compared to the purchasing power for that furniture when retailed even at ten times its cost price in the same neighbourhood. The salary of a twenty-year-old who speaks broken English is far lower than the money he generates for his employer, who caters to companies that outsource their business processes to him. Labour in a steel manufacturing unit is cheap, whereas the

---

[2] Agrawal 2017.

[3] *Daily Mail* 2016.

[4] Agrawal 2017.

[5] In 2000, India's richest 1 per cent owned 36.8 per cent of the country's wealth, while the share of the top 10 per cent was 65.9 per cent. Since then, they have steadily increased their share of the pie. In 2017, the share of the top 1 per cent is 53 per cent.

final product can be sold at a price commensurate to the high demand from infrastructure development projects. The salary of teachers, even in private schools, is meagre compared to the utterly exorbitant fees charged by some schools. The salaries of trained hotel staff, even in the most luxurious of hospitality establishments—and you can check any—are shamefully low compared to the room rates the hotel's guests are charged. The CEO of India's top IT firm earns 416 times the average salary of an employee in his company.[6] In every sector, profit margins in India are based on income inequality.

He had leveraged the cost advantage in India by getting the complex machinery designed and manufactured by a small waterworks company in Pune, using cheap labour at half the cost quoted to him by a manufacturer in Germany.

His was just one example among thousands of entrepreneurs in the country who are enamoured by the market opportunity here; they benefit from leveraging the income inequality, and are hounded by corruption and nepotism. The Indian middle class is dependent on the poor to keep itself afloat, and they have no desire to alter this. If the poor in India were not so desperately needy, how would the middle class convince them to work at the most abysmal wages? The unfortunate and gaping disparity in resources available to the poor and the middle class creates opportunities for cost arbitrage that are useful for the middle class' business. In fact, sociologist Dipankar Gupta writes that in India there is no middle class. He demonstrates that upwards of the middle class, social strata actually comprise the rich of Indian society—standing out not necessarily because of their accomplishments, but because those below them live in such desperate, unenviable conditions.[7] As I have written in more

---

[6] *Times of India* 2017.
[7] Gupta 2000.

detail earlier, for an individual to be perceived as 'higher' in the social hierarchy, there must be many others perceived as being 'lower'.[8]

I have also explained earlier the peculiar nature of politics in India, in which, again, success depends upon the continuation of poverty.[9] Politicians cannot win elections without wielding power over their minions. In villages, political power comes from the existence of a vast number of landless farmers, who are socially and economically in a despicable condition. And in both rural and urban India, the poor have neither the voice nor the will to oppose the drops of patronage coming their way.

Government officials, acting as agents of governance, often thrive on poverty as well as excess income. The salary from a government job in India is paltry, but the potential to earn through parallel means is enormous. Unless the official is altruistic and unusually committed to developing their specific sector, area or the country, the benefits of illegal earnings outdo the costs. However, to prosper, they need the coexistence of both classes—the poor and the wealthy. In India, government officials use their influence to wield power over the public, and cater to the whims of those who have money to pay them to get their work done. People with excess income have the spending power to pay off government officials, while government officials need the poor, needy and marginalized, whom they can easily bully, to get the wealthy person's work done.

Obviously, my central argument here is that accumulation of wealth in India is often at the expense of widening India's frightful income inequality. So then, I ask, why should it be in the interest of the wealthy to improve the condition of the poor? Why should

---

[8] See Chapter 7 titled 'Values'.

[9] Ibid.

we be surprised if the rich get richer and the poor even more impoverished?

Economic necessity often creates a tight network of relations for 'wheeling-dealing'. In India, the rich need the poor—the wealthy get major benefits from maintaining an economic structure that ensures the financial exploitation of the poor. The two ends of the spectrum need to coexist, with as much disparity between them as possible, for maximum profitability for those who are already wealthy. It is this tightly knit structure which I believe also provides an ideal breeding ground for corruption.

We should be careful with the assumed causality between poverty and corruption, but corruption does easily infest an established and well-oiled 'need-based' structure between the rich and the poor. Corruption is not just monetary. When juxtaposed with a pre-existing need-based structure, it becomes a gradual institutionalization of misbehaviour, which contributes to legitimizing that behaviour and socializing others into it too. It is a process—one that leads to an overall 'culture of corruption'.[10] In such a scenario, in which corruption operates as an institutionalized practice, individuals who are not corrupt would need to engage with the corrupt structure. In India, corruption has entered a pre-existing structure that provides financial gain to the group that holds the most power. The outcome could be anything—the corruption of one or several members within an organization, individuals acting on behalf of the organization, or the entire organization.

Chirag and I were told that we were lucky to have been granted an audience by the South Delhi Municipal Corporation's development councillor himself. Indeed, we were privileged beneficiaries of the long-standing symbiotic relationship between the Jindal Group and the local outfit. I had been introduced to

---

[10] Ashforth and Anand 2003.

the councillor by the company just a day ago. Now, in his office at the scheduled time, the councillor's attendants explained that their boss would be away for a short while to clear out an illegal occupation of the city's public space by homeless squatters.

Sitting in the damp room, I looked around at the walls lined with old, stained file-stacked cupboards. The table in front of us had more papers and a plate of fresh fruits, sliced up and waiting for the councillor. Across the table was a tired faux leather swing chair, its head covered with two faded pink hand towels, its arms cracking to reveal yellow sheets of foam.

The councillor, once he arrived, wiped off the sweat beads from his forehead with one of the towels on his chair, and dug his stainless steel fork into the sliced mango on the plate before him.

'Is this a commercial or a residential street in Green Park?' Chirag asked, pointing his finger at a map of Delhi spread open on the table.

'Depends on what you want it to be,' the councillor replied, munching on his fruit.

'The rules are not clear in the book,' said Chirag, gently pushing a fat print publication, pretentiously titled *Delhi Rule Book 2017*, across the table.

'Yes, these rules do get complicated. Come back tomorrow. I will ask my team to search our files and tell you.'

There was no news from the councillor the next day. Two days later, and after another hour's wait in his office, we were blessed to meet him again.

The councillor arrived, patting away the sweat dripping from his neck, and seated himself in his chair. Just then, an elderly woman entered his office unannounced, and placing her hands on the table, begged him in a high-pitched voice to help her stop her tenant from taking over her two-room apartment. She explained that her family members were all dead, and the tiny apartment was her only asset and source of income. It was her twentieth visit to the councillor and she needed his help to turn the goons out of her house.

After having his attendants dismiss the woman, the councillor turned towards us.

'She has no work . . . keeps coming and screaming in my office,' he remarked.

He then announced that the street Chirag had identified for his office location was for residential purposes only.

'I would highly recommend that you follow the rules, but if you absolutely insist on building a commercial establishment in a residential area, we can help you do that as well . . . of course, for a price,' the councillor explained.

'Will I get a receipt for the money I pay you?' asked Chirag.

The councillor laughed. 'No, no, there is no receipt!'

'Then what if someone from your office later tells me that my commercial establishment is illegally built in a residential area? I will have no proof that I paid for it,' Chirag asked, genuinely bewildered.

'In that case, choose another spot for your business,' the councillor advised with a straight face.

Chirag immediately resumed his hunt for the ideal property. The property owners Chirag met over the next few months were just as bizarre, never missing a chance to make a quick buck.

'Is this your property?' Chirag asked one of them, Mr Marwah, while visiting a posh ground-floor commercial property.

'Yes, it is,' answered Mr Marwah.

'What will the rent be?'

'Rs 2 lakh per month, plus a one-time broker fee to me.'

'If you are the owner, why do you charge a broker fee?'

'My brother and I own this place. He charges the rent and I take the broker fee,' Mr Marwah explained.

There is indeed a cost–benefit analysis that plays out in favour of the corrupt in India. Here, the benefits of corruption, minus the probability of being caught, even taking into account its penalties, are greater than the benefits of not being corrupt. Trust plays an important role too. When the state cannot be trusted, corruption becomes more appealing to the individual. If he has trusted, established networks and relationships, then the individual further increases the chance of getting the benefits of corruption and reduces the chances of getting caught.

A primary assumption of French sociologist Pierre Bourdieu's work is that there is a correspondence between social structures and mental structures, between the objective divisions of the social world and the principles that agents apply to it.[11] In the vast body of academic literature on subcultural delinquency theory as well, it has been proved that once individuals live in a group culture where violence is the norm, it is hard for them not to become violent themselves. Similarly, I believe there are social factors that work through the individual, and influence their disposition to make them corrupt. Dispositions can be so strongly determined by social context that it is hard for the individual to escape the behaviour within that context. When consistently reinforced in certain ideas and acts, it is difficult for an agent to step outside that culture. Hence, it is difficult, often impossible, for the individual to get something done without resorting to corruption in India because it is embedded in the societal structures around him. It is for these reasons in India that it is not uncommon to hear corrupt individuals say:

'Everyone is doing it and so I do it too.'

Or, 'I still think I did nothing wrong.'

From the need-based network between the rich and the poor, which favours the wealthy, a causal path leads to the group

---

[11] Bourdieu and Wacquant 1992, 13; Graaf 2007, 71.

behaviour of corruption within the network. That, in turn, affects the individual's mental state. Based on this argument, the reason Chirag did not succumb to corruption in India was that he was an outsider to the need-based network in India, as he had never lived here. His mental state was still conditioned by the ways of doing business in New Zealand. In India corruption is not merely an individual's faulty character.

There is less emphasis on the individual than there is on community relations and affiliations in India, in both society and the state, and I have demonstrated this in great detail in an earlier chapter. We are deliberately taught—at home, in school, and by society—not to nurture the skill of developing our individual values (which is ultimately sourced from an independent mental faculty). Society dreads a free-thinking individual that may chance to think contrary to the socially accepted norm. Here, society and corporations are aligned in their practices. They want obedient zombies, men here want subservient wives, and parents want children who conform to existing social rules. So much so that it makes individuals wary of developing a rational and independent mental faculty lest they upset the accepted societal structure and destroy the system. Corruption is part of our social structure, and it will continue to be as long as the dominant groups in society benefit from it. Till then, every independently developed individual moral compass which might point to a non-corrupt course of action will be a freak case and an exception.

In 2007, a survey by the research firm AC Nielson was carried out in Delhi about those aspects of society that had seen the least progress since Independence. In the survey, 82 per cent respondents said that it was corruption that needed to be eradicated.[12] Rapid urbanization, globalization and the struggle for resources

---

[12] *Times of India* 2007.

contrasted starkly with the masses of wealth accumulated by a few individuals. Everyone wanted as much wealth as others, angry about how a few had got ahead.

By 2010, the frustration amongst these citizens escalated at the revelations of extraordinary corruption in the organization of the Commonwealth Games in New Delhi, the issuance of 2G licence contracts to telecom companies, and the corrupt politico-business nexus. Some citizens began to organize themselves into small-scale movements against corruption and a few leaders emerged from civil society. Modern communication channels offered citizens unprecedented access to information, resulting in a more knowledgeable society and greater awareness about the conduct of government and business.[13]

In response to the public discontentment, the Indian government introduced a bill in the Parliament called the Lokpal Bill as a step to combat the problem. The bill stipulated that ordinary citizens could send complaints about corruption to the Speaker of the Lok Sabha (the Lower House of the Indian Parliament) or the chairperson of the Rajya Sabha (the Upper House). They, in turn, would forward certain complaints for further examination to an advisory body called the Lokpal, which would then send its report to the appropriate authority for action. The civil society leaders in India disagreed, arguing that the proposed bill did not grant the Lokpal any power either to initiate action or to receive complaints of corruption directly from citizens, and would hence be unsuccessful in combating corruption.

Social movements in the Arab countries at that time in my opinion further encouraged these Indians to raise their voices and demonstrate against the Lokpal Bill proposed by the government. In its stead, civil society leaders proposed a Jan Lokpal Bill drafted

---

[13] DiRienzo et al. 2007.

by them, which they asserted was the credible solution to ending corruption in India. They then went about mobilizing citizens nationwide in an organized way, transforming roused emotions into what they hoped would be a large-scale people's movement.[14]

A group of twenty, brought together by Arvind Kejriwal, a former Indian Revenue Service officer–turned–social activist, mobilized tens of thousands of anti-corruption activists for a protest against the Lokpal Bill on Delhi's Ramlila Maidan on 30 January 2011. The success of this event, the government's hitherto unwavering stand on the Lokpal Bill, and the example of the successful revolutions in Tunisia a few months earlier, as well as the ongoing revolution in Egypt at that time, convinced Kejriwal's group to step up their efforts. In Egypt, after eighteen days of protests, on 11 February 2011 the President ceded power. Simultaneously, in India, the anti-corruption movement across the country was launched at a scale that drew immense media and political attention. Anna Hazare, one of the members of Kejriwal's core group, went on a fast unto death at a public space, demanding that the government concede to a mutually agreeable solution with the group.[15]

A hunger strike is not an uncommon form of protest in India. Mahatma Gandhi famously employed it against British colonial rule in India in the early twentieth century, and since then, it has been used quite often—for example, when activist Medha Patkar protested against the construction of the dam over the Narmada river. It is, therefore, an old and culturally well-understood form of protest by Indians. However, Gandhi's approach to effective change was to act locally and stay rooted in one's own context by doing what one could, where one could and where one had

---

[14] Chatterji 2012, 96.
[15] Ibid.

a community. Patkar's movement against the Narmada dam also pivots on the same theory—rooted in the indigenous political culture, where action is local but has an effect at the power centre. This was not the case with India's anti-corruption movement, which organized itself strategically and consciously across cities as a nationwide urban movement via a much-publicized, centrally located hunger strike.

On 5 April 2011 at New Delhi's Jantar Mantar, a landmark symbolizing Indian scientific genius, Hazare went on a hunger strike, with images of Gandhi and 'Mother India' behind him. On the first day of Hazare's hunger strike, a dismal crowd of only a few hundred people gathered at the venue. However, Indian television channel editors, covering the rapid spread of people-driven social movements in Libya, Egypt, Syria and Bahrain, got the perfect image of public frustration in India too—the sight of a pained and fasting Hazare atop a raised platform in Jantar Mantar. The media amplified this protest of a hitherto little-known social activist through heady comparisons with Gandhian satyagraha.

As a result, over the following days, Indians from almost 400 cities joined the movement, believing that they too had finally achieved their own, well-deserved revolution in the spring, and hoping that the movement would ultimately result in the redistribution of wealth from their wealthier compatriots to them.[16]

Hazare broke his fast on 9 April 2011, the fourth day of the hunger strike, as soon as the government issued a notification in the Gazette of India on the formation of a joint committee for the drafting of the Jan Lokpal Bill.[17]

---

[16] Giri 2011.
[17] Government of India 2014.

Over the next two years, Arvind Kejriwal, the instigator of India's anti-corruption movement, created and expanded the Aam Aadmi Party (AAP) to ensure the direct political involvement of the anti-corruption brigade. In the 2013 Delhi Legislative Assembly elections, the AAP emerged as the second-largest party, winning twenty-eight of the seventy seats, making Kejriwal the chief minister of Delhi. But with no party obtaining an overall majority, it formed a minority government with conditional support from the Congress. An important part of the AAP agenda was to quickly introduce the Jan Lokpal Bill in Delhi, but it could not gather support from the other major parties. In a dramatic sequence of events, Kejriwal resigned only forty-nine days after coming to power in 2014. The following year, in the 2015 Delhi Legislative Assembly elections, the AAP came to power again after winning a majority—sixty-seven of the seventy seats—in the assembly.

Even though the annual Central Vigilance Report declared within a year that the number of corruption complaints against the government of Delhi had declined—969 in 2016 compared to 5139 in 2015[18]—nothing much has changed in the private sector. Businesses in India are still rife with the usual biases, extortion and exploitative behaviour. However, the politicization of India's anti-corruption movement, thanks to the creation and success of the AAP, has made the anti-corruption drive in the private sector a political issue as well. Political parties realized that the anti-corruption agenda had a strong grip on the emotions of the common Indian, so much so that the AAP could leverage those emotions to form a majority government in the country's capital.

Riding on this anti-corruption wave, in 2014, Narendra Modi won the elections and became prime minister partly on the basis of his promise to tackle corruption. But corruption

---

[18] *Hindustan Times* 2017.

is still thriving. The international anti-corruption organization Transparency International conducted face-to-face detailed interviews with a sample group of 3000 Indians between March and April 2016, and published the results in a public report.[19] The organization found that 69 per cent, or nearly seven in ten interviewees, had to pay a bribe to access public services.[20] The report ranked India as the most corrupt country in the Asia-Pacific.

Modi's 8 November 2016 decision to demonetize high-value currency notes of Rs 500 and Rs 1000—which represented 86 per cent of the money in circulation at that time[21]—was presented as an effort to rid the country of unaccounted wealth and to push towards a cash-free economy. Modi reiterated several times that the demonetization initiative was part of a larger plan to combat corruption, and that the resulting economic system would provide for a level playing field to empower the poor.

But in reality, the impoverished were the most adversely affected by demonetization. The most impoverished in India are unbanked and literally cash-less. They have no money for even one meal a day, and with a shortage of cash, they are the ones starving to death. They queue up at ATMs night and day. They do not have access to the digital economy, with no chance of logging on to the Internet and buying their meals online. Their lack of access to the digital economy is not their fault, but an institutional failure of wealth distribution efforts in India. Each of the hundred or so deaths that occurred while standing outside ATMs in the aftermath of demonetization was of someone poor—not wealthy.[22] The woman

---

[19] Pring 2017.

[20] Ibid.

[21] Manish 2016.

[22] Worstall 2016.

who gave birth while waiting in an ATM queue was not wealthy.[23] More than 90 per cent of the labour force in India is dependent on cash[24] transactions, and they were the ones left starving to death— not the millionaires. On the other hand, the rich sent their minions to withdraw cash from banks, the wealthier folks had their cash locked in investments, and the wealthiest lost some of their cash in the ensuing raids—these were the stories that the media picked up and published as success stories of demonetization. India's wealthiest either did not care or had privileged information so that they could stack up their cash in the 'right notes' in advance.

Ultimately, corruption wins in India. There is no real incentive for any power group—politicians or businessmen—to mitigate inequality or the corruption that rides on inequality. We have not arrived at such a situation by design. There has been no conniving plan that India's prosperity would be at the expense of exploiting our poorest, and keeping them poor. The development of our corrupt system has been organic, growing like a tree that expands and spreads its branches in the air, and digs its roots deep into the ground.

After eight gruelling months, Chirag set up his small business in central Delhi. When he had set out from New Zealand, he had not accounted for bribes in his budget estimates, and on the eve of his company's launch, that was the budget he had maintained. But there seemed to be one final threshold he needed to cross. On the day of the launch, he was faced with a group of unexpected visitors—transvestites in colourful saris, wearing fake gold jewellery, painted lips and thick black hair switches. They demanded money in exchange for blessings. Nowhere else in the world had Chirag heard of such a unique business model.

---

[23] *Financial Express* 2016.
[24] *News World India* 2016.

'Come on, young man, give us some *badhai*,' one of the transvestites said, while the other three rested their backs on the reception desk and clapped. 'Fifty thousand rupees for us all will be good.'

'Oh, but I have no money. The owner is away,' said Chirag.

'Tell the owner to come give us money!' another transvestite insisted.

'He is a terrible man, the owner. He does not even pay me,' Chirag replied.

'Listen boy, don't mess with us! The consequences will not be pretty! You go give the owner this card,' the transvestite threatened Chirag, thrusting a visiting card into his hands. The visiting card was in Hindi, and read:

Koyal Rawat

98716416xx

Guru Koyal and Party

Note: We warn you that in case any transvestite other than us is given badhai, you will have to pay us ten times the amount.

The ultimate accomplishment in India is not just the accumulation of wealth, but attaining that wealth honestly. The latter is a tall task, precisely because we are all part of the nexus of nepotism, corruption and extortion. The wealthy do not want to destroy this nexus, and the marginalized, such as Guru Koyal and Party, cannot afford to. The politicians pay lip service to an anti-corruption agenda, but that too, in reality, caters mostly to their own pursuit of power. The groups currently dominant in India have no incentive to mitigate India's gaping income inequality. The rich get richer only when the poor get poorer. We are stuck in a system that is unyieldingly corrupt and most treacherous to the poorest.

References

Agrawal, Nisha. 2017. Inequality in India: What's the real story? *World Economic Forum*, 2 July.

Ashforth, Blake E., and Vikas Anand. 2003. The normalization of corruption in organizations. *Research in Organizational Behaviour*, pp. 1–52.

Bourdieu, Pierre, and Loïc J.D. Wacquant. 1992. *An Invitation to Reflexive Sociology* (Chicago: University of Chicago Press).

Chatterji, Miniya. 2012. The globalization of politics: From Egypt to India. *Social Movement Studies*, pp. 96–102.

Daily Mail. 2016. As population soars, India battles to tame malnutrition. 2016. 7 January.

De Graaf, Gjalt. 2007. Causes of corruption: Towards a contextual theory of corruption. *Public Administration Quarterly*, p. 71.

DiRienzo, Cassandra E. et al. 2007. Corruption and the role of information. *Journal of International Business Studies*, pp. 320–332.

Financial Express. 2016. Pregnant woman delivers baby standing outside ATM machine kiosk. December 4.

Giri, Saroj. 2011. Where is India's Tahrir Square? *Open Democracy*, 17 February.

Government of India. 2014. *The Gazette of India*. http://ccis.nic.in/WriteReadData/CircularPortal/D2/D02ser/407_06_2013-AVD-IV-09012014.pdf.

Gupta, Dipankar. 2000. *Mistaken modernity: India between worlds* (Noida: HarperCollins India).

Hindustan Times. 2017. CVC report on dip in corruption shows people's level of satisfaction with AAP: Sisodia. 16 April.

Manish, Sai. 2016. 86 per cent of currency by value in India are of Rs 500 & Rs 1,000 denominations. *Business Standard*, 8 November.

News World India. 2016. The demonetisation, a crippled economy and the mayhem! 14 December.

Pring, C. 2017. Global corruption barometer 2016. *Global Corruption Report 2017*.

Times of India. 2007. Majority of Indians wish to be reborn in motherland: Survey. 14 August.

Times of India. 2017. India's rising income inequality: Richest 1 per cent own 58 per cent of total wealth. 16 January.

World Population Review. 2017. Delhi Population. http://worldpopulationreview.com/world-cities/delhi-population.

Worstall, Tim. 2016. India's demonetisation kills 100 people apparently—this is not an important number. *Forbes*, 8 December.

13

Decibels

The avant-garde building sits on the banks of a lake on the posh outskirts of Geneva, surrounded by the Swiss Alps. A curved linearity connects its various sections, with ascetic minimalism in glass and stone, green proselytism and postmodern interiors. Probably the most unlikely not-for-profit one could come across, the character of the World Economic Forum headquarters building is an apt reflection of the abstraction in the world today. On the other hand, the organization's humble mission statement— 'improving the state of the world'—is hardly representative of the power it wields on the most influential individuals across politics, business, arts and the sciences.

Essentially, this is what the World Economic Forum does: it chooses the most powerful people in the world for attending various confidential meetings all around the year. These individuals—partly because they consider it a status symbol to be among the 'chosen ones'—pay hefty sums of money as registration fees to come together and talk to each other about solving crucial world issues. It is like an elite restaurant with restricted entry that everyone wants to go to. The business model is brilliant and unfailing, its success unparalleled thus far. For three years, my job at the World Economic Forum was to bring together these individuals' diverse ideas and opinions to a single discussion table.

I felt that in many ways the success of the World Economic Forum was also a consequence of the failure of traditional channels of formal consultation and discussion, which international organizations like the United Nations, and various regional and bilateral political alliances, were expected to facilitate. Instead, the informal systems created by the World Economic Forum had attracted influential stakeholders and ensured that serious issues could be dealt with head-on during spontaneous and uninhibited conversations in confidential surroundings. These conversations brought to the table many new ideas. More often than not, these ideas then self-organized themselves into the mental schematics of the participants, who would return from these meetings, go back to their local ecosystems, and apply what they had learnt there.

Such was the power of conversations that I had experienced and learnt to appreciate.

After leaving the World Economic Forum, when I moved to Delhi, I was therefore excited about the noisy enthusiasm to express views and opinions here. One of the first things that I noticed was that everyone I met in Delhi had something to say about the state of affairs in the country, their own lives . . . and even my life. The people here, both rich and poor, laughed unrestrainedly. They were quick to fight as well, and brawls were not uncommon. Tears of joy and sorrow fell easily. People were not shy about calling out to each other loudly in public, neither were they embarrassed if their child bawled and screamed in public spaces.

Travelling in and out of Delhi, it also seemed to me that India's diversity needed no eyes. Climb a terrace in any neighbourhood, and you hear a unique medley of sounds, each exposing the locality's distinctive features. We are presented with a mix of dialects, languages, religious calls, cowbells and factory sirens which together tell us the state of affairs in the area. The music—impromptu creations, improvisations on the spot, not sets of Western-style rigid symphonies —can reveal the heritage of the land. The voices of the people, their different intonations, and what they laugh about, offer a glimpse of the region's character.

India is a unique case in auditory prowess. At 1.3 billion,[1] there are so many of us that our voices cross over each other's. Yet, we love to talk, argue, express our opinions, anger and joy in varying degrees across regions. We are not an intrinsically mellow society, nor disciplined and well-behaved in matters of expression. There is no other country in the world that has twenty-two constitutionally recognized languages! Besides, Census 2011 counted 122 major languages spoken in the country. Many of these belong to different language families—Indo-Aryan, Dravidian, Austro-Asiatic, Sino-Tibetan, Tai-Kadai and others—each distinct in its sound. We *are* the chaos.

We thrive on this multiplicity of voices. Our celebrations are joyous and cacophonic. Even in some of our most popular religions, such as Hinduism, Sikhism and the Sufi strand within Islam,[2] the celebration of God is noisy. Our entertainment— be it traditional forms from the Natya Shastra and puppetry or contemporary Bollywood—is designed to induce a grand stimulation of several senses at once. We often make the effort to verbally describe what we want others to believe we are— we are typically not ones to reveal ourselves slowly. Our voices

---

[1] World Bank 2016.
[2] See Chapter 10 titled 'Religion'.

are matched with sounds symbolic of our emotions, which we physically and deliberately create with material objects. We express our faith with the strength we invest in ringing temple bells, while on the roads, the amount and type of our frustration are duly conveyed in the manner and frequency of our car horns. The sounds of India are just as revealing of us as our words. So the ability to meditate—even though very much part of our heritage—is today considered awe-inspiring and viewed as an exceptional activity meant for spiritual people, because living amidst noise is accepted as the comfort zone.

Even in the past, Eastern philosophies have embraced chaos—or abstraction, diversity, illusion, noise, unpredictability, even conflict—in the environment better than the ancient Greek philosophies.[3] Let us take a few examples.

First, the Hindu concept of maya: Hindu philosophies from the Rig Veda, dating back to around 1500 BC—therefore being the oldest extant texts in any Indo-European language—believe the world to be an illusion, or maya. Maya means magic in Sanskrit—that the world does not exist and yet does, that reality is amoebic and ever-shifting according to context. The Rig Veda does not describe maya as good or always bad, but recommends technique and means to separate what can be perceived from that which cannot be perceived. It tells us that there will always be illusion and abstraction around us, not everything will be laid out in black and white for us to perceive immaculately, and that instead of being afraid of illusion, we must learn how to deal with it. Maya does not denigrate chaos and illusion, or try to bring order.

Another example is yoga, which helps develop our physical, mental and spiritual capabilities so that we can cope with the

---

[3] Albert 1995, 15.

abstraction surrounding us. The origin of yoga can be traced back to the pre-Vedic age. It was originally a meditative means of raising and expanding the consciousness from one's self to being coextensive with everyone and everything around us. It has also been discussed in Vedic literature, the Mahabharata, the *Prasamaratiprakarana* of the Jains, and the Buddhist *Nikaya* texts. It was suggested as a path to enlightened consciousness that enabled one to comprehend the impermanent, illusive and delusive, and separate them from the reality that is true and transcendent. Yoga is a way to be grounded despite the chaos in our external surroundings or in the inner self.

The Rig Veda, in its *samgachchhadhvam* and *samvadadhvam* verses, calls for people to come together and exchange their views and feelings freely, without inhibition.[4] There was no fear of a pandemonium or of contradictory voices. In fact, the rise and success of competing schools of thought such as Jainism and Buddhism, besides others such as Pancharatra and Kapalika, which ebbed gradually, and their coexistence with the Vedic schools, points to a society that allowed diversity of thought and speech. It was an era when intellectual freedom was encouraged.

Going further east, the trend continues. The Chinese poet-philosopher Lao Tzu reminded us that the Tao represents the omnipresent, forever-changing complexities that are all around us, yet elusive and inaccessible. The Chinese Taoists developed the philosophy that the intuitive knowledge of life can never be fully grasped as a concept, but can be understood only through actual living. Essentially, it prescribes going with the flow in life, not clinging to idea structures but changing and evolving because chaos is good and it creates infinite possibilities. The details of

---

[4] Rukmani 2011, 184.

these philosophies—especially the Chinese and Buddhist ones—
are beyond the scope of this essay, but pointing these out suffices
to show that Eastern philosophies did not staunchly oppose chaos.
They did not attempt to subdue chaos into order. They accepted
the complexities of the world as a given, and suggested techniques
for us to manoeuvre through them.

But societies in Europe have, instead, craved order. In the
stories of Babylon and the ancient Hebrews, Apollo's ascendance
over Dionysus, the human role on Earth has been defined as
building order out of chaos, needing to tame chaos to make
us evolve from barbarism to civilization. Ironically, science has
shown otherwise—that the universe actually evolved from an
equilibrium state or order into chaos.[5] In ancient Greece, the
world was perceived as a fight or an *agon* between the two forces
of reason or law, and chaos or nature. The Greeks called the first
force *nomos* and the second force *physis*. Chaos is what there was
before there were gods. For example, in his verses about the birth
of the gods, the Greek poet Hesiod wrote in the eighth century
BC that chaos was the divine primordial condition, which was the
origin of the gods and of all things.[6] The Greeks believed that the
gods came to bring order to the world, and that the gods liked
order and hated chaos.

Hence, for the Greeks, the disciplines of mathematics,
architecture and music—as examples of nomos—followed strict
sets of rules to impose order upon nature. Mathematics brought the
infinite under control, architecture brought space under control,
while music brought noise under control with set symphonies
(unlike the Indian tradition of spontaneous *jugalbandi* based on

---

[5] Nicolis and Prigogine 1977.
[6] 'Theogony' is a poem written in ancient Greek, composed by Hesiod in
   700 BC, which describes the origins and genealogies of the Greek gods.

ragas). Many centuries later, this fascination for bringing order to chaos has persisted.

As another example of nomos and the need for order, Europe created the concept of a modern nation and gifted it to the world. Nation states were presented (and still are) as a way of transforming societies from barbarism to civilization, from chaos to order. The English political philosopher Thomas Hobbes can be considered the first political philosopher to establish the idea of sovereign states in his work *Leviathan*, published in 1651, in which he wrote that the government should be established on an anti-religious basis. This was roughly at the same time the treaties of the Peace of Westphalia were signed, which decreed that the sovereign ruler of a state had power over religion as well.[7] Hobbes's absolute state was one based on fear—a fear of chaos and disorder. He advised that our only recourse was to surrender our natural rights to an absolute monarch who would protect us from chaos, but for that, we would have to obey him absolutely. Much later, after the French Revolution, the first modern nation state was created. Thereafter, most modern nations emerged after wars and struggles for freedom from tyrannical, colonial or dictatorial powers, with a seemingly missionary mandate for harmony. And so these modern nations—in the East and the West—have by definition taken on the goal of unifying the primordial mess.

---

[7] The end of the Thirty Years' War, fought throughout Europe from 1618 to 1648 between the Protestants and Catholics, laid the legal foundation for the nation state. The war involved many small German states, the Austrian Empire, Sweden, France and Spain, among other places in Europe. The Catholics were unable to overturn Protestantism, and the treaties that ended the war, called the Peace of Westphalia, decreed that the sovereign ruler of a state had power over all elements of both the nation and the state, including religion.

In a country as diverse as contemporary India, our ancient traditions of learning how to deal with chaos (instead of suppressing it into order) are tough to carry forward now. For example, in India today, there is a chance that every opinion on an issue may be equally legitimate depending on the sociocultural context it refers to. Unlike societies that are more homogeneous in socio-economic, anthropological and cultural matters, in India, we are increasingly surrounded by multiple truths. Several truths can coexist, depending on the perspective you see them from. Often, these opinions are magnified by the media or by locals themselves, and our country's millions vociferously take different sides on the matter.

Further, citizens with diverse backgrounds—and we have plenty of those in India—often have different individual preferences and beliefs. Lopsided development—which is the case in India[8]—has a compounding effect on the diversification of tastes, beliefs and opinions. For instance, the rich get richer, often with increasing levels of education and exposure to new ideas, whereas the poor have fewer chances to develop their full potential, thus broadening the socio-economic gap and at times the communication gap.

A nation state, however, is based on an aspiration for collective equilibrium. In a collective equilibrium, not every disparate voice is part of the final decision. In a country as diverse as India, politicians have feared that the citizens' increasingly divergent individual preferences and beliefs, if left uncontrolled, will create political chaos. They are afraid that unbridled freedom to express opinions will make it harder for voters to remain in harmony with each other, and to ultimately submit themselves to a single

---

[8] See Chapter 12 titled 'Money'.

leader. Thus, freedom of speech in India has never been abundant. Curbing expression is nothing new.

As I will explain now with a few examples, there were restrictions set by various governments in power—the Congress governments since the days of Nehru, as well as by the Left government in West Bengal, and continues even now.

In 1950, a leftist weekly journal in English, *Cross Roads*, started by journalist Romesh Thapar, published views critical of Nehruvian policy. The journal was banned by the Madras state, and the following year the Nehru administration made an amendment to Article 19(1)(a) of the Constitution against 'abuse of freedom of speech and expression'.[9] This was the very first amendment made to the Constitution of India, and it included the provision to restrict absolute freedom of speech and expression in the country.

Later, this amendment was used by Prime Minister Indira Gandhi during the Emergency in 1975 to cripple the freedom of the press. Few periods in India's history can ever be as dark as the years of Emergency, and its abject disrespect for our freedom of expression.

The trend continued. The Congress government under Rajiv Gandhi was quick to ban Salman Rushdie's novel *The Satanic Verses* even before Ayatollah Khomeini issued a fatwa against it in Iran.[10]

The Hindutva extremists have been notorious in this regard too—in 2006, M.F. Husain was forced into exile by a series of

---

[9] The Constitution (First Amendment) Act, 1951 was moved by the then Prime Minister of India, Jawaharlal Nehru, on 10 May 1951, and enacted by Parliament on 18 June 1951 (Also see Rajan 2005, 21–22).

[10] *New Yorker* 2012.

court cases filed against him by them.[11] Ultimately, the greatest Indian artist of our times relinquished his Indian citizenship to become a citizen of Qatar.

The eastern part of India has suffered the same fate. The Communist government in West Bengal banned Taslima Nasrin's novel *Dwikhondito* in 2003. In the south, politicians J. Jayalalithaa and M. Karunanidhi did not protect the novelist Perumal Murugan when he was coerced in 2014 by a group of caste vigilantes in Tamil Nadu to stop writing.[12]

In India, the worlds of Bollywood and the press enjoy the same legal status and rights as far as constitutional freedom related to the expression of ideas is concerned. This is contrary to, say, the United States, where a 1915 Supreme Court decision established that the legal status of cinema was not a part of the press of the country or an organ of public opinion. Films in the United States are, therefore, not protected by the US constitutional guarantee to free speech, as is the case in India. Yet, Indian films have been far more liable than American ones to prior censorship. In the United States and also in the United Kingdom, an independent film classification body made up of industry committees with little official government status decides movie ratings. In India, however, the Central Board of Film Certification (CBFC) is a government body, which, for the past seven decades now—no matter which political party has been in power—has been known to cut up movies or ban them.[13]

---

[11] Guha 2016, 34; *The Hindu* 2011.

[12] Yamunan 2015. Later, in July 2016, the Madras High Court ruled against the state intervention.

[13] See legal advocate and author Abhinav Chandrachud's view on the issue (Print 2017). Moreover, in countries such as Australia and Singapore, the movie rating agency is also a government body, but these agencies censor movies far less frequently than in India.

Just a few of the many examples of this: the plot of *Aandhi* (1975) seemed to be loosely based on the life of Indira Gandhi, and the film was banned when the Congress government, led by Indira Gandhi, was in power.[14] In the recent documentary *Argumentative Indian* (2017), based on conversations with Nobel laureate Amartya Sen, the CBFC asked for four words or phrases—'cow', 'Gujarat', 'Hindutva view of India' and 'Hindu India'—to be bleeped out.[15] The reasons for film censorship in India—ranging from being prudish to obtusely ideological—can be astounding.

Successive governments in India have sought to restrict freedom of expression in varying degrees. The Modi government reimagines India as an ancient territory having a homogeneous Hindutva identity. This specific form of nationalism was, as I have mentioned earlier in this book,[16] posited by pro-Independence activist Savarkar in the early years of the twentieth century, developed further in free India, and often used to deal with dissenting voices.

For instance, in February 2016, Kanhaiya Kumar, the former president of the Jawaharlal Nehru University Students' Union was arrested by the Delhi Police and charged with sedition for allegedly raising anti-national slogans in a student rally. The rally was actually organized to protest the 2013 hanging of Mohammed Afzal Guru, a Kashmiri separatist convicted for the 2001 Indian Parliament attack. Elsewhere, the state government of Uttar Pradesh set up 'anti-Romeo' squads in 2017 to keep a check on any public display of affection.

---

[14] *The Hindu* 2013.
[15] Volokh 2017.
[16] See Chapter 8 titled 'Nationalism'.

In the World Press Freedom Index, India has consistently been ranked abysmally low. In the first year of the publication of the index in 2002, India was placed at eighty out of 139 countries. Since then, its performance seems to have only worsened. India's latest move in 2017 has been a slide to three ranks lower from the previous year, to be placed at 136 out of 180 countries.[17]

Ramachandra Guha, in his book *Democrats and Dissenters*, deplores the loss of the freedom to express ourselves in India. He points to the rise of identity politics and the ease with which any group of people can complain that its sentiments have been hurt or offended by a statement or product. Guha writes that freedom of expression is threatened also by the disinterest of politicians—no major or minor Indian politician or political party has ever supported writers, artists or film-makers against thugs and bigots.[18]

I believe that one of the greatest threats to our right to speak freely is our tendency to be subservient to any authority that asks us to compromise on our freedom. We are prone to believing that doing so is necessary for us to transform from our supposedly 'barbaric' selves to more 'civilized' beings. In the face of authority, we do not trust our own selves and let go of our sense of judgement.

Why do we do so? Perhaps because centuries of colonial rule have made us guilty about expressing joy, anger, sorrow, desire— we had been told by our colonial rulers that it was 'barbaric' for us to do so. When the Europeans came to India, they brought with them their need for order. We were asked to cover up our bodies (like wearing a blouse under our sari to cover our naked

---

[17] Reporters Without Borders 2017.
[18] Guha 2016, 33.

breasts) as well as our emotions. Their rationale was the same as our politicians' today—freedom of thought and expression makes a public hard to control.

But the foundation of India has been the freedom to express even dissenting voices. Kautilya opposed the Nandas of Magadh when the latter were complacent in the face of Alexander's invasions. The mutinous soldiers of Barrackpore and Meerut led to the first war of independence against the British in 1857. During the long and bloody freedom struggle from the British that ensued, our freedom fighters, each one of them, were all dissenters. Even at the time of our independence, Dr B.R. Ambedkar disagreed with Gandhi, and gave India its Constitution.

I cite these examples from history to draw a stark comparison with recent years. It is worth wondering what has happened to our spirits now. How did our dissenting voices, which have historically risen against forces squashing our freedom, become so enfeebled?

When Indira Gandhi declared the Emergency and censored the press in 1975, we were distressed for a while, but then became inured to it and went about our lives. The majority of us sits by and watches when talented artists, writers, film-makers and members of the press are persecuted by religious groups, political parties or the authorities. In 2016, after the initial shock, we ultimately shrugged off our anguish about Kanhaiya Kumar's arrest. In 2017, we have been told what we cannot eat after the government ban on the sale and purchase of cattle for slaughter, and we obey. Often, we cannot express in traditional and social media views contrary to those of the establishment, and we go with that. We have surrendered, given up the fight to differ. When our freedom to freely express our emotions is curbed by an authority, we briefly worry, but soon after, we calm down by telling ourselves that this restraint must be for our own good.

We have been 'brainwashed', first by the British and thereafter by our politicians. In neuroscience, the phenomenon of 'brainwashing' has been proven—research shows that repeated transmission of the same message eases the replacement of an old belief structure by a new one in our brain.[19] The technique of brainwashing has been used in ancient sexual initiation rites, rhythmic singing in primitive societies, and in evangelical speeches in many parts of the world. Now, it can be seen in political rhetoric the world over as politicians repeat a particular message constantly in their speeches to induce a change in attitude among their audience. The rhetoric that has been hammered into our heads by anyone who has wanted to govern India is that we Indians need to mind our expressive ways. This is part of the psychological foundations upon which contemporary Indian society is now being built.

And so we accept to be stopped short of speaking up, writing and expressing, or creating works of art that reflect the soul. We are left under-confident and suspicious of our own natural tendency to uninhibited expression. Our films— which tend to be an explosion of emotions, songs, dance and elaborate fights—are considered to be good 'art movies' when they are more restrained. On the other hand we find it odd, but ultimately accept the chopping of all sex scenes by the CBFC, a government authority which advocates that adults cannot express their sexuality even in their bedrooms. Why? Because we, the people from the land of the Kamasutra, are too barbaric to know whom to have sex with and when, so our expressions of love and desire need to be controlled.

---

[19] Albert ed. 1995, 6.

Ultimately, the contrast is glaring: on the one hand, Indians have thrived on unbridled self-expression, while on the other, the freedom of expression allowed to us is consistently and dangerously restricted.

When I moved from Geneva to Delhi, I observed that people in India liked to talk. But after a few years here, I also discovered a unique pattern of conversation starters I had never experienced anywhere else in the world. The first set of questions I was usually asked by someone I met socially for the first time would be: 'Where do you live?', 'What do you do?' Both questions were often asked in the same breath. With my response, my interrogator would have sized me up, placing me mentally in the hierarchy of social status. Did I belong to 'high society' and therefore deemed good enough to be befriended? I was used to people in Europe being friendly without getting on to personal territory during initial conversations, but in Delhi, it was quite the opposite.

Contrary to my education, which had taught me that 'name dropping' was anathema, in Delhi, if you knew a well-known person even remotely, then you had the licence to announce him or her as your 'close friend' in public at the first opportunity.

Then came the point in the conversation when the other person spoke about his or her own self. I had been taught to be understated, to reveal little, and instead be gradually revealed to the other person in the conversation. Instead, those I met would immediately jump into a monologue of—I only later deciphered—a rather exaggerated version of their life story.

Meeting someone for the second time around was even more bizarre. The trend was to seem forgetful about the people you have met. I was only later explained this simple logic—if you recognize the person immediately (even if you actually do remember them), it would mean that you don't meet enough people in a day, and therefore you are socially or professionally (or both) unsuccessful.

And if both parties do recollect meeting each other earlier, the answer to the innocent question 'How are you?' must unfailingly be 'Terribly busy'. To be not busy here, I learnt, signified being unwanted and therefore unimportant. In every other country I had lived in, such a question usually elicited a more optimistic or at least a more emotionally neutral answer.

There is certainly no right or wrong way of conducting an appropriate conversation, and comparisons of cultural moorings in this regard can be brushed aside as, at most, amusing. However, my only—and intensely depressing— discovery in the social circuits of Delhi was that ideas and hypocrisy in a conversation were two sides of the same coin. And my only solace lay in the fact that these interactions were perhaps specific to their own local sphere, and not representative of the rest of India.

Over the past three years of living in India, I studied a larger and more diverse sample size of people and their conversations. I found, of course, plenty of honest discussions and disagreements as well as genuine aspirations to act in accordance with deeply held commitments. Many did engage in fascinating deliberation and dialogue because they were open to the possibility of other opinions.

But I also observed something else. I realized that the pretence—in cases where it existed—of upholding a certain virtuous 'image' played an important (and perhaps necessary) part in conforming to the dominant vision of the way 'we ought to be' in a country as diverse as India. This brings us back to the argument I earlier made about our guilt at being 'barbaric'. Indeed, to be self-interested, lazy, unfaithful and deceitful is considered barbaric, and so we are coerced by our own collectivity (society) to conform to more 'civilized' ways. But when we are unable to conform to these so-called civilized ways, we merely pretend to others that we do.

I also discovered that this apparent pretence is not necessarily always bad for society. As every 'hypocritical' public utterance declaring the pretence of an unpractised virtue, the strength of that virtue is reinforced, albeit deceitfully. For example, uttering lofty words about business ethics would sometimes be a lot of eyewash to cover up corrupt practices. Expressing pride at working hard to run a thriving business could be a massive exaggeration of the reality. Long charades about fidelity in marriage could, in reality, be nothing short of a cover-up for an arrangement full of deceit. Those who went to great lengths to talk to me about the virtues of living in a joint family, I would discover later, were the ones who were most miserable and guileful in that set-up. In certain social contexts in India, I found that making public statements like this was the best that could be done. In some other cases, the pretence—of being ethical, persevering, faithful and so on—served as a constraint to the deviant behaviour, sometimes leading people to appreciate and eventually perhaps be transformed into the version of themselves they had pretended to be. In this way—for good or bad reasons—social pretence had a moderating effect on the diversity of thought and actions in Indian society. I have written earlier about our desire for preserving traditional community values.[20] This, in reality, can be very hard to do. And so, what many might decry as hypocrisy towards values in Indian society—where people preach and practise different things—has at times been useful in maintaining some sort of societal harmony. At the same time,

---

[20] See Chapter 7 titled 'Values'.

let us bear in mind that this silver lining of pretence is only a slim one.

So how else have our dissenting voices been enfeebled? I have discussed earlier in this chapter how the project of building a nation requires a certain collective equilibrium among citizens, not chaos. Various governments in India have taken measures to control freedom of expression because they fear the diversity and audacity of the voices in our country. Politics has emphasized that more or less everyone needs to accept, believe and practise certain core values—which often change in a democracy, depending on the political leanings of the government in power—that become the defining traits of the nation, at least for that time.

Further, we form a collectivity called 'society' that often puts pressure on individuals to abide by certain ethics, morals and behaviour patterns, which make up a 'proper' code of conduct. Nationhood and proper social conduct, we are told, are the paths we need to take to move away from our barbaric ways and become civilized like the West. Individuals fear that non-compliance to these dominant values, ethics and morals established by politics and society might lead to dire consequences. In our history and all around us today, there are enough examples of punishment meted out to dissenters not just by the government, but also by society.

This is precisely what leads to the other side, the ugly side, of hypocrisy. In India, the diverse and rapidly evolving contexts that individuals live in preclude the slightest possibility of everyone honestly believing, voicing and practising the same set of values at any point in time. It is not possible for such a vast, diverse population to speak in the same voice. Ironically, while being most in need of honest expression as a virtue, politics and society in India produce the conditions that in fact undermine that virtue. This results in a never-ending cycle of lies and more lies because the only way to ensure political and social harmony is for individuals to compromise as much as possible to conform to these dominant values, ethics, morals and behaviour patterns. When individuals fail to conform, they can unceasingly lie, leading to unending deceit, corruption and betrayal.

In a society that loves to talk, silence is not an option. Conversations that could have been chaotic, diverse and therefore constructive can become platforms for people to zealously prove themselves—truthfully or not—as conformists to the expected dominant behaviour. But this hypocrisy need not continue if the grip of political and societal authority on what we say is loosened.

References

Albert, Alain, ed. 1995. *Chaos and Society* (Amsterdam: IOS Press)

Guha, Ramachandra. 2016. *Democrats and Dissenters* (Gurgaon: Penguin India), p.33.

New Yorker. 2012. The disappeared: How a fatwa changed a writer's life. https://www.newyorker.com/magazine/2012/09/17/the-disappeared.

Nicolis, G., and I. Prigogine. 1977. *Self-organisation in Non-equilibrium Systems* (New York: John Wiley and Sons).

Print. 2017. The problem with India's censor board is its morally conservative outlook. 1 October.

Rajan, Nalini. 2005. *Practising Journalism: Values, Constraints, Implications* (New Delhi: Sage Publications)

Reporters without Borders. 2017. India: Threat from Modi's nationalism. 15 July. https://rsf.org/en/india.

Rukmani, T.S. 2011. Intellectual freedom in ancient India: Some random thoughts. *Sanskrit-Vimarśaḥ* http://www.sanskrit.nic.in/SVimarsha/V6/c14.pdf.

The Hindu. 2011. Requiem for M.F. Husain. 10 June. http://www.thehindu.com/news/national/ Requiem-for-M.F.-Husain/article13059657.ece.

The Hindu. 2013. Friday review: *Aandhi* 1975. http://www.thehindu.com/features/cinema/cinema-columns/aandhi-1975/article4742988.ece.

Yamunan, Sruthisagar. 2015. What is behind Dravidian parties' silence in
    Perumal Murugan issue? *The Hindu*, 14 January.
Volokh, Eugene. 2017. Forbidden words in a documentary about Amartya
    Sen. *Washington Post*, 13 July.
World Bank. 2016. https://data.worldbank.org/country/India.

14

Aesthetics

Until I returned to live in India as an adult, I had never owned a sari in my life. Within the first week of my arrival here, I scooted off to the only sari maker I knew. I had visited him earlier in the year as a passive shopping companion to a girlfriend. Sanjay Garg was a reticent and withdrawn thirty-five-year-old man, so reclusive that anyone who wished to purchase his saris had to trek up to his home, an airy two-storey bungalow located in the midst of utter wilderness almost an hour's ride out of Delhi.

His saris were woven on the loom, mostly lustrous silks from all over the country. Each piece was so unique that it even had its own name marked on its tag.

'I don't think I have seen you around here before,' remarked Sanjay on seeing me seated cross-legged on the rug in his shop surrounded by saris.

'You will see more of me from now on,' I replied. 'These saris are gorgeous.'

'Then you must visit Jaipur, my hometown, and see the saris there. That is real Indian designs,' he added, in faltering English.

I had picked three of Sanjay's plainest saris. Much to the chagrin of my women colleagues, I wore the traditional Indian attire loosely with the most oversized shirts and blouses. A traditional garment, the sari was meant to be draped gracefully, not in the obtuse 'comfort wear' manner I wore it. But the sari was emblematic of the deep relationship between heritage and the daily lives of those colleagues who wore the garment. They were well-meaning and concerned that I would portray a 'bad character' the way I wore it.

However, I soon realized that the sari was a garment of great diversity. There were a range of draping styles influenced by regional identity, personal taste, and most of all by weather and occupation. The women of Coorg in Karnataka tie their sari pleats at the back, leaving their hands free to pick tea leaves on plantations in the mountainous slopes. The Maharashtrian sari is especially long— 9 yards instead of the typical 6—so women can wear it in the traditional men's dhoti style and work comfortably on farms. The traditional sari in Bengal is made of cotton because the soil in the region is so rich that it produces the finest-quality cotton. Moreover, the weather in Bengal is humid, so cotton is considered a more comfortable material than silk, and women wear it in a distinct style that covers the shoulders and the bust because traditionally they did not wear a blouse. Meanwhile, the warrior culture of Punjab and the cold weather in Jammu, among other reasons, makes it inconvenient to wear the sari at all in these regions.

'Taste' in the context of the sari has been defined and redefined over the centuries—it has been mentioned many thousands of years ago (as *nevi)* in the Rig Veda, and (as sati) in the Ramayana and the Mahabharata.

Since those ancient times, the garment has reinvented itself continuously, influenced by the 'taste-makers' of different eras who defined what beauty and propriety, meant. In late medieval times, the royalty and aristocracy set the trend in the design and drape of the sari. Now that role has been delegated to politicians, actors and socialites. Of these, the influence of leading actors in films played the strongest role in defining culture, even though very little of that influence was truly long-lasting and took years to percolate down to the public.

However, I felt that there were other mechanisms at work, far greater than the influence of celebrities, which defined the Indian aesthetics of today.

I found that the taste of the masses was being defined primarily by each individual's personal circles of interaction and influence over extended periods. Within community and family networks, there were always the 'influencers' and the 'influenced'. The elders in the family would chastise the younger generation into wearing the sari in a certain regional or cultural style, just as my colleagues had tried to influence my style. These roles were fluid and mutable, each one influencing the other so that taste operated like a meme. Preferences were dictated and influenced by societal, religious and familial norms, as well as by economic factors, awareness and culturally defined ideas of propriety. It was through lenses such as these that the broader levels of aesthetic influence, such as those from cinema and celebrities, filtered in.

Indian aesthetics, I realized, was a vast topic, encompassing everything from architecture to art, music, food, clothing and much more. I chose to seek the answers to my questions about Indian aesthetics by following the trail of the sari.

My interest in the 'sari chronicles' led me to believe that cultural historians in India (and elsewhere) traditionally paid less attention to material culture—such as what we wear and why we do so—than to ideas, leaving the material realm to economic historians. Economic historians then neglect the symbolic aspects, and typically analyse matters such as the amount of an individual's income spent on purchasing that item. The few studies of material culture, or the physical aspects of a culture that surrounds people, that *do* inspect the symbolic aspect focus mostly on the classic trio of topics—food, clothes, housing. These studies often analyse only the history of their consumption, try to draw conclusions about their symbolic role in displaying or achieving status, and explore issues related to identity, often emphasizing the influence of the media in stimulating the desire for these goods.

Instead, I marvelled at how people were easily typecast based on the garment they wore. The vocabulary of the motifs, material and drape of the sari could apparently reveal not just regional identity but also economic class, and indicate if the wearer was 'decent'! Where did these contemporary stereotypes come from? What constituted taste and aesthetics in contemporary India? I was more interested in understanding the aesthetics of the real India. Here, 'culture', I found, was often used to refer only to 'high' culture. This term was then seemingly extended 'downwards' to include 'popular' culture. Instead, was it possible to expand the notion of 'culture' sideways to refer to objects—such as the humble sari—worn by every class in India, to find clues to what defined Indian aesthetics?

To find out, I took Sanjay's passing suggestion far too seriously, perhaps foolishly so. I set off on a five-hour drive out of Delhi to the city of Jaipur, touted to be India's design capital. En route, I realized that ironically, there is no equivalent word for 'design' in the Hindi language. The closest word, *shilp*, means 'craft', and for lack of such a word, the country's premier design institute, the National Institute of Design, is officially called Rashtriya Design Sansthan in Hindi![1]

---

[1] Author's interview with Abhimanyu Nowhar, founder of Kiba Design, 4 July 2017.

It was 11 a.m. but still early in the day when I arrived in Johri Bazaar, the liveliest fashion market in the heart of Jaipur. I walked down the empty streets, imagining what they would look like in a few hours. Just then, a puff of dust blew into my eyes. A boy was sweeping a shop, sending dust on to the road two steps below and into my face.

'Hey, take it easy, boy!' I exclaimed.

'Oh, you need to step aside,' he said, looking up at me, broom in hand.

'But why are you dumping all the dust on to the street?' I asked, dusting off my face, perplexed that he was keeping his shop clean but clearly not caring about the street right outside.

'*Yahan bas aisa hi hai* (this is how it is here),' he replied, pointing to the large open drain at the crossroads close by.

'Okay . . . so what are you selling in your shop?' I asked.

'Saris,' he said.

'What is so special about your saris?' I asked, amused.

'You see, none of our saris are simple. They have the most embroidery in the whole of Johri Bazaar,' he explained, indicating the glittering ware-stacked floor to ceiling on all walls of his fifteen-square-metre shop.

By the time the sun was blazing down, crowds of pedestrians were swarming amid motorcycles laden with clothes strapped into large bundles, crammed horse carts, and an occasional loudly honking tempo. People would stop every few minutes to touch the silks and chiffons on the mannequins along the open shops. Adding to the cacophony, the shopkeepers were trying to entice the crowds, promising attractive prices for the textiles, saris and lehngas on sale. This was Lalji Sand Ka Rasta, Johri Bazaar's main fashion street with a name as unique as its wares, and a sea of glittering chaos.

'Can I see something without embroidery?' I inquired at one of the larger sari shops.

'Madam ji, without embroidery there is none,' the salesman replied.

The garments sold here were mostly in silk, tissue, chiffon, kota cotton-silk, flashing bright colours with gold threadwork all over. The colour contrasts were not timid either—a deep red cropped blouse over a cream-and-gold lehnga in tissue, teamed with a dupatta in green, pink and gold. Or a pink-and-gold lehnga embellished with emerald green motifs only on the skirt.

'Who has designed these?' I asked a shop owner, pointing to a burgundy-coloured satin skirt draped on a mannequin by the entrance.

'We have no designer, baba, it is our tailor upstairs who makes these,' he said, pointing to a winding stairway in the corner going up to what seemed like a loft. 'People in India want lots of gota and colour. They like their clothes to be full of gold work all over . . . *chakachak!*'

After every few shops on Lalji Sand Ka Rasta, there were arched gateways unexpectedly leading to large marble courtyards. Perhaps calm and airy a hundred years ago, the courtyards were now congested with more shops on the remaining three sides, all selling wedding saris embellished with gota and coloured sequins in designs as frenzied as the ambience itself.

By the end of the day, my feet were sore with all the walking, my hair grey with dust and traffic fumes, and my eardrums ringing with the hullabaloo. I might have even dreamt of glitter on silk that night.

The following day, I chose to venture out to calmer quarters. I drove to the village of Sanganer, located about 15 kilometres to the north of Jaipur.

At first it resembled a rustic Indian idyll: a few mud houses and some brick-and-mortar ones painted white, broad, dusty roads with no motor vehicle except mine in sight, buffalo and goats bounding around, women in colourful saris fetching water from the pump, and men sitting by the roadside smoking bidis. As soon as my car halted, I could hear the birds chirp until some cows started mooing. The quietude belied Sanganer's reputation as the centre for the much-celebrated Rajasthani block-printed cloth. A resident of Jaipur had earlier explained to me that in the sixteenth century, Prince Sanga, one of the sons of Raja Prithviraj, ruler of the kingdom of Dhoondhar, had founded Sanganer, and under his patronage and that of the successive rulers of Dhoondhar, paper-making and block printing on cloth became two of the major industries of this hamlet. Today, all that remains of that royal patronage are the families of artisans who once catered to royalty—they now take the traditional art forward, supplying their wares to the many export houses that visit Sanganer so it can be sold to the world.

Parking my car in a side lane of this quaint town, I walked towards a cloth dyeing ground spread across roughly two hectares of land, bordered by the river on one side and low stone walls on the other. Inside, there were five large sinks dug into the ground, of which three had yards of cloth dipped in chemically treated water so that they soak up the colour. The owner of the dyeing ground, Sandeep, walked up and explained it all to me.

'Beyond the sinks . . . that vast expanse of land you see there?' Sandeep pointed to a few hundred metres away.

'Yes, yes,' I replied, noticing the stretch of several hundred metres of brightly coloured cloth in the sun.

'Out there, hundreds of metres of freshly dyed cloth are drying.'

'Can I see the finished product?'

'Madam ji, why don't you come to my house? We do block printing there,' Sandeep offered. 'You can see the finished product.'

I agreed and followed him as he walked across the road.

It was around two in the afternoon. After a meal, Sandeep's family had got back to work on the textiles on the first and second floors of their three-storey home. At that hour, only his aunt was in the mood for tea, and I agreed to accompany her. As we sat together on a charpoy sipping tea, she explained how six generations of the family had been block printing on cloth in this very house. Earlier, they made cloth for kings, and now their cloth was sold all over India and to Indians abroad.

Downstairs, there were about two dozen men at work. They were busy at a narrow table about 50 metres long, tightly spreading reams of cotton cloth freshly dyed in bright pink, indigo, purple and shades of green.

'We are Rangrej,' explained Sandeep.

'What does that mean?'

'Rangrej is our caste. We are people who colour cloth in the sinks outside,' he said. 'They are Neelgari,' Sandeep pointed to the men spreading the dyed cloth on the table. 'And those over there . . . you see them, the ones printing the motifs on the cloth with their blocks of wood?'

I nodded.

'They are of the Chippa caste,' he continued. 'The son of a Chippa is always a Chippa,' he added and laughed.

'So you can only do the work that your father did? A baby born in the Rangrej caste cannot grow up to become a Neelgari?' I asked.

'It is rare, but it is happening,' Sandeep said. 'Nowadays, people are marrying across castes here. There are hundreds of castes.'

I looked at the bundles of finished block-printed cotton cloth stacked in columns. The motifs ranged from flowers and creepers to animals and human faces as well as figurines.

'Utterly complex, winding and intricate designs,' I remarked.

'These are our traditional designs, from the days of the maharajas,' a workman standing beside me said.

Sandeep interrupted with, 'Have you seen the new Rs 2000 note issued by Modi?' referring to the currency issued by the Indian government in November 2016, after the Rs 500 and Rs 1000 rupee notes were demonetized.

'Yes, I have.'

'That note is American design. But the design we make here in Sanganer is Indian,' he said with pride.

The traditional ware sold in the calm village of Sanganer was just as embellished with complex motifs of geometric designs, flowers and creepers as those in the frenetic lanes of Johri Bazaar in Jaipur. Local aesthetics—or the perception of beauty—did not show much influence of the sights, sounds and smells in their immediate surroundings. Silk or cotton, wedding attire or regular clothing, 'plain' was looked down upon with disdain, and 'simple' was clearly undesirable in both of the two contrasting environments.

I spoke to people in Delhi and found that the more patterns sewn into the design or the threadwork, the better the dress is considered. A classic, simply cut salwar kameez without any work is unlikely to be found worthy of praise. A plain sari risks being disdainfully looked down on as 'simple'. On the ramp and off it, clothes in India, especially for women, are 'effortfully' intricate, not effortlessly chic. In fact, even in other mediums, the love for embellishments is evident. The detailed Islamic calligraphy embellishing the walls of Delhi's Jama Masjid is unforgettable. Be it the tombs of the Mughal emperors, the temples, or the palaces on the border of Delhi and Rajasthan, the most celebrated architectural masterpieces of the city flaunted distinct styles of scrupulously intricate works of murals and frescoes, carvings and mosaics. The greater the abundance and intricacy of the designs, the more spectacular the structures were considered to be.

A few months later, I travelled east to Kolkata and its outskirts, hopping across more than three dozen shops selling traditional attire. The motifs on the *Dhakai jamdani* handwoven cotton saris were distinctly different from what I had seen in the south or the north, but a full body of work all over the sari was a tradition. Floral designs ran amok on the Baluchari sari, with the *aanchal* extending to one quarter of the entire length of the garment, resplendent with scenes from mythological texts. I also found here various *butti* and *patta* designs on tussar silk, and the intricate *kantha* stitch dazzlingly filling up a six-metre sari.

In each place I went to, the length and width of the sari varied with the region and quality of yarn. Materials such as muslin, cotton and silk cotton with zari woven in a range of techniques were embellished with embroidery, print or paint, with different motifs and designs—from human to animal figurines and from birds to floral patterns.

I visited several towns in the south of India—silk weavers in Madurai and large showrooms in Chennai. Intricate gold motifs were woven on the side border, the field (the body of the sari) the aanchal (end panel), or on the entire sari. The small shacks in Tirupati also sold similar aesthetics in different quality of silks.

When I lived near the temple of Lord Venkateshwara atop the Tirumala Hills. I found that here, and in other temples in India, the gods are also adorned. The Meenakshi temple of Madurai stands out with its wondrous collection of colourful statues of deities in traditional clothes and jewellery. In the sculptures at the Khajuraho temples, erotic imagery—women performing fellatio on men, men performing cunnilingus on women, men having sex with men, women having sex with women, men with many women, women with many men, and even men and women with animals—are detailed in the extreme, and each figure wears traditional jewellery, even if they don't have much clothes on.

In fact, an essential component of the daily ritual in temples is the placement of jewellery on idols. During festivals, idols of gods and goddesses are often elaborately decorated and resplendently ornamented with crowns, necklaces, earrings, armbands, bangles, girdles and anklets. The great Sri Lankan Tamil metaphysicist and art historian Ananda Coomaraswamy says that whatever is devoid of ornamentation is 'naked' and 'unqualified'.[2] So a god without ornamentation is invisible (*nirguna*), but when he is adorned, he is 'endowed with qualities' and visible (*saguna*). For women to be seen without ornaments—a pair of bangles, simple earrings and a chain around the neck—is therefore considered inauspicious. In Indian traditions, there are sixteen rituals of beautification (or *solah shringar*) prescribed for a bride, and of these, ten pertain to adornment with jewels from head to toe, because, having been ornamented, the bride now becomes a personification of the goddess.

In the past, the maharajas, in their role as divine monarchs, proclaimed power and wealth not only by extending their kingdoms and armies, but also by the blazing turban ornaments, necklaces, armbands and bangles they adorned themselves with. These symbolized divine kingship.

In religion, literature and poetry in India, clothes, jewels and gems are used as metaphors for character, beauty and physical attributes. This is also evident in our sculptures and paintings. The art of adornment with jewels is even prescribed in ancient texts like the Kamasutra, which declares that the arts and sciences women must know should include knowledge of gold, silver, jewels and gems, and the art of stringing necklaces and making ear ornaments.[3]

---

[2] Coomaraswamy 1939 and 1943.
[3] Burton 1883, 44.

Certain ornaments even today define social relationships such as marriage and status, caste and community. Certain jewels and gemstones are considered powerful amulets against the negative effects of planets. They adorn the strategic marma or pressure points in the body, which are closely linked with physical, mental and spiritual well-being. Energy is believed to travel in the body along these points, and so it is believed that wearing a particular piece of jewellery on these points opens up the pathways and facilitates the movement of energy within the wearer. Even now, if you look at Indian high-end luxury designer wear, it is usually dripping with gold embellishments on clothes as well as accessories.

But India is a land of heartbreaking contrasts. On the other end of the socio-economic spectrum are the tribals, who are the most socio-economically as well as politically disadvantaged group in our country.

I travelled to remote parts of Chhattisgarh and Odisha for about two weeks each month for work. On one of my trips, I discovered that in Sambalpur, a five-hour drive from Bhubaneswar, there were homes where silk was woven on a pit loom. The family sat around a bamboo loom in a room often decorated like a temple, with an anointed shrine and hand-painted motifs on the floor. On the loom, narrow design bands of *rudraksha* beads were made with simple string heddles. Weighted eyes were tied together for each row in the pattern, threaded over the top of the loom, with a sequence of rings woven in tightly, which they pulled down tight over a circular wire. A simple loom could render such complex patterns.

However, I found that many of the weavers in Odisha and Chhattisgarh belonged to tribal communities, which found it difficult to sell their wares in the market. They lived in secluded areas, lacked the know-how to market their product, and suffered because of the general bias that handicrafts made by tribal populations were of inferior design and quality. Handicrafts were most often purchased by those belonging to higher castes or living in urban pockets as artefacts, an object of wonder to be displayed at home, or sometimes as an act of solidarity to support backward communities—but rarely as a product good enough to be used regularly. I realized that in India, relations with lower castes and the tribes are most often theorized in religious, political or economic terms, but too little attention is given to the aesthetic dimensions of the response to 'otherness'. There is a distinct aesthetic response—consisting of a disconnect in taste and trust— to those who are denigrated by political and social oppression. What I mean is that we do not connect with the tribal population on their taste in design, and we do not trust them for the quality and manufacturing technique of their product either.

Our sense of aesthetics, I found, also had a cops-and-robbers relationship with modernity. On the one hand, it is believed that only our ancestors had a genetic, innate propensity for appreciating and creating beauty, and that modernity has now chased that out of our reach. It is commonly lamented that modernity has turned our villages into dung heaps and our cities into sewers, because we live in a country infested by fairness creams and mass commodification of everything from Ganesha to Gucci handbags.

On the other hand, I discovered that with all its new technologies and global connectivity, modernity has boosted the industry producing cultural items. Brocade manufacturing in Benares and the surrounding areas, for instance, has gradually incorporated mechanical devices such as punched cards to supplement manual skills. While retaining the intricacy of the original handcrafted process, these mechanical supplements have speeded up the production process and reduced errors. Modern processes such as jacquard weaving on power looms and metallic transfer printing have been introduced. There has been experimentation with motifs, asymmetrical layouts and non-traditional imagery, borrowing visual elements from other textile traditions and international fashion houses.[4] How we interpret these changes is a matter of personal 'taste'. One of India's foremost contemporary philosophers, Sudipta Kaviraj, writes: 'What modern art achieves is not a sense of beauty, but an intelligence.'[5] He defends Indian modernity by pointing out that our symbols have perhaps become more complex, cluttered and asymmetrical, but they continue to remain powerful.

'Marrying our crafts with modernity has its own challenges,' Ashdeen Lilaowala told me over the phone. During my research on Indian aesthetics, Ashdeen was introduced to me by a friend. I knew of him already as a textile designer, but now I discovered him as an author and researcher who had travelled through Iran, China and India to trace the routes and origins of traditional Parsi embroidery, using it in contemporary wear in his craft and writings.[6]

'Challenges such as?' I probed.

'Respect for deadlines. Traditional craftsmen do not work around timelines! Moreover, one of the most frustrating situations is when you give them a very specific shade of a colour to embroider, and they do the embroidery in a completely different shade with the excuse "sahib ji, *bas unnees-bees ka farak hai*".

'The problem is that many buyers accept these discrepancies. They feel that this is craft and so it is all right for the aesthetics to vary,' Ashdeen told me.

---

[4] Bhuyan 2016.
[5] Chakrabarti 2016.
[6] Lilaowala and Cama 2013.

We live in a symbiotic environment, and a lot has come to Indian traditional aesthetics within this environment despite and because of the constraints of transferability between modernity and tradition. How a commodity is produced and where it is produced determines its look and feel. In all the traditional designs I had seen produced in different far-flung parts of India, and then promoted as high fashion in Delhi, I felt that the lack of connect between the producer and the wearer is what made the garment work. The producer of that garment had probably never stepped out of a village and did not know the context in which the craft would be consumed. If he knew, he would probably have made his wares differently.

In fact, everywhere in the world, I have found that our sense of aesthetics is shaped by financial, geographical and other constraints and our perception of the environment around us. It is not the immediate surroundings, but our observations, deductions and experiences over a lifetime that shape our idea of 'beauty'.

Perceptions are influenced by the environment we surround ourselves with over considerable periods. Because of the environment I have been surrounded by for several years it is my perception of an object that results in my assessment of it as 'utterly complex'. The complexity would lie in my interpretation of what I have seen. It is the judgement made by my senses. My brain has been conditioned by my experiences and surroundings over the years. As soon as I sight an object or organism, my brain contiguously assesses it in regard with mental notes taken from earlier observations and deductions, and gives a verdict on its utility, beauty, value and so on.

One evening, just as I was wrapping up a long working Saturday, I got a call. 'We will be at your place tomorrow at 9 a.m. sharp,' Sanjay told me on the phone.

'What for?' I asked, puzzled. I had not met or heard from him after my first visit to his remote abode.

'I love your pictures on Facebook and how you drape your saris; I am shooting my look-book for the season and would like to have you on our cover,' he said.

The sari is omnipresent, changing its form according to the times and personal tastes, and now through channels facilitated by modern technologies, I thought as I agreed to the proposition.

I have written on modernity in great detail in an earlier essay in this book. However, when it comes to aesthetics, I feel that modernity in India has had another effect—of facilitating the intermediation of the arts. Intermediate artists position their audience between the medium and the discipline. They remove the confines of traditional forms of art and instead expand art to other mediums such as body art, installation art, environmental art, textiles and crafts. They explicitly think in and communicate with their medium, such as bodies, brushes, cameras, language, space, digits and guitars. We can now interpret Danto's argument that 'art indeed is ended, because it is omnipresent' differently, because we can affirm that art has not disappeared because of a lack of success, but it has penetrated—facilitated by the agents of modernity—many more aspects of our life. Thus, the staples of material culture—clothing, food, habitat—can be considered mediums of art. The uniqueness of motifs on saris, its textures and falls, can be assessed in the same way we would assess a work of art.

This I see as an immense change in our overall approach to aesthetics, especially because classical Indian and Western aesthetic theories have differed precisely on the issue of medium. While most Western aestheticians consider art to be enduring visible objects such as painting or sculpture, Indian aestheticians consider the *natya* performance—religious dance theatre—to be the paradigm work of art.[7]

Classical Indian aesthetic theory explores the art of naṭya through the idea of rasa, a term that means taste or aesthetic emotion. There have been important debates concerning the number of rasas—the principal ones being delight, laughter, sorrow, anger, fear, disgust, heroism, and astonishment—and their relationship to more transient or subsidiary emotions called *bhava*s—erotic, comic, pathetic, furious, terrible, odious, marvellous, and many more. It also debates whether rasa is located in the work of art itself. Or, as Tagore and Gandhi later discussed, is it located within the audience of the art? Tagore, in fact, had a fascination for the self-contained life of a glow-worm. He felt that art too was like a glow-worm—capable of internalizing the light of the universe to emit a glow, not borrowed but created from within, with which it could transcend the universe. The rasas thus have an important influence on the link between aesthetics and the environment, which begs the question: Is it human feeling that irradiates the environment around us? Is it, after all, our own emotions that give aesthetic meaning to the objects surrounding us?

The earliest discussion of the rasas in India, in about 300 BC, was taking place at about the same time the Greek philosopher Plato, in his theory of mimesis, proposed that art imitated an idea, which makes art an imitation of reality. He writes that art of all kinds becomes things that are twice removed from reality (he calls poetry an imitation thrice removed from the truth!). In this way, Plato reconciles to linking—somewhat vaguely—aesthetics to reality or the environment, even if a few times removed. However, Plato's contemporary, Aristotle, firmly defended art and aesthetics

---

[7] Chakrabarti 2016.

in his rich body of work called *Poetics*. According to him, the arts depict universal truths in more palpable forms than history, which concerns itself only with facts.

However, the theories that counter my argument, that our aesthetics are shaped by the accumulation of our life experiences, are in the eighteenth-century philosophical writings of Anthony Ashley Cooper of Shaftesbury, the works of Francis Hutcheson, and in later (and the most important) works by the German philosopher Immanuel Kant. These writings assert that our aesthetics develop separately and distinctly from the environment that surrounds us. They believed that our appreciation of beauty is objective, and is only related to the object of appreciation and has nothing whatsoever to do with our surroundings, ambience and experiences.

A hundred years later, during and after the First and Second World Wars, psychologists were also involved in the debates around aesthetics and environment. They researched how our moods, choices and aesthetics are influenced by conditions such as crowding, chaos, war and peace in our surroundings. During this time, a man considered the doyen of functional psychology, John Dewey, wrote in *Art as Experience*[8]—a book that is considered one of the most important contemporary theoretical works on aesthetics till date—that aesthetics is intrinsically linked to one's experience with the surroundings. Dewey's view is that aesthetics restores the continuity between the refined experiences aroused by art and the experiences of everyday life. Another American philosopher, Nelson Goodman, shared Dewey's conviction, replacing the question 'What is art?' with 'When is art?'[9] By this, Goodman meant that the same object viewed at different points

---

[8] Dewey 1934.
[9] Goodman 1978.

of time in our life would arouse in us different assessments of its beauty based on the accumulation of our life experiences at that time.

I, of course, concur with Dewey (and Goodman), as he wrote that 'the career and destiny of a living being are bound up with its interchanges with its environment, not externally but in the most intimate way'. Dewey insisted that life goes on through our interactions with our environment. It engages all the senses, which then catalyse our aesthetics. Everywhere in the world, I have indeed found that how people live, what they eat, and what they wear is as much an anthropological summation of their environment as it is a mirror of their individual history.

In every era, social revolutions, political trends and wars have left a mark on how we dress. Our attire can be an intimate window into the psychology of social change. There are many examples of this. The combination of student protests, contraceptives and second-wave feminism in the US and Europe during the 1960s and 1970s did away with gendered roles in society, and also in fashion. When young women could choose when to be mothers and how to express themselves sexually, they rebelled against the demure scarf and stockings, and instead introduced to the world the miniskirt.

Even earlier, the post–Second World War era in the UK had knickers made of military-issue silk maps and air-raid outfits. This was when British women buried their corsets and gowns and instead began to wear garments that gave them more mobility while maintaining a sense of elegance and style. In continental Europe as well, clothing reflected the many ways in which the war had affected countries socially and economically. In Africa and Asia too, it has been distressing yet fascinating how imperialists have intervened in local dress practices through trade and education in the past.

In India, at different times, clothing has been influenced by socio-political situations. One example among hundreds is the story of the humble blouse. In the nineteenth century, most women did not cover their torsos in southern India, while some went bare-breasted under saris in Bengal.[10] During that time, too, European ladies laced themselves tight in corsets and dresses that covered them neck to toe—only the silhouette, strangled into an hourglass shape, marked their femininity. No wonder the British were aghast at the perceived indecorum of Indian women walking around naked under a sari. And so it was the British who added the blouse to the sari, along with their own ideas of European propriety. Perhaps the blouse has been Britain's most powerful export to India, one that has outlived the influence of the crown.

In independent India, the first and earliest wave of some sort of a 'pan-Indian aesthetic' in garments was established by stalwarts such as the cultural activist Pupul Jayakar, and the Ahimsa silk shawl–clad erstwhile Rajput prince Martand Singh, fondly called Mapu, in the 1980s. It was an era when old verities vanished and new ones raised their heads, when the Congress hegemony ended by 1989. As the seeds for an economic revolution in India were being planted, Singh and Jayakar too led a revolution in the field of Indian textiles at that time. They were not designers. They were astute historians, researchers and revivalists, conserving and popularizing near-forgotten Indian arts. They brought together various Indians motifs and techniques of production, putting the spotlight on Indian weavers and showcasing them in garments, literature and pan-Indian textile exhibitions called Vishwakarma in India and all over the world—the Grand Palais in Paris, Tokyo, and the Metropolitan Museum in New York, to name a few of the magnificent venues.

---

[10] Chatterji 2016.

As Indian trade and business opened its doors to the world in the 1990s through a policy shift—from a closed, state-controlled economy to a market-driven one—people's lives changed. They became more connected with the world outside India in the products they consumed and sold, as well as in their exchange of ideas, knowledge, aesthetics, tastes and culture. This first wave of Indian aesthetics rode on these social and political changes in the country. Jayakar and Singh's efforts and their Vishwakarma exhibitions were a turning point in the history of Indian textiles, because no one had previously married dying Indian crafts and couture and turned it into a pan-Indian aesthetic, an aesthetic that India would be known for even internationally.

The second wave in Indian aesthetics came about in the new millennium, with the stitched garment. Previously, it was almost all about the unstitched sari. But now, designers such as Tarun Tahiliani, Ritu Kumar and J.J. Valaya started experimenting with the stitched garment. They brought about a fashion movement, using a bit of craft and creating something modern. By the beginning of the new millennium, most sectors of Indian industry had been successfully liberalized. India was now open to the world. Indian tastes were being influenced by products from abroad. Our desires and aesthetics were changing to something where we could stand out, yet be one with the world. In tandem with these changes—neither causing them, nor because of them—Indian designers established new references, tailoring lehngas, cholis, kurtas and salwars. The proportions they catered to were different, and so were the silhouettes they created. They used plenty of motifs, often in threadwork. The more the kalamkari, the more 'beautiful' the garment was considered. The most enduring effect of this second wave of Indian aesthetics has been the establishment of the notion that simple is dull. These were the designers, later joined by the talented couturier Sabyasachi

Mukherjee, who draped Indian Bollywood actors dancing on the silver screen in shimmering, gold-embroidered lehngas in front of the Indian masses, who liked what they saw. This aesthetic—of shimmer and gold all over a garment—has transposed itself from the couture stores of Delhi to the lanes of Johri Bazaar in Jaipur.

We are now in an era that is searching for India. There is a feeling that we have gone too far away, and too soon. We have lost much of our ancient knowledge in the sciences and mathematics, and we do not know any more how to read Sanskrit, the language in which most of the treasures of our ancient wisdom are written. Who are we as Indians? Are we lost in the glitter and gold of global influences? Have we lost our core?

Searching for answers, we are at the ebb of a new revivalist wave—a third wave—in Indian aesthetics. Led by designers such as Sanjay Garg, the old crafts of India are being brought back into the mainstream. The sari is once again in the limelight, with a renewed conviction that it belongs to the loom. Often, the motifs are woven in, not embroidered, thus showcasing the power of the loom. The aesthetics are minimalistic. The silhouette of the blouse and the drape of the sari have changed dramatically. The blouse and the sari are worn loose, comfortable and airy, rejecting the erstwhile tight, restrictive sari ensemble.

Wearing the sari draped casually, teamed with a loose blouse and loafers or boots, is a contemporary statement of sorts by Indian women standing up to the men in their desire to go out and work. It is not yet a reflection of changing times, but of these women's desire to change their status. In this sense, the socio-economic circumstances that caused this change in dress are not the same as those that caused a fashion shift in the post–Second World War era of hardship, when British women gave up their corsets and gowns for garments that gave them more mobility to go out and work with the men.

We would expect economic growth to go hand in hand with the emancipation of women. We would imagine that the expansion of the economy would provide more opportunities and conducive environments for women to work if they wish to. But in India, it has been the other way round. Between 2004 and 2011, when the Indian economy grew at a healthy average of about 7 per cent, there was a devastating decline in female participation in the country's labour force, from over 35 per cent to 25 per cent. The rising educational enrolment of women contributed to this fall in workforce numbers, but so did factors such as lack of employment opportunities for women and increased household income.[11] This is a disturbing trend—and one that is long-term, not transitory—because it means that the freedom of women to earn their livelihood in India is being curtailed.

Therefore the pushback from many women comes not just in the form of words, but in their dress too. They dress for comfort, often to send out a message of 'ready-to-work' easy confidence and that they too are at par with the men.

It is impossible for an Indian to follow merely one culture—the one in the immediate surroundings at a specific moment, or, say, the one they were born into—among many, and be immune to the rest.

We are defined by what we surround ourselves with over extended periods. For each of us, therefore, being surrounded by an incredibly fast-changing society, which includes thousands of diverse local cultures, influences the manner in which we live and even our dress and tastes. Our personal history, socio-economic as well as political changes in the environment, the social constraints we are confronted with, regional affiliations, cultural moorings, as well as our own interpretation of the complex changes in our

---

[11] Verick 2014.

unparalleled, heterogeneous society all shape our individual tastes and aesthetics. This shapes who we are, our likes and dislikes, our aspirations and hopes. We are thus, each of us, a product of the complexity that such diversity and change in India bring.

References

Bhuyan, Avantika. 2016. The Benarasi brocade and a monument of weaves. *Business Standard*, 26 February.

Burton, Richard Francis, trans. 1883. *The Kama Sutra of Vatsyayana* (Benares: Society of the Friends of India).

Chakrabarti, Arindam, ed. 2016. *The Bloomsbury Research Handbook of Indian Aesthetics and the Philosophy of Art* (New Delhi: Bloomsbury Publishing).

Chatterji, Miniya. 2016. Unpeeling the history of the blouse. Huffington Post India, 21 August.

Coomaraswamy, Ananda K. 1939. Ornament, *The Art Bulletin* 21.4, pp. 375–382.

Coomaraswamy, Ananda K. 1943. *Christian and Oriental Philosophy of Art* (North Chelmsford: Courier Corporation).

Dewey, John. 1934. *Art as Experience* (New York: Minton, Balch & Company).

Goodman, Nelson. 1978. *Ways of Worldmaking* (Hackett Publishing Company).

Lilaowala, Ashdeen Z., and Shernaz Cama. 2013. *Threads of Continuity: The Zoroastrian Craft of Kusti Weaving* (Mumbai: Parzor Foundation).

Verick, Sher. 2014. Women's labour force participation in India: Why is it so low? International Labour Organization, http://www.ilo.org/wcmsp5/groups/public/---asia/---ro-bangkok/---sro-new_delhi/documents/genericdocument/wcms_342357.pdf.

Part V

CONCLUSION

15

Freedom

What is the difference between Anna Hazare fasting to draw attention to his ethical position against corruption and a homeless person starving because he lacks the means to get food? Both these people are living in a politically free country. Neither is gaining good nutrition and both are in pain. But the difference is that while the former is exercising free will, the latter is not free because he has no choice. Only the latter is enslaved to his condition of starvation.

If a young man who is the heir to his father's business chooses not to pursue an education he is exercising his choice. Another man who has no money and does not have the choice to study is enslaved to the deprivation of education. The former is free, while the latter is not.

A woman who chooses, without any external pressure, not to earn her livelihood—for motherhood, lack of interest, or any other reason—has freedom. A woman who is either forced to work due to financial constraints or any other reason or forced not to work is enslaved.

When we think of freedom, we usually think of civil and political rights. But for a person who is hungry, or is having to take on a burdening loan because there is no governmental health care, freedom means the freedom from that hunger or debt or the kind of insecurity that causes him to kill himself. For a person who wants to study but is held back by finances, freedom is getting an education. For a woman who is prohibited from going out to work, freedom means having the choice to pursue her aspirations outside the domestic setting.

The birth of India was marked by political freedom, which meant freedom from external government coercion—and nothing else. It did not mean freedom from hunger, exploitation and disease. There are many other forms of freedom that are needed to guarantee a fulfilling life. We cannot evolve if we are not free to do so. Only if we are granted free movement can we explore. If our sexual freedom is curbed, we can certainly not procreate. I have written in the first part of this book about how humans are instinctually predisposed towards survival, evolution, exploration and procreation. But a prerequisite for us to abide by these instincts is freedom.

I would therefore argue that the crucial difference between freedom and slavery is a person's voluntary action, as opposed to compulsion. Elaborating this argument, I have raised a few questions in the second part of this book: Are we really free if bound by law (especially as the law is subjective anyway, changing from one country to another)? How can we exercise individual free will if we are pressured to conform to certain societal values we might not believe in? In the second and third parts of this book, I have discussed the idea that in India, politics, society, corporations and religions have become contraptions of our own making that restrict our 'absolute freedom'. We created these institutions, which have now laid out rules that frame our life. The collectivist voice of these institutions tells us, 'No, there is no absolute freedom. You need to enslave yourself to gain a livelihood, and society holds the right to limit your individual freedom.' Should we listen to this collectivist voice and drop the delusion of our 'freedoms'? Should we suppress our instincts to freely evolve, explore and procreate as per our choice? Should we accept that our freedoms are whatever society decides they are?

My quest for answers to these questions has not been merely an intellectual exercise. I am no economist sitting at my desk and commissioning research reports to then write about the report's conclusions from a bird's-eye view. Instead, my academic training has equipped me to scientifically investigate and objectively study my intimate experiences and involvement with India. What I have experienced and felt in India has been the key to the comparisons I have made with the experiences and feelings of others in India and abroad. It has made me read about various approaches to the same issue, because surely, there are several perspectives other than mine towards a country as vast and wild in its beauty as India. These are the reflections that I have, in all naked honesty, poured into this book.

In doing so, I have been well aware that my ability to recognize and follow my instinct has been a gift of my education at home, at school and of my explorations as a young adult in the world. But I have also long realized that while this gift has empowered me with volition, it has been my volition and the consequent life choices I have made that have almost made me feel apologetic towards the society of the country that I belong to.

The instances are many, and I have referred to some of them in this book. My rejection of religious rituals (while fully welcoming others following them) from the age of six onwards was supported by my parents, but not by society. I have, till date, not been forgiven for absconding at age nineteen on the day of a 'surprise' arranged engagement to a man I hardly knew. A few years later, in a country where boys need to study primarily to get a job, I am still told by members of the extended family to 'take it easy'. On the other hand, when I have quit the 'right jobs' which seemingly increased my social status in order to pursue my heart's desire I have been made to feel sorry and nervous by the people around me. When I lived across the world with my long-term Muslim partner, I was ostracized by my family for a few years. And when my partner and I parted ways after more than a decade of being together, it was smugly concluded by uncles and aunts that the reason was religious differences (though it was not!). Much later, when I married a man I loved who happened to be several years my junior, I was advised by friends to keep the age difference a secret. 'Don't say and they won't be able to tell,' a girlfriend a few years my senior told me. When, at our own wedding, my husband and I freely expressed our joy at being with child, not many were pleased.

Economist Amartya Sen's perspective of 'substantial' freedom, as he writes of it, is concerned with becoming 'fuller social persons, exercising our own volitions and interacting with and influencing the world in which we live.'[1] But in reality, volition took me—as it does many other young girls in the country—on a tough path that has only threatened my social relationships.

In my opinion, it is not the legal framework of the Constitution, nor the religious scriptures and certainly not society that can prevent us harming one another. It is our education that teaches us to respect the right of another man to live and that prohibits us from harming or killing him. Unless we have this respect, no amount of rules curbing our various freedoms can save man from man. But if we, *one*, have this respect, and *two*, are able to exercise our rational faculty in our actions, even if society's arbitrary rules ask us to harm another man, we will choose to disobey. Of course,

---

[1] Sen 1999, 14–15.

the human mind is not infallible. We are not always capable of thinking rationally, and might make the wrong decision. But when rationality fails, respect for the other intervenes.

In essence, another man's survival requires that those who are free must also be rational and educated enough to respect one another's lives. These two preconditions are essential. This is why no matter how many legal or societal rules we create to control our freedom, if we as a nation do not nurture respect, rationality, and the ability to independently think and judge, as well as implement our volition, we will continue to kill or harm each other on the slightest pretext.

Rationality and freedom are therefore two sides of the same coin. We can only be rational when we think with a free mind, and when we are rational, freedom can win. One does not really exist without the other. So a rational mind does not work under compulsion. Once it perceives the situation, it cannot be subservient to anyone else's orders or controls. Such a mind can therefore be perceived as dangerous to political harmony. If a person equipped with such a mind cannot be cajoled, manipulated or forced even at gunpoint, how can a political leader have their orders obeyed?

It is for this reason, as I have pointed out in detail earlier in this book, that freedom of expression in India has been curbed—in more or less ways—by many successive governments even after we gained political freedom.[2] After all, can there be any greater irony than the fact that in 1951 the very first amendment to the Constitution of India included the provisions to curtail freedom of speech and expression?[3]

---

[2] See Chapter 13 titled 'Decibels'.

[3] The Nehru administration made the amendment to Article 19(1)(a) of Constitution of India against 'abuse of freedom of speech and expression' in 1951 (See more on this in Chandrachud 2016).

If encouraging rational thinking amongst our people is detrimental to an Indian political leader's tenure in power, what incentive does he have to encourage quality education in India?

I refer here to the kind of education that opens up the mind with questions rather than closes it with answers learnt by rote; the education that teaches us to respect each other as human beings, and not pull one another down even when scrambling for the same resources; the education that persuades us to stand with our head held high despite all our perceived flaws and not idolize a stereotype; the education that asks us to think for ourselves and speak our opinion, not pander to those of others.

For political leaders to remain in power, it is in their best interest that citizens abstain from such an education, whether formal or informal. Parents must be told not to nurture independent-minded children, for which society must work hand in hand with politicians and parents to ensure that the ability of our children to think rationally and independently is forever stunted. Schools must continue to encourage learning by rote, as that is a sure-shot way to produce clones who will be programmed to learn—without applying their mind—everything they are told. Such citizens would be easiest to provoke with political rhetoric.

I am by no means suggesting a great conspiracy on the part of political leaders to stunt the mental faculties of our citizens. My point here instead is that the sort of political leadership that has developed in India might have little real incentive to encourage an education that will promote rational and independent thinking. Expanding on this, my larger point is that citizens under such a leadership are not free. Our minds are slaves to the dictates of others. We will not question the rules laid down by politics, society, religion, or the boss who demands work 24/7. And the issue is not about being a slave to a 'good' cause (be it political, social, religious, professional, etc.) versus a slave to a 'bad' cause. The issue is freedom versus slavery.

If freedom is to be upheld, then individual rights need to be upheld, guaranteed and protected by the political system. However, despite all the rules in the Constitution that explicitly intend to do so, this has not been easy to implement in India.

For instance, the Indian Constitution equally empowers both free thinkers as well as the offended, who can pursue criminal charges against writers, artists, film-makers editors and reporters who may have allegedly hurt their sensibilities. Both groups have an equal claim to protection by the Constitution. An artist has as much freedom to paint what they wish to as any Indian citizen who claims to have been religiously offended by that artist's painting. It is this dichotomy that has long been the focal point of conflict between the free thinkers and those who are offended, both of whose rights are protected by the Constitution.

Although India is a secular state, the growing number of 'easily religiously offended' groups wants the government to prioritize religion over secularism and human rights. There is also an increasingly condescending attitude—in both urban and rural milieus—towards liberal and secular elements. There is a single view of how to be a citizen that is being propagated, which is that one must believe the line that the government takes. The message being sent out by the ruling party is that we must think in 'a way that is in the national interest'. But if a large number of people think that national interest is in upholding Constitutional values and the unity of different parts of the population, then that is in conflict with the government's belief that there should be a Hindu nation. Then the people's freedom to hold their own beliefs is hugely under threat. The freedom to converse, the freedom to think, is under attack.[4]

---

[4] Author's interview with Karuna Nundy, 14 July 2017.

Recently, in a major blow to our right to free speech, the government in 2016 argued before the Supreme Court in favour of retaining criminal penalties for defamation—and the court upheld the law. While lamenting the misuse of government power, we must also realize that the role of the government is not easy in India either, balancing various public opinions and sentiments within the framework of the Constitution that does not always help in this regard. Politicians of the world's largest democracy are not always acting on their selfish agenda to garner more votes in the elections (though they do so often). The dilemma created by the Indian Constitution, which protects the agents of freedom of speech as well as those who might be offended by that speech, is a difficult one. Ultimately, the actions of the Indian government on free expression—whichever way it weighs—have often also reflected the dominant opinion of the people.

As a consequence of this constitutional dilemma, as well as the political populism for votes, freedom of expression has suffered at different times and in varying degrees in India. Despite gaining political freedom, and indeed, ever since then, societal and government intolerance of free expression have peaked and ebbed. Such intolerance suffocates and discourages open discussion typical of a liberal, democratic society. Ultimately, a culture of fear to hold open, liberal discussions develops, which is the perfect breeding ground for extremist views of every kind to grow covertly. This leads to sentiments of hatred all around, and a mob culture ready to strike anywhere. Is this the India that we want to present to our children?

In the essay titled 'Decibels', I have pointed out how the curbing of freedom of expression has been an enduring problem in India, and not a passing one in just our present times. I would add here that we must not get lost in the ongoing blame game regarding which political party or government has worsened our lack of freedom. We need to instead wonder, how are so many of us joining the 'easily religiously offended' group? We are not a theocratic state. Then why are increasing numbers of Indians ridiculing or mistrusting their liberal and secular compatriots? We need to recognize that the curbing of freedom of expression is a worrying long-standing trend in a secular democratic nation that claims to constitutionally protect fundamental rights and secular values. How do we put an end to this trend before it is too late?

We must realize that societal 'rules' and all the laws established by the state have often failed miserably in protecting our freedom to lead a dignified life or even the freedom to live. As I have mentioned in my essay on religion in India, faith in religion provides tremendous hope to survive, but by the same token, it is also an overpowering force that can sway people towards differences. Both society and our legal framework have fallen victims to this force.

Off and on, there have also been instances in (politically free) India's history when politicians have purposely supported and propagated religious nationalism, or chosen not to act either during or after communal clashes. The US Commission on International Religious Freedom is an independent US government advisory body that monitors religious freedom worldwide. Its 2016 Annual Report explains that

> India is a multi-religious, multi-ethnic, multi-cultural country and a secular democracy . . . However, the Indian government has long struggled to maintain religious and communal harmony . . . In 2013, in Muzaffarnagar, Uttar Pradesh, violence between Hindus and Muslims killed forty people, at least a dozen women and girls were raped, and

more than 50,000 were displaced. In Odisha in 2007–08, violence between Hindus and Christians destroyed churches and homes, displacing nearly 10,000 and killing around forty people. In Gujarat in 2002, violence between Hindus and Muslims left between 1200 and 2500 Muslims dead. The 1984 anti-Sikh riots killed 3000 Sikhs.[5]

Many cases stemming from these incidents are still pending in the Indian courts.[6] According to Supreme Court lawyer Karuna Nundy, the reasons for this are multiple. One, the police is answerable to the state government, which cripples the police's ability to act freely to control communal riots. Two, in the event of a pogrom, the police, for a certain period, has likely stepped back and observed or even gently facilitated the killing. So during the 'golden hour' of evidence—which is the time and place where the crime has occurred—no evidence has been gathered. Three, witness protection programmes in India are in dire straits. 'The witness is the least valuable person in the local thana,' says Nundy. 'And so when you are up against some big communal political community, it is justice versus your life, and that slows down the entire case further.' And four: 'Usually when an opposing government comes to power, they control the CBI, and then drive it to become suddenly active on a past case that may have occurred during the previous government. There might be an active and honest judge who would thereafter take forward the independent evidence gathering efforts,'[7] says Nundy.

---

[5] USCIRF 2016. Also see *Reuters* 2017.
[6] USCIRF 2016.
[7] Author's interview with Karuna Nundy, 14 July 2017.

If governance systems and their guardians—our politicians—fail to calm such violence and are at times the perpetrators or supporters of it, how can we entrust them with the greatest responsibility of protecting our freedom to live? If the laws of our land, which the political elite has enshrined in our Constitution, cannot stop people from killing each other, and don't even allow the meting out of justice in such cases, on what basis do they claim to know better than us common folks about what to do when free? Even today, ask any politician (or members of their clan and families) about the benefits of governance in India, and they will tell you that in a country where 25.6 per cent of the people are illiterate, the masses do not have the intellectual or emotional bandwidth to take informed decisions about what to do with their freedom and therefore need to be guided by societal norms, religious doctrines and legal frameworks. The truth is that much to the benefit of these politicians who want to stay in power, if the masses are lacking in terms of education—formal and informal—they are less likely to take rational decisions that defy the agenda of the ruling political, societal, corporate and religious elite.

Communal violence, even if a common feature in India,[8] has grown neither progressively nor continuously, spurting excessively once in a while. The situation today is not the worst we have seen, yet, undeniably, it has deteriorated in recent times. In 2015, according to India's Ministry of Home Affairs, India suffered a 17 per cent increase in reported communal violence, with 751 reported incidents as compared to the 644 reported in the previous year.[9] In addition, there were at least 365 major attacks on Christians and their institutions in 2015, compared to 120

---

[8] Engineer, Dabhade and Nair 2017; Khan 2017.
[9] *Economic Times* 2016.

in 2014.[10] In 2017, India has risen to the fifteenth rank on the Open Doors World Watch List of the fifty countries in which it is hardest to live as a Christian.[11] Also, statistics show that as of 2014, only 5 per cent of marriages in India are inter-caste.[12]

As opposed to communal riots, which might make it to a sensational newspaper headline, there are individual cases of intolerance-induced violence that appear routine.

Mohammad Akhlaq, a fifty-two-year-old Muslim man in a village close to Delhi, was lynched by a mob in September 2015, after rumours that he had eaten beef and was storing cow meat at home.[13] Meanwhile, Kannur, in Kerala, has been a hotbed for political violence for several decades, witness to a number of deaths across party lines. Police data between 2000 and 2016 shows that of the sixty-nine political deaths in this district, thirty-one were of Hindus from the BJP or the RSS.[14]

In Jharkhand, two cattle traders, thirty-two-year-old Mazlum Ansari and fifteen-year-old Imteyaz Khan, were caught by a group, beaten and left hanging from a tree in March 2016.[15] In 2017, a twenty-three-year-old RSS worker in Tamil Nadu was brutally hacked to death in broad daylight allegedly by the Communist Party of India (Marxist). The victim was an accused in a case related to the murder of a Democratic Youth Federation of India worker in 2013.[16] On 10 July 2017, seven Hindu pilgrims died in a deadly assault in Anantnag, a Muslim-majority region in

---

[10] *Hindustan Times* 2016a.
[11] Open Doors USA 2017; World Watch Monitor 2017.
[12] *The Hindu* 2014.
[13] BBC News 2015; *Indian Express* 2015.
[14] Scroll 2017.
[15] *Hindustan Times* 2016b.
[16] *The Hindu* 2017.

Kashmir.[17] In 2000, an attack on the same pilgrimage also killed thirty people, most of them Hindus, and was blamed on the Pakistan-based militant group Lashkar-e-Taiba.

The list goes on, and will go on.[18]

There are people being attacked, beaten up and murdered on the basis of various accusations or political interests. Article 48 of the Indian Constitution restricts or bans cow slaughter in twenty-four out of twenty-nine Indian states as of 2015.[19] This, indeed, is a law in India, even though it economically marginalizes the people who work in the beef industry, which includes slaughter for consumption, hauling items, and producing leather goods.

Let us be clear that murders and lynching have happened before, under all governments. Communal and political violence in India has occurred across all political regimes. The old slogan 'unity in diversity' should be practised and preserved by all government and political parties.

Hegemony is power with legitimacy, and it is the majority groups that are hegemonic today. A gay man can be harassed or killed by a mob, because his murderers would have measured homosexuality by societal values (despite and because of these being ever-changing), and found it shameful, abnormal or just 'wrong'. A woman can be bullied, harassed and raped by a group of men because she would be considered according to societal norms to be wearing the 'wrong' length of skirt. These members of majority groups are immune or deadened to the respect for another individual's freedom to live a dignified life. They are not

---

[17] *Guardian* 2017.

[18] *Milli Gazette* 2017.

[19] Under state criminal laws, individuals can face up to ten years in jail or a fine of up to Rs 10,000 for the slaughter or possession of cows or bulls or the consumption of beef (*News in Asia* 2016).

educated—despite any number of degrees—in a way that they can think rationally and independently for themselves either. How else can one explain the continual killing of human beings? Even the laws of the Constitution have failed to save man from man— this is a country where homosexuality has always been a legally contentious[20] issue.

Freedom in India is therefore subjective, dependent on where you live, which family and caste you were born into, your gender, religion, sexuality, source of livelihood. The guarantee of freedom for our marginalized communities—be it on the basis of religion, gender, sexual orientation or economic status—has always been the most fragile. This will not change, no matter how many laws are drafted, religious doctrines invoked, and societal norms established, unless all our children—regardless of their background—are educated to be rational, independent-minded individuals who respect one another. It is possible to create various kinds of freedoms by pursuing such an education facilitated by home, school and society.

Because at the end of the day, it is important to ask: What is the defining characteristic of our nation? Is it the territorial boundary or the collection of Indian people in all their diversity? If it is the former, we can focus on only political freedom, but if it

---

[20] Section 377 of the Indian Penal Code makes sex with a person of the same gender punishable by law. On 2 July 2009, the Delhi High Court held that provision to be unconstitutional with respect to sex between consenting adults. However the Supreme Court of India overturned that ruling on 11 December 2013, stating that the court was instead deferring to Indian legislators to provide the sought-after clarity. At the time of writing this book, the Supreme Court had agreed (on 2 February 2016) to reconsider its judgment, stating it would refer petitions to abolish Section 377 to a five-member constitutional bench, which would conduct a comprehensive hearing on the issue.

is the latter, we do need a larger framework of 'freedoms' in India to be truly free.

References

BBC News. 2015. Why India man was lynched over beef rumours. 1 October. http://www.thehindu.com/data/just-5-per-cent-of-indian-marriages-are-intercaste/article6591502.ece.

Chandrachud, Abhinav. 2016. Of curbs to free speech. *The Hindu*, 27 July.

Economic Times. 2016. Communal violence up 17 per cent in 2015. 24 February. https://economictimes.indiatimes.com/news/politics-and-nation/communal-violence-up-17-in-2015/articleshow/51125252.cms.

Engineer, Irfan. Neha Dabhade, and Suraj Nair. 2017. Communal violence in 2016. *Matters India*, 7 January.

Guardian. 2017. Attack by militants kills at least seven Hindu pilgrims in Kashmir. 10 July. https://www.theguardian.com/world/2017/jul/10/attack-by-militants-kills-hindu-pilgrims-kashmir-india.

Hindustan Times. 2016a. 2015 worst year for Christians since Independence, 8,000 attacked. 19 January. http://www.hindustantimes.com/india/2015-the-worst-year-for-christians-since-independence-study/story-WmObF2tsphJPVq2mqBDesK.html.

Hindustan Times. 2016b. Cow activist, 4 others held after 2 Muslim cowherds hanged to death. 20 March. http://www.hindustantimes.com/india/five-arrested-after-two-muslim-cowherds-hanged-to-death-in-jharkhand/story-KcHi7nNS22Y6CXAych5eBJ.html.

Indian Express. 2015. Dadri: Mob kills man, injures son over 'rumours' that they ate beef. 25 December. http://indianexpress.com/article/india/india-others/next-door-to-delhi-mob-kills-50-year-old-injures-son-over-rumours-they-ate-beef.

Khan, Shahzaib. 2017. India's age of extremism. *Indian Express,* 14 July.

Milli Gazette. 2017. How much more blood is needed to outrage you, Madhu Kishwar. 31 May.

News in Asia. 2016. US expresses concern over rising intolerance and communal violence in India. 30 July.

Open Doors USA. 2017. World Watch List. https://www.opendoorsusa.org/christian-persecution/world-watch-list.

Reuters. 2017. Intimidation, death threats stalk gang-raped Muslim women after India's religious riots. 9 February.

Scroll. 2017. How many BJP-RSS workers have been murdered in Kerala? Depends on whom you ask. 6 October. https://scroll.in/article/853061/how-many-bjp-rss-workers-have-been-murdered-in-kerala-depends-on-whom-you-ask.

Sen, Amartya. 1999. *Development as Freedom* (New York: Alfred A. Knopf).

The Hindu. 2017. RSS worker killed in Kerala. 13 November. http://www.thehindu.com/news/national/kerala/rss-worker-killed-in-kerala/article20368163.ece.

The Hindu. 2014. Just 5 per cent of Indian marriages are inter-caste: Survey. 13 November. http://www.thehindu.com/data/just-5-per-cent-of-indian-marriages-are-intercaste/article6591502.ece.

United States Commission on International Religious Freedom. 2016. http://www.uscirf.gov/sites/default/files/USCIRF%202016%20Annual%20Report.pdf.

World Watch Monitor. 2017. India's religious freedom failings 'enshrined in constitution'. 15 March.